FOLKLORE RECYCLED

FOLKLORE RECYCLED

Old Traditions in New Contexts

Frank de Caro

UNIVERSITY PRESS OF MISSISSIPPI • JACKSON

www.upress.state.ms.us

The University Press of Mississippi is a member of the Association of American University Presses.

First printing 2013
∞
Library of Congress Cataloging-in-Publication Data

De Caro, F. A., 1943–
  Folklore recycled : old traditions in new contexts / Frank de Caro.
    pages cm
  Includes bibliographical references and index.
  ISBN 978-1-61703-764-1 (cloth : alk. paper) — ISBN 978-1-61703-765-8 (ebook) 1. Folklore—United States—History and criticism. 2. Folk literature, American—History and criticism. 3. Literature and folklore—United States—History and criticism. 4. Folk art—United States—History. I. Title.
  GR105.D42 2013
  398.20973—dc23   2012050640

British Library Cataloging-in-Publication Data available

CONTENTS

ACKNOWLEDGMENTS

My wife, Rosan Augusta Jordan, coauthored chapter 2 of this book, and I give her my many thanks for having worked on this material with me. Her research into Americans in Mexico, which she has been engaged in for a number of years, was also influential in shaping my chapter 6. Chapter 2 previously appeared, in somewhat different form, in the *Journal of American Folklore* (volume 109 [1996]: 31–59), and I thank the American Folklore Society for permission to use it here. Quotations from the minutes of the Louisiana Branch of the American Folklore Society that appear in that chapter are used with the permission of Tulane University, in whose library archives those minutes reside (from the Louisiana Folklore Documents Collection, Louisiana Research Collection, Tulane University). Chapter 1 previously appeared, in somewhat different form, in *The Folklore Historian* (volume 23 [2006]: 3–18); my thanks to the editors of that journal for originally publishing this material and for permission to use it here.

Margaret Eiluned Morgan, granddaughter of Dwight and Elizabeth Morrow, whose work is discussed in chapter 6, has kindly assisted me in securing permission to use illustrations that originally appeared in her grandmother's books. Some of the information I give about her grandparents is derived from personal communications from her, and I thank her for her interest and assistance.

My thanks to the several institutions that provided illustrative material and whose rights and permissions are indicated in appropriate places in this book and also to the individuals who similarly provided or gave permission to use illustrations. My thanks also to Dr. Leslie Blake for her brief comments on chicken pox in the Caribbean.

At the University Press of Mississippi Craig Gill and Katie Keene were both encouraging and helpful, and I thank them for their input, as I thank my editor, Deborah Upton, for her careful attention to my manuscript and for her many improvements.

FOLKLORE RECYCLED

INTRODUCTION

Folklore's Messiness

◇◇

Although my own personal favorite definition of "folklore" holds that folklore is "what elderly English vicars study on afternoons when it is too wet to play croquet,"[1] more serious definitions focus on the parameters of its social and cultural contexts. They see folklore as a mode of communication that relies upon certain kinds of *processes*, of orality and tradition, and as the expressive culture of certain *groups*, of the "common people" or of preindustrial society or of the remnants of preindustrial society, or of the collective understandings of a defined *group* (loggers, Mennonites, Slovak Americans).

This book will not, however, dwell on such definitions, which are generally overlapping and which folklorists can sometimes discuss for rather long periods of time. It will deal with what might be called folklore's messiness, with the porousness of the usual contexts in which folklore flourishes (and in terms of which folklore *is* defined, hence my beginning with a brief consideration of definition) such that folklore becomes transmuted or transported into other, non-folk contexts, artistic, intellectual, and otherwise. Insofar as folklore—in its original, "pure" form oral and traditional—can be transcribed, described, mechanically or electronically recorded, filmed, abstracted, or insofar as folk performances can be moved to venues different from their usual, normative, historical contexts, or insofar as folk materials can be performed by the non-folk, folklore can be assimilated in varying degrees by those who stand wholly or partly outside particular folk contexts, outside the contexts of oral tradition and folk culture. Folklore can be incorporated into novels and movies. Traditional folk craftspeople can appear at popular crafts fairs to make traditional quilts or hide-bottom chairs for nontraditional consumers. Professionally trained singers can sing traditional folksongs at Carnegie Recital Hall concerts.

That is, folklore can be manipulated, exploited, and otherwise used by those normally outside the context in which that folklore is performed and transmitted. Thus a New Orleans brass band (which normally plays in the streets at funerals and during the annual parading season of the

social-aid-and-pleasure clubs) plays at a racetrack converted to an enter-
tainment/ educational venue as the New Orleans Jazz and Heritage Festival.
The idea of the quilting bee becomes part of an animated cartoon commercial for paper towels in which elderly and presumably folksy ladies sew
together layers, apparently, of soft and absorbent paper into "quilted" products. The folktale "Cinderella" (passed down by word of mouth for centuries
at *veglia* and other storytelling occasions) becomes a Walt Disney animated
film or a children's storybook or a stylish *conte* for French aristocrats.[2] Although folklorists are interested in folklore because they seek to understand
and promote the meanings and social and cultural positioning of folklore,
others have conceived interests in folklore for a variety of artistic, personal,
and ideological reasons; such interests, though they may be purely or partly
intellectual, can lead to other forms of reuse and recycling.

Certainly in contemporary society different kinds of folklore are apt to
be known in different ways; some are more or less accessible in their usual,
folkloric contexts to those outside the folk tradition. Commonly, however,
folklore is not experienced in its usual performative contexts but through
some sort of recycling: as literature and elite art, in special performance
venues, as tourist symbols, elite decorative objects, or nationalistic propaganda.

Contemporary folklorists need to see the study of such re-situation of
folklore—to use a term coined by Roger Abrahams and Barbara Babcock
and which I and a coauthor have used extensively elsewhere[3]—as very important, indeed nearly as important as the study of folklore's prime contexts
themselves. Re-situation/recycling is where the members of contemporary
Western society are most likely to encounter folklore—or at least those
forms of folklore which, unlike the urban legend, do not actually circulate
in contemporary cultural contexts—and it is imperative to have an understanding of how folklore is presented and perceived through non-folk
media in the contemporary world. To do so not only broadens folklorists'
understandings of culture but also creates or strengthens ties to scholars in
other fields of culture studies. By expanding the interest in folklore in culture, folklorists call more attention to the considerable significance of folklore beyond actual folk contexts and ultimately to folklore as a fundamental,
key mode of human communication that has many ramifications and that
needs to be more fully appreciated by cultural commentators generally.

The term folklorism (German *folklorismus*) has been developed to refer
to the "life" folklore has beyond folk contexts, but though American folklorists are certainly familiar with the term, they have paid comparatively little

attention to folklorism, whereas European scholars have been those primarily exploring its ramifications. (Regina Bendix notes that as "American folklorists began to develop an interest in the study of folklore *in* its context, some European folklorists began to deal with what might be called folklore *out* of context."[4]) There is, however, some disagreement over the parameters of the term folklorism and of its connotations. Some definitions seem neutral, whereas others have been more value laden; some broad, others more narrow. Herman Bausinger's characterizations, that folklorism is "the use of material or stylistic elements of folklore in a context which is foreign to the original tradition," that it is "the process of a folk culture experienced at second hand,"[5] is among the more direct statements, as is that of Hans Moser, who defines the term as "second-hand mediation and presentation of folk culture."[6] These definitions are in accord with each other. In saying that "Folklorism is the conscious recognition and repetition of folk tradition as a symbol of ethnic, regional, or national culture," Guntis Smidchens introduces other elements, however, implying that folklorism necessarily has a symbolic element, one tied to particular groups of people at that.[7] Barbara Thornbury says that "Folklorism is folklore on display, mainly for purposes of tourism or cultural preservation,"[8] implying that certain, particular contexts are necessary or usual as conditions for folklorism. Regina Bendix thinks that differences in the cultural contexts they each study has led Europeans (whose historical experience has "included a distinct peasant class" and "overt propagandizing"[9]) to be more aware of certain kinds of "use" and "alteration" of folklore that seem less relevant to Americans.

Some conceptualizations of folklorism have given the phenomenon a decidedly negative cast. Linda Dégh, for example, sees folklorism rather specifically as "commercial exploitation of uprooted and displaced folk art,"[10] her choices of wording suggesting theft and illegitimate wrenching out of context. In the United States Richard Dorson's coining of the term fakelore had considerable influence.[11] Although his term was not synonymous with folklorism—it referred to, really, the invention of folklike "traditions" and passing them off as genuine folklore—it did cover some aspects of folklorism (taking Bausinger's "stylistic elements of folklore" and working with them in some way), and some have used the term more loosely than did Dorson himself. Certainly the use of "fake" in this terminology implies deceit and illegitimacy.

What exactly folklorism covers, then, may not be agreed to. To say that, as does Vilmos Voight, "The concept of folklorism for us means the transmission of folklore into non-folklore"[12] suggests that the incorporation of folklore into their literary works by writers—a process long of interest to folklorists—is a kind of folklorism, and Dégh speaks of "literary folklorism."[13] Yet few American folklorists at any rate have connected this time-honored literary practice to forms of folklorism, preferring such terms as re-situating or, simply, thinking in terms of how writers "use" folklore. Although the term folklorism can be very useful and underlies some of what will be said in subsequent chapters, it will be used sparingly here. Not only is there disagreement upon its parameters, but there are instances in which folklore comes to spill out of its historic contexts in ways that do not necessarily mean that it becomes transformed into something else: intellectual interest in genuine folklore for ideological reasons, for example, may project new meanings on to the lore without literally taking it out of its natural context.

In general the "uses" of folklore by those outside the scope of folk traditions appear in the course of a number of cultural and intellectual endeavors, including the use of folklore in literature; the production of "folk festivals"; the development of "applied folklore"; the context of nationalistic, ideological, and political movements and practices; revivals; commercial undertakings; and tourism (to name only some of the most prominent of these endeavors that have received attention from folklorists).

FOLKLORE AND LITERATURE

Folkloric material's shifting into non-folk contexts is hardly a new process and in fact we would know much, much less about folklore before the nineteenth century had folk texts not been taken over by written, especially literary, ones. Indeed writers of literature have been particularly taken with folklore—some of which contains similarities to literature; hence the term oral literature to refer to some kinds of folklore. And students of folklore, probably because many of them have also been scholars and critics of literature, have long been interested in folklore in its literary relations. Folklore's becoming intertwined with literature in part is a result of folklore's general tendency to be in a dynamic state of flux because of its fluid, unwritten nature, so that adaptation into written forms is a natural step. The social closeness of folk and non-folk media and the existence of social groups that rely on both in related contexts in many cultures have also been major factors in crossovers from one to the other. Indeed we might say—if we are oriented toward the superorganic and like to think of folklore as having a life of its own—that folklore rather naturally recycles. Roland Barthes and Umberto Eco both work with the idea of the "open text," the fact that some literary texts have been created to be especially open to variant readings and permutations.[14] Perhaps folklore, with its usually greater fluidity than written texts, is the ultimate in open textuality, allowing for a kind of inter-textuality in which content and even form are available for a constant or at least regular shifting.

One could argue that the study of folklore in literature has preoccupied folklorists to the extent that folklorists have expended considerable energies in this endeavor while paying comparatively little attention to how folk-lore has been re-situated into other important contexts. The purpose of this book is to look at a few of those contexts and to urge other commentators to look at still others because to do so is of central importance to folkloristics today, when intertextuality plays such a key role in cultural dynamics and when so many of us encounter folklore not in performance but embedded in other media. The folkloristic paradigm has shifted to ethnographic and contextualist approaches, notably performance-oriented ones, a contextual approach, which Dorson saw as a "growing movement among energetic younger folklorists."[15] While the study of folklore and literature has come to seem a bit of a scholarly backwater, an area of study venerable but lacking in the way of intellectual pizzaz, it would be more useful to look at examin-ing the folklore and literature relationship as a sort of prelude for seeing how folklore becomes re-situated in modern and postmodern culture more generally, as a starting point for appreciating how far folklore has made its way beyond its natural habitats and why it has made that journey.

Writers have been users of folklore for a variety of reasons,[16] and their reasons may give us insight into why folklore appeals as an aspect of cul-ture suitable for adaptation or ideological borrowing generally. For example, folklore has often been associated with particular social "layers" or segments, such as the peasantry or the common people or rural groups. Thus folklore can come to be seen as embedding a worldview held by some bygone or ex-otic Other, and writers who seek to portray that Other may look to folklore to smoothly convey the perspectives of a certain group. Or folklore, insofar as it has been viewed as a "survival" from some past mode of existence, may be used to bring that past into the literary present. Certainly the love that eighteenth- and nineteenth-century British literary figures showed for the ballad—not only collecting ballads but writing numerous literary imitations of the poetic form of the ballad[17]—stemmed in part from a desire to pen-etrate the Middle Ages, the period from which ballads were presumed to come and a period that clearly was intriguing but much of which remained little understood at the time.

Assuming that folklore, despite widespread diffusion, has particular local connections has enabled regional writers to make use of it as local symbol or for "local color." The presumed mystical associations that folklore conveys has allowed for the inclusion of, for example, myths and ghost legends, to suggest in literature connections to other realities beyond the "real." Given the importance of proverbs in African culture, African writers like Chinua Achebe have been able to use proverbs as statements of traditional values and cultural authority. Because in American material culture the quilt has been a widely made and used artifact and because quilts have been made primarily by women, American writers, especially women writers, have been able to focus on the quilt as conveying semi-secret female messages.[18] Indeed, the idea of folklore as a conveyor of knowledge not generally understood by elites or by modern society has been used by writers such as Thomas Pynchon, whose *The Crying of Lot 49* not only displays interest in urban legends but fixes upon webs of secret knowledge. Similar conceptions of folklore as this or that have led political and social thinkers, local planners, and advertising executives as well as writers (and other artists, for surely composers and visual artists have appropriated folk materials) to borrow from folklore what they think they need.

FOLK FESTIVALS

Of course, even folklorists, who seek to understand the social roles of folklore in its usual contexts, are themselves responsible for lifting folklore out of its usual cultural contexts. In collecting folklore and publishing folk texts, in writing about folklore and in teaching about it or presenting it in museums, folklorists give the lore an existence outside its normal contexts. Although they have fully learned to do so only over time, folklorists do try to respect the original contexts and to explain them when they present folklore in print or through other media. They do aim for creating understanding of folklore as it exists and functions in culture. That is, "functioning as 'culture brokers'" folklorists endeavor to translate "the values and practices of the folk into forms and events understandable to the general public."[19] Yet once the folklore has been, so to speak, extracted into a book, a film, or a museum exhibition, it does come to a public as somewhat disembodied culture and open to understandings that differ from those of the folk who actually circulate the lore in tradition, though folklorists may endeavor to explain original meanings to students, readers, film viewers, and museumgoers.

"Folk festivals" have been a venue in which folklorists have particularly endeavored to present recycled folk traditions to a public and a venue to which they have given a great deal of thought. The term folk festival covers wide territory, but for folklorists it often refers to a public event at which folklorists present and explain performances put on by folk musicians, craftspeople, narrators, and the like, who have been encountered through fieldwork and who are seen as representatives of authentic tradition. The production of folk festivals in the United States is by no means only a recent phenomenon. Bascom Lamar Lunsford's Mountain Dance and Folk Festival began in Asheville, North Carolina, in 1928; the American Folk Song Festival was organized by Jean Bell Thomas in Kentucky in 1930; the White Top folk festival—closely examined by David Whisnant[20]—in Virginia in 1931. Sarah Gertrude Knott's National Folk Festival began in St. Louis in 1934. Americans certainly have had plenty of time to get used to the idea of traditional performers being presented outside their own cultural contexts (with the close involvement of professionally trained folklorists being a more recent development). The Festival of American Folklife (more recently called the Smithsonian Folklife Festival), presented on the National Mall in Washington, D.C., through a division of the Smithsonian Institution, is probably the premier such event today and, indeed, the subject of much-read scholarship by Robert Cantwell, Richard Bauman, Patricia Sawin, and others (while Barbara Kirshenblatt-Gimblett has also written recently and cogently on the broader implications of staging culture, in exhibitions as well as other venues like folk festivals).[21]

As early as 1980 Charles Camp and Timothy Lloyd were looking at the reasons why folklorists stage or otherwise participate in folk festivals, although they framed their discussion in terms of reasons for perhaps wanting *not* to participate.[22] Nonetheless, they did provide a well-formulated list of folklorists' rationales for putting on or participating in festivals. Festivals give reinforcement to folk participants and their cultural self-awareness and give them "popular attention and respect." They provide information and understanding about folk culture to a public that may not have other sources of knowledge. Thus festivals can be "an effective means for the accurate presentation of folk culture," while they can also celebrate it. And in educating the public about folk culture, they also encourage its support and study. Camp and Lloyd, however, are critical of such festivals because they may "convey a narrow-headed idea of what folklife is" and because those presenting it have often failed to explain such important things as "tradition, context, transmission, and function," elements that folklorists see as essential to the construction of folklore. And others such as Cantwell and Kirshenblatt-Gimblett would come along to further question the nature of festival and other means of presenting folk cultural forms to a public outside the historical conduits of the folk.

Whisnant's examination of the White Top folk festival in Virginia considers many aspects of this once-annual event, ranging from the reasons behind its founding to the roles it played in both preserving and distorting southern mountain traditions. The festival grew out of the same sort of cultural interventionism that motivated the founding of "folk schools" in the southern mountains. The creators of the festival were particularly disturbed by what recording companies and radio seemed to be doing to the traditional folk music of the southern mountain region and hoped to "moderate the destructive impact of modernity upon the lives of traditional musicians . . . and to correct the misleading images of their music being foisted upon a credulous public by commercial record companies and the radio barn dances which were proliferating throughout the 1920s." A festival "would bring the performers out of their isolated surroundings and place them before an appreciative audience" and could be more effective in educating an audience about traditional music than the books of scholars, which had a more limited impact. Of course the motives of early festival promoters did vary. One of the White Top promoters, John Blakemore, sought to promote a hotel, while another, Annabel Morris Buchanan, was more a romantic purist and cultural preservationist. A third, John Powell, not only hoped to use traditional folk music as the basis for classical compositions but was much involved in ideologies that put mountain music at the heart of "Anglo-Saxon" racial purity, connecting race and culture. Whisnant sees the White Top festival ultimately as a force that provided "not the presentation of a preexisting [cultural] reality but . . . a manipulation of it,"[23] as the organizers stressed certain musical forms over others and even promoted performance forms that had no basis in local culture, such as the English morris and sword dances that musicologist Cecil Sharp had introduced earlier to the United States. Nonetheless, though the potential problems inherent in festivals such as White Top might be many, the folk festival has created an important venue for the use of traditional folklore outside its usual contexts, which in part accounts for the continuing critiques that folklorists and others have undertaken of folk festivals.

In writing about the New Orleans Jazz and Heritage Festival (Jazz Fest, which has continued to attract vast numbers of people to its productions each spring) Helen Regis and Shana Walton note:

> *Festivals have long been seen as conscious community displays, often showcasing versions of community ideals rather than lived experience. In this idea of self-conscious display, festivals have become a site for cultural critique. That is, because the festivals are consciously produced by people who have the power to create and craft such exhibitions, folklorists, anthropologists, and cultural studies scholars have deconstructed the events, examining what is chosen to be displayed, who consumes the displays, and what social/cultural purposes are being accomplished.*[24]

Regis and Walton suggest that though Jazz Fest, which has its almost fanatical adherents, has developed a culture of its own, it offers those who attend an opportunity not merely to observe traditional performers but to imaginatively merge with traditional folk cultures: "By learning how to make Cajun carnival masks, conversing with [folk participant] Susan Launey about alligator locomotion, honoring the living ancestors of American popular music, second lining behind a social and pleasure club, and chanting with the Mardi Gras Indians, one becomes a part of the folk."[25]

That is, the folk festival, with its live intermingling of traditional performers with those who are outside particular folk traditions, is a kind of recycling of folklore, which—though on one level it may merely present an audience with the occasion for observing, appreciating, and learning about traditional performers—provides certain opportunities for imaginative reconstruction of the folk (which give festivals both their appeal for the public and concern for their critics). Folklore gets recycled in the festival context for a variety of reasons, of course, including the ideological. For example, Emily Satterwhite, one of several recent critics of the Smithsonian Folklife Festival, suggests that visitors to the Appalachian section of the festival in 2002 "imagined the region as the (white, rural) roots of 'real' America, a reservoir of an ordinary and legitimate American culture," a conception not unlike that promoted in the 1930s by John Powell of the White Top festival. She goes on to note that "appeals to nationalism are . . . pervasive in festival rhetoric" despite "the counterhegemonic implications of the festival's goals of cultural inclusiveness"[26] promoted by, among other things, the increasingly popular international aspects of the festival.

APPLIED FOLKLORE

In recent years folklorists have moved increasingly into a variety of "public sector" endeavors (sometimes working on the production of folk festivals) and into applied folklore, a field in which the uses of folklore outside usual contexts are at least partially explored by those who study and understand those contexts. Applied folklore has been defined in this way: "We define applied folklore as the utilization of the theoretical concepts, factual knowledge, and research methodologies of folklorists in activities or programs meant to ameliorate contemporary social, economic, and technological problems."[27] In applied folklore, folklorists do not become social workers but do bring their expertise to social problems and social and cultural policy making, endeavors explored by, among others, the authors of the short studies published in the aptly named volume *Putting Folklore to Use*, edited by Michael Owen Jones. For example, Marjorie Bard argues that folklorists have important contributions to make in aiding America's homeless population because folklorists, as fieldworkers and ethnographers, are in a strong position to understand the culture of homelessness (whereas social welfare providers typically ignore the actual milieu of the homeless). She suggests that folklorists' familiarity with dealing with oral narration enables them, through textual analysis, to provide novel understandings of the actual experience of homelessness.[28] David Shuldiner recounts how he utilized his skills as a folklorist to stimulate dialogue with elderly people, indeed a population folklorists have historically worked with because the elderly have been assumed to be living repositories of cultural tradition. By getting them to talk about such subjects as local history, the immigration experience and traditional arts and music, all subjects of interest in folklore studies, he enabled them "to assert their sense of self and community belonging, as reflections of their continued vitality and engagement."[29]

Jones himself has been interested in a folklore perspective on organizational behavior, contending that "Folklorists' knowledge, skills, and abilities are needed to help diagnose organizational problems as well as to enhance communication, promote creativity, and maintain a climate of social support."[30] He notes that specialists in organizational behavior—a field which has many practical applications, notably in business—have only recently begun studying the traditional and symbolic aspects of organizations, and of course folklorists specialize in studying the traditional and the symbolic. To better understand these aspects, something folklorists may facilitate, can bring benefits to organizations and those who belong to them. Sara Selene Faulds suggests that folklorists' field techniques and folkloristic concepts can aid in the planning of public spaces through the study of how people use their environments.[31] And David Hufford, a professor at the Pennsylvania State College of Medicine, has repeatedly pointed out how folklorists can help medical practitioners; for example, by providing knowledge of folk medical practices and of folk concepts of disease and healing.[32]

Applied folklore certainly can involve bringing folklore into nontraditional environments; it is, however, much more concerned with how folklorists' skills and knowledge (such as their ability to carry out intensive fieldwork and to bridge communication gaps across cultures) can be transferred to situations beyond the study of folklore as such. It is less directly involved in providing a knowledge of folk traditions. The broader field of public sector folklore, which may involve the dissemination of knowledge about folk traditions through public agencies or museums, is more relevant to that task (and this book), though the extent to which public sector folklorists have influenced the broad public understanding and use of folklore has been limited.

NATIONALISM, IDEOLOGIES, AND POLITICS

We would do well to remember that the beginnings of the modern *study of folklore* were bound up with a wish to use folklore in arenas beyond folklore's natural contexts, notably in the cause of nationalism, national literatures, and national identity. The name of Johann Gottfried Herder is one frequently invoked by folklorists as the great early modern pioneer in turning intellectual interest toward folk materials. Though Herder was certainly many things—"philosopher, philologist, litterateur, anthropologist, social theorist, folklorist, preacher and poet"[33]—his considerable interest in folklore stemmed primarily from his interest in something else: championing the cause of German literature. Folklore was for him something usable outside its existence as folklore, however interesting folklore might be in itself. Herder sought not merely to break with an Enlightenment centered chiefly in France but also to engineer a reaction against a French neoclassical literature that was the paramount literary influence on the continent of Europe. But if much of French literature consisted of stiff imitations of classical models, German imitations of French imitations were even further removed from the vitality of Latin and Greek originals. German literature was cut off from German culture and needed to be redirected to its own Germanic beginnings.

Herder believed that societies evolved through uniform stages of development, beginning with a poetic stage when a society remains relatively uncomplicated and cohesive; at this point an individual "race" is closest to its basic roots and definition of itself, to its basic essence. As the society develops, however, it necessarily becomes more complex and in need of structural developments that take it into prosaic and philosophic stages, stages necessary for development but which take the culture away from fundamental cultural tropes. Herder sought to redirect German literature precisely toward the cultural essence that characterized the earlier stage of German "racial" development. To find that cultural essence he turned to medieval romances and the folk ballads then being given early scholarly attention by such people as England's Bishop Percy, whose *Reliques of Ancient Poetry* Herder found influential, and in the supposedly simple social milieu wherein ballads and folksongs continued to be created and passed on. In that milieu of folklore the poetic stage continued to exist; the folklore could be used to recapture something of use to writers who would in effect extract it from its actual context. To take the idea a little further, folklore could be used to reveal certain basic, underlying fundamentals of a culture to members of the culture who had nonetheless lost touch with them and thus be used in cultural revitalization.[34]

The influence of Herder's ideas proceeded in at least two directions. On the one hand, it stimulated folklore scholarship, leading to intellectual attempts to understand the nature of folklore and to appreciate it as an important aspect in the interpretation of culture. On the other, it led to an appropriation of folklore by writers, artists, cultural nationalists, and others, who came to see folklore as symbolically important to their endeavors and of use in carrying those endeavors out. Though folklore might have various artistic uses, its expressing underlying cultural fundamentals was particularly important as national identity became more important to artists as well as to others. These two approaches, the scholarly and the aesthetic, have sometimes been closely interconnected.

The famous brothers Jacob and Wilhelm Grimm, though certainly cultural nationalists in their way, represent an immediate move toward the more scholarly approach to folklore. They may speak poetically of their tales as relics of the past when they describe them in terms of vegetation imagery:

When the heavens have unleashed a storm, or when some other natural disaster has battered down a whole harvest, we may well find that in some sheltered corner by the roadside, under hedges and shrubs, a few ears of corn have survived. When the sun begins to shine again, they will grow, hidden and unnoticed.[35]

But their surviving ears of corn, that is their folktales, they saw as historical documents to be looked at for knowledge of the past. As one commentator says, "Songs and tales were basic to their study of philology. . . . To Jacob and Wilhelm they [the tales] were a strong and vital part of mankind's half-forgotten past."[36] That they were interested in intellectual understandings of history is perhaps seen even more clearly in Jacob Grimm's *Deutsche Mythologie* in which he, for example, notes that still current folk customs of hanging wreaths on and performing ring dances under certain trees demonstrates the ancient German reverence for holy trees, or that the Thuringian custom of dressing a "lettuce-king" in green each Whit-Thursday sheds light on ancient religious concerns for fertility and the return of the seasons.[37]

But Herder's cultural nationalism also developed in less scientific ways with a variety of implications for folklore as seen and used nationalistically and politically, and it is these implications that are more relevant to this book or at least to the premises that underlie it. Unfortunately, Herder's emphasis on German nationhood appealed to Nazi interests in racial purity in the period during which the National Socialists were in power in Germany, and folkloristic thinking was used to lend support to Nazi racist theorizing, a movement that in turn led to dreadful atrocities perpetrated upon those insufficiently "Aryan" or "Nordic." Racist ideology, supported by folkloristic conceptions, justified atrocity. There has been considerable recent debate on the extent to which German folklore scholars aided and abetted this development, but certainly there was also considerable popular interest in such topics as Germanic mythology as a base for German national identity during the Nazi period. To cite a single example of such interest, there was the collecting activity of Karl Theodor Weigel, who began as early as 1912 to record, via sketches and later photographs, a variety of what he presumed to be ancient German symbols painted on or incised into house beams, furniture, and folk implements. These were presumed to communicate an ancient symbolic language that gave insight into the worldviews of the German people and their "racial soul." But museums of the period attempted to suggest, for example through costume displays, connections between ancient Germanic tribespeople and the National Socialists,[38] while Heinrich

Himmler himself corresponded with those involved in folklore about their interests.[39]

The Nazis have hardly been the only group in recent times to use folklore for political reasons, though these attempts have had varying relationships to nationalism. In early twentieth-century China, for example, intellectuals who sought to revive Chinese culture looked to folklore in the context of the New Culture Movement, finding in folklore an aspect of culture that was Chinese but not tainted by association with old, rejected Confucianist culture. Sandra Eminov writes, "The notion that the folk possessed a special, long-ignored oral literature that preserved uniquely Chinese virtues and traditions was an idea which captured the imagination of the new intellectuals."[40] Though folklore might sometimes be criticized as a repository of "superstition," it obviously had its uses, and later Mao Tse-tung and the communists found folklore useful in attempts to identify with the common people. In the Soviet Union, though in the 1920s there were calls for the eradication of folklore as reflecting the interests of the ruling classes (tsars, for example, were important characters in folktales), Maxim Gorki "made a powerful appeal for folklore," seeing its close connection to the people, its optimism about the aspirations of the masses, and its artistic value. He "opened the eyes of the party leaders"[41] that folklore could actually advance communism, and Lenin came to see folklore as a form of "monumental propaganda," and traditional singers were actually directed to compose songs reflecting approved communist ideas; folklorists collected with an eye to finding material that best embodied Marxist ideology. In the Soviet Ukraine, it was recognized that folklore could democratize literature and that folklore "underscores the prominence of the laboring masses in all matters that pertain to artistic creativity,"[42] positioning folklore as a means for promoting a Marxist aesthetic.

What is probably the most celebrated and perhaps most pervasive use of folklore for nationalistic reasons is, of course, what happened in Finland in the nineteenth century in the creation and promotion of that country's "national epic," the *Kalevala*. This great poem was in effect constructed by Elias Lönnrot out of oral folk poems that had been collected in the region of Karelia by Lönnrot and others. Their motives were patriotic ones. In the face of Russian annexation of Finland, they sought to create an awareness of Finland as a nation with a great culture by proving that Finland had a glorious past, that Finnish as a language could support great literature (whereas the country had virtually none), and that it could in fact serve as a national language (the upper classes spoke Swedish). Through the fiction that the

Kalevala was a unified epic from ancient times, these cultural nationalists succeeded in producing a national symbol and a national focus of expression. As William A. Wilson writes, "Rising Finnish self-esteem in the second half of the nineteenth century can be traced directly to the publication of the *Kalevala*."[43] Of course the *Kalevala* went on to become a potent national symbol ("the less it was read," Wilson notes, "the more it was cited"[44]) used for the purposes of propaganda in an independent Finland, used to stimulate the idea "that Finland should develop into a strong, militaristic nation"[45] (with notably anti-Soviet and anticommunist tendencies) and to promote the notion of a "greater Finland" with borders beyond actual political boundaries. There was a grand celebration of the centennial anniversary of the *Kalevala* in 1935 with a variety of events and programs, although there was also an annual "Kalevala Day" with student marching groups and singers gathering around the statue of Elias Lönnrot, the epic's great editor, in the capital.

The *Kalevala* "movement" of course involves both literary reconfiguring of folk materials and their political manipulation, literature and folklore both playing important roles in nationalistic political movements. In another, modern African context, David Kerr notes that folklore has been "usurped" through "the staging of traditional songs and dances to praise the achievements of post-independence politicians," though he primarily has given attention to another "political" use of folklore, which involves literary recasting, notably the creation of popular performances based on folk forms as part of attempts to promote social development in African villages. In Zambia he was part of a project aimed at using traditional "plots and motifs, along with . . . songs, formulae, proverbs . . . to feed the theatre traditions"[46] being worked out at a university. However, attempts were also made to put traditional forms to use in terms of social development. He discusses, for example, the adaptation of a *nthano* (tale with song) about a young wife who neglects cleaning her home and is confronted by a visiting mother-in-law who encounters, as a result of the neglect, an infestation of bedbugs to promote the work of village health councils. Here the folklore becomes recycled as popular performance for quite immediate "political" purposes involving social change.

Ideological uses of folklore need not be tied very closely to either politics or nationalism (although both have been especially powerful forces influencing interest in folk materials). Simon J. Bronner has argued that Americans made a variety of ideological uses of folklore in the late nineteenth and earlier twentieth centuries that were tied to political and nationalistic conceptions only indirectly, if at all. The folkloristics that developed, particularly in England, toward the end of the nineteenth century was evolutionary in its theoretical bases, folklore being seen as "survival" from earlier, more primitive stages of a culture that had now evolved into the more civilized; culture had left the early stages behind but carried folklore remnants into modern times. The past was "usable" as a prelude toward understanding the present, and folklore was "usable" in providing insight into the nature of the past. Such a view, "decentering civilization toward the present," would appeal to nineteenth-century Americans, not only because it gave study a utilitarian cast but also because their attachment to progress would cause Americans to appreciate a conception of the study of culture that suggested a way to observe and evaluate social and even industrial progress. Folklore could be used as a yardstick for measuring "the remarkable material progress of America as a culmination of the civilization process,"[47] something of interest not only to scholars but also to the general public.

Thus at the Chicago World's Fair in 1893 a prominent display of folk artifacts along the midway called attention to the "people 'who have shared least in the general advance'"[48] of progress, thus highlighting the magnitude of the advance. It was no accident that University of Chicago professor William I. Knapp, president of the Chicago Folklore Society, would call attention to Chicago as the "centripetal maelstrom" of American progress, or that folklorist and ethnologist Otis T. Mason, when he spoke at the Fair, saw the city as "the epitome of creativity,"[49] in contrast to the more conventionalized and imitative productions of folk tradition. Americans of the period also used African American folklore to "measure . . . how far blacks had come or could go" (100). The general public were made very aware of black folklore, notably spirituals, folktales, and superstitions, and these became emblematic of black "cultural difference," but they could also indicate levels of progress. The dignified spirituals, for example, "could be reassuringly heard as signifying the promise of black adoption of white religious virtues," although they could also be used to underscore the goodness of the romantically conceived old plantation (a topic dealt with in chapter 2). The Uncle Remus tales of Joel Chandler Harris, which became extremely popular, created an image of slavery times that was accommodationist in depicting a kindly black man passing on his cultural treasures to whites. Booker T. Washington urged the collection "in some museum the relics that mark its [the race's] progress," and the founding of a folklore collecting group at Hampton Institute, the renowned black institution of higher education, in part stressed that they were dealing with cultural materials that were, in the words of A. M. Bacon, the group's white mentor, "now happily passing away."[50]

REVIVALS

Folk materials have also undergone "revivals" in a number of contexts. "Revival" is a problematic term. Among other inherent problems with the term, it can refer to both the adaptation of folklore to new contexts as during the North American folksong revival, and it can refer to efforts to revitalize existing cultures in situ, as with attempts to revitalize Scottish Gaelic culture or Cajun culture and language in Louisiana. In the United States the most widely known revivals have involved the appropriation or adaptation of folk materials, folksongs, and folk narratives, to new, non-folk contexts.

In the United States in the twentieth century, for example, folksongs came to play a significant role in left-wing political movements (thus tying revivals to other political contexts noted in the previous section). Although the earlier American communists took rather little interest in folklore, the coalition of left-wing groups that was called the Popular Front, which was formed in 1935, showed an expanded interest in American culture, and many involved in the Front became "interested in the popularization of folklore and its promulgation as the culture of the American people." Folksongs were not associated with the "bourgeois" tunesmithing of Tin Pan Alley but could be seen as "a product of the American cultural experience associated with the rural lower classes" and hence "might describe much of the roots and aspirations of the masses."[51] Folksongs could thus be projected as a form of the expression of the people, a "guiding light" for communing with something basic in the culture of the American masses, and Popular Front members formed such organizations as People's Songs and People's Artists and founded *Sing Out!*, the publication that played such an important role in the folksong revival, though its ideological underpinnings were later diminished. Indeed, what later developed was what Robert Cantwell has called "the politically more innocent folk revival of the next decade," when the *Folkways Anthology of American Folk Music*, produced by Harry Smith, in particular "reframed [folk music] as a kind of avant-garde art."[52] A more politically ideological background certainly had an effect on this later folksong revival and continued to shape it to some extent, but it had its own nonpolitical and commercial dimensions with bohemian coffee house venues, campus folksong clubs, and televised hootenannies (as folksong–singing events came to be called).[53] In itself it was an important American example of folklore being recycled outside traditional folk contexts, a great variety of people recreating folk forms in new ways and places for various reasons. Ellen Stekert's classification of the participants in the folksong revival of the 1950s and 1960s into the traditional singers who made appearances for nontraditional audiences; the emulators (Stekert originally called them imitators) who learned a traditional style of performance; the utilizers who adapted folk material to "accepted city aesthetics"[54]; and those who created a new aesthetic that merged traditional music with a variety of other influences remains a useful configuration in looking at the ways in which such "revivals" utilize and adapt the folk (although the later storytelling revival followed a different projectory). Though what Neil Rosenberg terms the "great boom" of the folksong revival lasted only a few years, the revival had a significant impact on American society and culture and surely was a notable example of traditional folklore carried outside its original, historical context. (The great boom lasted probably from 1958, when the Kingston Trio's recording of "Tom Dooley" was a hit song until the late 1960s when "singing about social and political problems was no longer adequate" during "years of [actual] political activism," and "political events overwhelmed the revival."[55])

The "revival" of folk materials, however, need not be political or ideological. Not only did the politics of the folksong revival tend to dissipate, but the storytelling revival of recent decades, for example, does not share in the politics that at least helped to initiate the folksong revival, though it certainly also involved the recycling of traditional folk material into new, nontraditional venues. This complex North American movement involved the emergence of a number of persons who came to develop repertoires of orally told narratives, in many cases relying upon traditional folktales for their material, folktales inevitably drawn from, at least initially, printed collections of traditional tales. In some ways this movement traces back to late-nineteenth-century attempts to introduce traditional tales into library and school contexts, not for adult listeners but for children, in itself an important reuse of folklore. Such "storytelling came to be regarded as an important pedagogic tool,"[56] and a National Storytelling League was founded for teachers in 1903. In the 1960s, however, "a more dynamic style of storytelling" began to appear (sometimes those who had started out as librarians or teachers moving on to become the performers). Storytelling festivals, notably in Jonesboro, Tennessee, and in Toronto, were established and became major venues for narrators.

Kay Stone argues that the basic differences that can be perceived between traditional narrators (who come out of contexts in which the oral tradition has persisted and who do continue to exist and sometimes have interacted with and influenced phases of the storytelling revival) and nontraditional and what she calls neo-traditional narrators is a matter of the relationship that prevails between teller and audience. She further notes that the neo-traditional narrators, though they may not be "historically or culturally connected to a long-standing narrative community" nonetheless are the "stepchildren" of that oral tradition who have developed a sort of oral tradition of their own. Their relationship to traditional tales has varied over the years, but the recycling of traditional stories, especially magic tales, has been an important element in their endeavors: "the *Märchen*, both traditional and newly created, retained a central position in neotraditional performances. Gradually, more and more tellers turned away from traditional tales . . . . Still, fairy tales continued to be told by many performers."[57] This storytelling revival certainly calls attention to the complexity of the relationship between traditional folklore and its reuse by those outside of actual folk contexts.[58]

COMMERCIAL USES

The use of folklore for commercial reasons is surely a worldwide phenomenon, though given the American penchant for business, there certainly has been considerable American exploitation of folk forms for the purpose of making money (Priscilla Denby coined the term "folklure" to apply to this process, though that word never achieved much currency[59]). Among the most obvious have been the commercial exploitation of proverbs and proverbial sayings, such as Wolfgang and Barbara Meider have noted, particularly in connection with advertizing "headlines"; that is, the short ad slogans that aim to initially capture our attention.

> *This is where the proverb is useful, often even in its original form. The proverb "Good things come in small packages" certainly was an appropriate headline for advertising a 35mm camera, and the statement "To see it is to believe it" quite literally invited the reader to come and take a look at another camera.*
>
> *. . . A last example from the Burlington (Vermont) Savings Bank has not just one but three proverbs as headlines: "The early bird gets the worm," "A stitch in time saves nine," and "A penny saved is a penny earned" . . . The advertisement actually uses the proverbs in the old didactic fashion, attempting to convince the reader of the necessity for saving.*[60]

Commonly, advertisers will also use proverb patterns for headlines and adapt and parody proverbs for ads: "Different Volks for different folks" ("Different strokes for different folks") to stress a variety of car models, for example. Other commentators have pointed to the use of proverbial language in advertising (and Mieder and Mieder note a long tradition of illustrating proverbs, including in modern comic strips and cartoons).[61]

Similarly, Linda Dégh has discussed the prevalence of elements borrowed from the traditional Märchen in television advertising:

> *Giants, dwarves, fairies, witches, mermaids, anthropomorphic objects and personified principles appear on the television screen to enlighten the viewer on the value of certain commodities as often as the clowning of comedians. . . .*
>
> *In [one] commercial, Cinderella scrubs the floor with ammonia while her sisters, dressed in fine garb, leave for the dance. She scrubs and scrubs, then waxes and rewaxes, until her Fairy Godmother comes to her rescue. She hands her a bottle of "Mr. Clean," an effective floor polish which shines the floor without waxing. . . .*
>
> *Mr. Clean himself also appears in a leading role. This benevolent genie with shaven head and gold earrings . . . looks as if he had been summoned from the peripheries of the Arabian Nights. Sleeping Beauty is also a popular consumer persuader; in one ad she prompts the viewer to buy the softest bedding and lingerie ever produced. In another commercial, Prince Charming is unable to kiss Snow White awake until clean-shaven and emanating the right fragrance of Palmolive Rapid Shave. The talking mirror of the Wicked Stepmother is also utilized; it reveals the name of the moisture cream that made Snow White's beauty superior to hers.*
>
> . . . .
>
> *According to the elf who dwells in the Hollow Tree, the secret of Mr. Keebler's Pecan Sandies is that they are baked by elves.*[62]

Sometimes the commercial factors affecting the recycling of folklore have been particularly direct and obvious. As was noted above, one of the promoters of the White Top folk festival in Virginia sought to use the festival to help in the establishment of a planned resort hotel in the area, and the encouragement of tourism and its commercial impact has often been at least a factor in the maintenance of various festivals.

Many of the manifestations that enraged Richard Dorson to coin the term fakelore stemmed from commercial endeavors of one sort or another. Certainly two of America's most widely known "folk heroes"—Paul Bunyan and John Henry—owe their celebrity to having been plucked from folklore and projected into other media, in part for commercial reasons (though the dividing line between commerce and art is sometimes a fine one, as in a capitalist society artists and their promoters surely seek to turn a profit).

As a folk figure, Paul Bunyan, the logger of prodigious strength and accomplishment, appeared in the oral tall tales of American lumbering camps, and there were early twentieth-century collectors of these tales to attest to their folk origins.[63] However, in 1914 W. B. Laughead produced a pamphlet containing stories about Paul Bunyan for the Red River Lumber Company (which had offices in Minneapolis and Chicago and in California) as an advertising and public relations vehicle for the company. Although it was not initially a great success, perhaps because it kept relatively close to the language and perspective of loggers, Laughead kept producing Bunyan pamphlets for the company and one he did in 1922 "caught on beyond the advertiser's fondest hopes."[64] Not only was the initial printing of 10,000 copies soon gone, but it kept being reprinted nearly every year into the 1940s until more than 100,000 copies were in print, given away by the company to promote its products; at one time one of the company's lines was called Paul Bunyan's Pine.

Then Paul Bunyan began to appear in print in forms other than Red River Lumber's advertising pamphlets. In 1916 Ida Virginia Turney published a sort of chapbook of Bunyan stories she said she had collected in Oregon (though they seem to bear the mark of Laughead's hand). In 1924 Esther Shephard published the first full-length book of tales about Paul, while James Stevens brought out a similar volume. His ultimately sold 75,000 copies, and he later did a second Bunyan book. Literary critics like humor scholar Constance Rourke took note of both Shephard and Stevens, who were essentially popularizers attempting to produce material for a reading public, although several serious writers, beginning with Robert Frost in 1921 and including Carl Sandburg, W. H. Auden, and Louis Untermeyer (who produced a lavishly illustrated, boxed volume of Bunyan tales for the Heritage Society), turned to Paul Bunyan as a subject. Beginning with an article in the magazine for high school students, the *Scholastic*, in 1926, Paul Bunyan has appeared in a variety of publications for younger readers. Bunyan thus went from folk figure to one exploited for commercial advertising to one used both by commercial and more literary authors.

John Henry, the "steel driving man" who died in a great contest with a machine (and whose story is recounted more fully in chapter 1) had a development not unlike Paul Bunyan's: moving from folk ballad and legend to novels, a Broadway show, radio broadcasts, and juvenilia. As a folklorist,

Richard Dorson resented the confusing of actual folk tradition with popularizations based, often tenuously, on folk tradition and the passing off of the one as the other. And he stood aghast at another American trend of the 1920s, 1930s, and 1940s, the invention in print of figures presented as folk heroes who had virtually no basis in oral tradition, figures like Annie Christmas, invented by Louisiana regionalist Lyle Saxon and a friend after a night of drinking in the French Quarter.[65] This seemed to Dorson a form of fakery and he labeled it accordingly as fakelore. Yet even such invention of tradition (a subject studied in terms wider than folk tradition by Eric Hobsbawm and his collaborators, who have in mind a process considerably broader than Dorson's concept of fakelore and indeed a process that does not necessarily involve any sort of fakery or even what folklorists would label folklore[66]), whatever its relation to folklorism, is a use of folklore, not of specific oral traditions perhaps, but of broad folk themes and of the very idea of what folklore is and what it means. Alan Dundes has argued that fakelore is a rather old process, including such developments as Alan MacPherson's creation of the Ossian poems in the eighteenth century and passing them off as the work of Scottish oral bards, and he traces the process to, again, nationalism. Fakelore, Dundes says, comes into play particularly when a nation has an inferiority complex and thus a need to have and, if necessary, produce hoary traditions to call its own.[67] That is, it comes particularly out of nationalistic considerations. But its ramifications go beyond that, and the appeal of "tradition" is not simply a result of nationalistic yearnings, though certainly it may be tied to place and to cultural or political group.

TOURISM

Tourism is a complex phenomenon including a great variety of kinds of travel. Cultural tourism is in itself complex and not well defined. Tourists in part travel to experience cultures not their own ("le différent," as the winner of a French contest said to explain what one expected of a voyage[68]), and that experience may be a very superficial one or a more profound one. Folklore often has come to be seen as characteristic of a particular place, whether an entire nation or something smaller like a region or a town or village. Hence it may become emblematic of experiencing that place, of encountering what is different and "typical" of that place. Because folklore may be seen as something that enjoys a particular cultural fundamentalism, to experience it is to experience something particularly "authentic" in and about a place (although, in fact, as Bausinger suggests, this may lead instead to "the inevitability of the inauthentic"[69]). Hence certain musical performances, or types of costume, or folk artifacts, or even dramatic performances like passion plays may become important in travel to a place and in how places are promoted by the travel industry and by the culture industry. In New Orleans certain kinds of traditional street parades are featured in travel brochures and can even be staged for visiting groups outside their usual contexts (actual performers may complain that at the same time local authorities are promoting these folk manifestations of authentic culture for tourism purposes, often they are impeding their performance in their usual, historical contexts through unrealistic permitting procedures or even police harassment). In the tourist center of Taos, New Mexico, at one time local merchants decorated the trash can placed helpfully outside a place of business with replicas of *retablos*; that is, the folk paintings of saints characteristic of the area's Hispanic population (and presumably reflective of local culture and of encountering it). In one region of Germany cowbells came to be seen as iconic of the place, and in recent years 80 percent of cowbells are made to sell to visitors, as opposed to 20 percent for cows.[70] (Indeed "folk art" and "folk crafts," whether produced for tourists or other contexts, particularly lend themselves to marketing, each category consisting as it does of objects that can be sold in galleries, in souvenir shops, or through catalog sales. Bed coverings in traditional American quilt patterns are available in various forms through catalogs, often mass produced in foreign countries. Takeoffs on the "flash art" signs of a bygone America may be sold in shops. All sorts of "visionary" pieces or just plain amateur work may be presented as "folk art" in the marketplace, as may be a great range of depictions of folklife. Although such work may be a far cry from what folklorists would consider folk art, some conception of what "folk art" is comes to be carried over into the new context.)

Demetrios Loukatos points out that the role of folklore in tourism is hardly a new one, tracing current touristic interest in such things as Greek handicrafts back to earlier tours aimed at benefiting from cultural knowledge. Further, he suggests the complexity of folklore and tourism by noting that touristic interest in folklore can benefit local cultures in promoting cultural revivals:

The interaction between visitors and "hosts" . . . takes on a special character at the time of folkloric events, and thus enhances respect for tradition in a significant way. In "modern" times young Greeks were beginning to look down on the customs and songs of their grandparents when they saw, to their astonishment, that young tourists liked to watch traditional village occupations, took photographs of each other beside looms or fishing boats, listened to the melodies of ballads and laments, and even joined in popular dances.[71]

So, the interaction of what Loukatos terms "ethnological folklore" and "tourist folklore" ("specially staged out of place and out of time"[72]) is complex and involves mutual influences. We cannot always easily separate folklore from folklorism and there is much to be said for looking at both, and not only in touristic contexts.

The subsequent chapters of this book are not intended to provide a complete history or discussion of folklorism or of the multitudinous ways in which folklore is, in our modern and postmodern worlds, de-situated from folk and re-situated into non-folk contexts in the recycling process whereby folklore is "used" by the non-folk. Rather, they provide considerations of several instances in which this recycling process has taken place to provide a sort of background for further looking at the process itself. Folklore has many features that make it appealing to those who discover it outside its natural contexts or who would recycle it in other contexts, wherever they find it, and assign it meanings (though they may assume that such meanings are inherent and their meanings may bear a relationship to original, folk meanings). Attempts to recycle folklore may be obviously commercial (proverbs or stories used to promote a product, the appropriation of the term folk art to assist in marketing crafts or paintings, the advertising of local customs to lure tourists to a region); aesthetic (the reuse of folk plots in plays or novels, the addition of references to folk mores in a literary work to provide local color); largely intellectual (appropriating folk heroes to provide national identity, using folklore as a documentary source to support theories about the past or about strange realities); or even quite personal (becoming familiar with local folklore to find a sense of belonging). Whatever the motives, the folkloric meanings, real or imagined, become central.

Though folklore is international in scope, and though the "same" stories or customs or sayings may be found widely distributed, folklore is sometimes assumed to be a very local phenomenon. As such it can be a focus for local identity and for tourism (a factor that plays an important role in this book's first chapter). This first chapter, "'Authentic Local Culture': The Open Textuality of a Folk Tradition," looks at a recent literary work, Colson

Whitehead's novel *John Henry Days*, thus beginning with the time-honored "folklore and literature" connection. However, the novel itself raises a number of questions about how folklore is re-situated; it examines, though through fiction, a whole range of folklore recycled, looking at how the John Henry story persists in memory and through reinvention and in strategies for promoting tourism and local identity and in individual lives; this chapter is not intended as a study only of how folklore is relevant to literary meanings but of how folklore inevitably exists in a number of contexts and, indeed, gets recycled constantly into new ones. Given the amorphous nature of folk tradition, the concept of the open text (borrowed by Roland Barthes from Umberto Eco) may be a particularly useful way of looking at folklore generally.

If folklore can become the focus for something like a local festival and a tourist economy through a connection to local identity, so too can it feature in ethnic identity and other forms of regional and personal identity. Even those involved in the "serious" study of folklore may come to that study for personal reasons and their folklore collecting activities may use folklore not only to understand it intellectually but also to satisfy a number of personal issues, including identity and status. The second chapter, "'In This Folk-Lore Land': Establishing Race, Class, and Identity through Folklore Studies" (co-authored by Rosan Augusta Jordan), looks at folklore collecting activities in two different time periods, the 1890s, when the Louisiana Folklore Association, a branch of the national American Folklore Society, was active in New Orleans; and the 1930s, when noted local author Lyle Saxon led the Louisiana affiliate of another attempt to collect and study folklore on a national level, the Louisiana Writers' Project. Although these were in part attempts to study folklore and to take folklore seriously, clearly those involved in these endeavors were concerned with issues of personal, race, and class identity, and they used folklore as a means of establishing identities, in fact less concerned with intellectual understandings of folklore than with how folklore could be used for establishing and explaining who they themselves were in relation to it.

Indeed, another writer associated with Louisiana (though more famous for his work in Japan and discussed here more for his work in the Caribbean) approached folklore in a similar way. Lafcadio Hearn wrote about folklore to spread knowledge of culture, and he also used folklore for reasons having to do with personal identity, an endeavor that ties him to both the Louisiana Association folklorists and Lyle Saxon. We might assume that popular nonfiction writing—essays and journalism were Hearn's forte—would at least attempt to merely document folklore and inform readers about folk-lore rather than to "use" folklore for ideological or aesthetic or personally aggrandizing purposes. However, his journalistic writings in the latter part of the nineteenth century provide an interesting example of a writer with particular personal intentions in writing about Creole folklore. Hearn has been seen as a folklorist, or a sort of proto-folklorist, who introduced the reading public to the folklore of Ohio, Louisiana, the Caribbean, and par-ticularly Japan. But he was a perpetual wanderer whose interest in folklore was in finding a personal anchor for his own floating self, and he presented folklore as a means of satisfying these personal needs. The third chapter, "'Unrivalled Charms': Folklore, Nonfiction, and Lafcadio Hearn," looks at Hearn's journalism from this perspective. Though in a sense it returns to considering literary uses of folk materials, it looks not at the imaginative literature like fiction and poetry in which context folklore has usually been considered but at how even what may seem to be straightforward nonfic-tion can recycle folklore in a manner that involves a personal agenda.

What may appear to be attempts merely to document folklore can in-volve a variety of perspectives, ideologies, and intentions that in fact present folklore in reshaped forms. Photography may seem to be an art form that merely "presents reality," though students of photography have long recog-nized the medium's power to present reality in particular ways. Folklore and folklife have been a popular subject for photographs, and the fourth chap-ter, "Photographing Folklife: Document, Symbol, Propaganda," looks at how those who have photographically documented folklore in one American state have used folklore for a variety of artistic, political, and other ideologi-cal purposes.

Romantic visions of folklore as something charmingly quaint, or as col-orful representation of place or group, or even as a means of expressing fun-damental, perhaps otherwise lost, human perspectives have certainly shaped how folklore has been recycled. Nationalistic perspectives have often been romantic ones, and tourism's agenda for folk materials may push the sort of romanticism that would draw people to travel to particular places. Ro-manticism is certainly at least an element in seeing folklore as a repository of knowledge lost to or ignored by the modern world. Chapter 5, "'The Age of Fire and Gravel': 'Occult' and 'Alternative History' Uses of Folklore" looks at the use of folklore as a document containing information unknown to most of us—information about cataclysmic events in ancient times, about visits by extraterrestrial beings, about extraordinary and unknown parts of the earth. Romanticism is at least an element also in American expatriates' attempts to come to terms with foreign cultures. Chapter 6, "Americans and the Folk Arts in Mexico: Tourism, Fine Art, Architecture, Interior Decoration, International Relations," looks at how those Americans discovering Mexico in the 1920s and 1930s (and in later time periods also) looked to the folk arts for emotional, aesthetic, and intellectual links to the foreign country in which they found themselves, including a push for using folk art for interior decoration and architectural inspiration and looking to the folk arts as a tool in promoting international relations.

Folklore clearly has multiple appeals for those who stand outside particular folk traditions and who then choose to "use" folklore. Its putative connections to place—to nation or *Heimat* or village—render it appealing for establishing nationalistic sentiments or regional identity or sense of place, whether for the purposes of tourism, politics, or personal belonging. Its presumed connection to groups—ethnic, class, or place-based—makes it a natural symbol for affiliation or disaffiliation with a group or with some social entity associated with a group. Perhaps particularly in times of change, folklore's seeming fundamentalism renders it a key element in heritage, evoking nostalgia, a sense of stability in the midst of flux, or potent feelings of belonging. Aspects of its familiarity (a plot, familiar language, a design) tell marketers that it can be used to sell us things, if products can be tied into its meanings. Because it has meanings (whether or not these are original to its folkloric context or assigned by others or are some combination of original and putative meanings), writers and photographers and artists of various kinds can use it to extend their own aesthetic intentions. Folk creations—songs or tales or dances or artifacts—can be recreated outside their usual contexts, either by folk performers and artisans themselves at such venues as educational or celebratory festivals or by revivalists in a variety of situations. Those who seek "hidden" knowledge can assume that folklore encodes understandings otherwise lost to us in terms of interpreting history and human existence and spirituality. There are those who have, because folklore has been seen as somehow "childlike" or perhaps even as wholesome and wise, "worked to fit [folklore] into public school curriculums, children's camp song repertoires, and other didactic entertainment for the young."[73]

All of this is merely to return to the point that folklore has many "uses" outside its historical cultural contexts and, as such, many meanings and levels of cultural significance. Indeed, in the postmodern world most of us will encounter folklore not within the bounds of particular traditional contexts at all, but elsewhere. Folklorists need to pay close attention to these nontraditional contexts where folklore comes to be recycled, for they play a powerful role in shaping and being shaped by how folklore is perceived by most people. Perhaps folklorists should see this complex recycling process as a sort of continuum. At one end of the continuum (if only because folklorists have spent a long time and a lot of effort exploring it) is the incorporation of folklore into literary works—by Chaucer and Shakespeare; by Hawthorne and Atwood.[74] At the opposite end (opposite if only because, unlike the study of folklore in literature, it is a fairly new development in folkloristics) might be put recent attempts to look at how folklore fits into mass cultural contexts (though such attempts by authors like Linda Dégh and Ronald Baker look not merely at how the mass media "uses" folklore but also at how the mass media become new conduits for transmitting folklore, a factor that suggests a very complex process indeed).[75] Between these poles (if that is what they are) lies a wide range of folkloric recyclings. Indeed, the very history of folklore studies needs to be looked at in terms of how it has been shaped by attempts to use folklore for a variety of purposes. But whether we speak of folklorism or ideological or literary "uses" of folklore, this is an area of interest that requires careful and considerable ongoing attention. Linda Dégh asks, about folk narrative in particular, "What makes modern . . . society maintain its interest in folktales? . . . What are the successful media devices that carry the tales and adjust them to up-to-date needs?"[76] Neil Rosenberg suggests that we need to ask questions about how folklore revivals address "issues of politics, theory, and aesthetics."[77] Ellen Stekert says that "we must also ask ourselves what the [folksong revival] movement means."[78] These questions are all part of the larger matter of understanding the de- and re-situating, the recycling of folklore beyond traditional folk conduits and part of the lovely messiness that results.

"AUTHENTIC LOCAL CULTURE"

The Open Textuality of a Folk Tradition

◇◇

Anyone noticing the title of Colson Whitehead's novel, *John Henry Days*, referencing as it does John Henry, one of the most celebrated figures in American folklore, might assume that it would attract the attention of folklorists.[1] Closer examination of this novel reveals that it is certainly an interesting, indeed an absorbing novel that "uses" folklore. It is, however, much more than that. It is a work of fiction that provides a discourse on how folklore in America is viewed, exploited, recycled, transmitted, transformed, and made symbolic. In its very use of folk materials the novel examines how folk materials are used in a number of contexts, giving the reader a fictional look at what folklorists, communities, the media, the government, commercial interests, and others "do" with folklore. It treats both the history of a folk tradition and the history of folklore scholarship and is very much a consideration of larger issues relating to folklore as reinterpreted in the modern world, a provocative look at the modern re-situation of folklore into other modes of communication and at some of the consequences and implications of such folkloric recycling. It is a prime example of folklore's being recycled but also examines—through the slightly refracted prism of fiction—how and why folklore gets recycled in some of the ways with which *Folklore Recycles* as a book is concerned. That is, it calls our attention to a number of the reasons why and manners in which folklore gets re-situated in new contexts.

· · ·

As the novel begins, a number of people with interests in John Henry converge on two rural West Virginia towns, Talcott and Hinton, on opposite sides of the Big Bend Tunnel where John Henry—the American "folk hero" who is at the center of a large body of traditional song—is said to have lost his life in a fabled contest against the power of a steam drill. They are coming for the first annual John Henry Days, a civic festival set to mark John Henry's connection to the area: representatives of the U.S. Postal Service, using the occasion to launch the American Folk Heroes series of stamps;[2] public relations operatives promoting the festival as a means of stimulating tourism; a band of media flacks lured to the festival by the p.r. people; Pamela Street, the daughter of an obsessive collector of John Henry materials, whom the town hopes to persuade to sell her late father's collection to fill a planned museum; and a stamp collector named Alphonse Miggs, who specializes in railroad stamps. The residents themselves are pushing John Henry and their alleged connection to him: the ambitious mayor who originally approached the p.r. firm; the motel owners who accommodate the out-of-town visitors and who hope for a wave of tourism; the locals who come for the steel-driving contest, or to sell food or John Henry figurines, or have a day of solidarity and fun; a local boy who entertains the visiting dignitaries at a welcoming dinner by actually singing a version of the ballad, an act that ties the song to the modern context of tourism, public relations, and newly minted festival. That is, from the outset of the novel and as the novel develops, the reader is made aware of a number of ways in which a traditional folksong and the "legend" surrounding it take on new meanings and uses beyond their traditional, historical contexts.

Various flashbacks take us to other times and places, when John Henry enters into the lives of various people. We see Guy Johnson, one of the two actual folklorists to have published books on John Henry in the 1920s and 1930s, as he visits Hinton to undertake fieldwork. A 1930s saloon blues singer who includes the song in his repertoire encounters a white blues collector and record producer. Paul Robeson makes an appearance as he unhappily plays in the Broadway show based on Roark Bradford's John Henry novel. In the 1940s a young girl in Harlem shocks and outrages her obsessively genteel mother by buying sheet music for the John Henry ballad at a seedy establishment. A Brooklyn street hustler tries to get money out of J. Sutter, one of the journalists who shows up in Hinton for free food and drink, by singing the song for him. And in several chapters John Henry himself figures as he works on the tunnel and looks ahead to the planned contest with the machine, a contest that holds both his victory and his doom.

Whitehead is not simply interested in the many permutations of the folklore of John Henry, and his novel develops a number of interrelated stories and pursues a variety of thematic threads, including the personal growth of the journalist J. Sutter and of Pamela Street and the theme of dehumanization by machines.

Pamela is weighted down by her father's John Henry obsession, for which he neglected her and her mother and ultimately himself. The physical existence of his collection, locked away in a New York storage vault, is a continuing reminder of this unhappy past. J leads the empty life of a nomadic puff-piece journalist who is weighted down by his having decided to break a mythical record for continuous attendance at publicity-generated events at which he receives free lodging, food, and drink. Already wearied by the pace of this, he seems wearied, too, by the essential meaninglessness of the actual events he covers and by the pointlessness of his quixotic quest, which is perhaps only possible because he seems to have no emotionally significant connections to other people, a situation made clear by the fruitless sexual relationship he carries on back in New York with a woman called only Monica the Publicist. By the end of the novel both Pamela and J are in different places in their lives as a result of their encounters with each other, the John Henry tradition, and the evolving festival occasion.

And rising out of a meaning that has long been associated with the John Henry story itself, Whitehead pursues another theme, that of human beings engaged in combat with a machine and fighting to beat that machine, though the world has moved on from the crude industrialism of the steam drill to the postindustrialism of the electronic age. Pamela once worked for a software company, an experience which was not only itself dehumanizing, employees cut off from each other while glued to computer screens, but additionally those employees were in a sort of race with the imminent arrival of a program called the Tool, which supposedly would revolutionize the company's endeavor and, like the steam drill, put numerous skilled workers out of work. The journalists covering John Henry Days are fixated on something called the List, which they believe to be a computer file that determines their continuing to receive invitations to cover the events they do. Clearly Whitehead is concerned with questions of dehumanizations of life, especially those that are economic in origin, and with the tension between human beings and their machines, however far society may have progressed from the age of the steam drill. The theme inherent in the ballad of a man contesting with a steam engine has long lent itself to thoughts of how machines may dehumanize us, and Whitehead's novel is the latest and the most brilliant recycling of the story to emphasize such a theme.

Indeed, the local landscape of the Big Bend Tunnel region is still haunted by the economic dehumanization of earlier times. A ghost literally haunts one of the rooms of the local motel—in fact that occupied by Alphonse Miggs, who winds up being a bringer of death—but the whole landscape is haunted by death and suffering, that of the black workers like John Henry who built the Big Bend Tunnel. The novel wants us to remember these men, actually many of them ex-slaves, some buried nearby in forgotten, never-marked graves. But except for John Henry (who of course may not even have been a real person and whose name simply combines the most common first-names recorded for ex-slaves), they and their heroic labors in the face of dangerous and very difficult circumstances *are* largely forgotten, like so many of the African Americans who built the American nation for little pay and less regard. Ironically, they built the tunnel for a company owned by white elites. Ironically, their tunnel did not even survive and caved in to be replaced by a different, still-used tunnel. Ironically, it is the mostly white inhabitants of Talcott and Hinton who may benefit now from the heroic deed of black John Henry and the sacrifices of his African American fellow workers.

The folklore of John Henry, then, serves the author in a variety of ways, as folklore has served other writers for centuries. In creating his own art out of the John Henry story, Whitehead examines how that story resonates for many people, how it has come to have a variety of meanings and uses, how it has evolved in many contexts and through various modes of presentation in public and private domains within and beyond the oral tradition. At a press conference J. Sutter once attended, an academic-turned-rock-musician sang a song about the concept of the open text:

> *Roland Barthes got hit by a truck*
> *That's a signifier you can't duck*
> *Life's an open text*
> *From cradle to death.*
> [337, emphasis original, punctuation added]

The concept of open text stems originally from Umberto Eco's *opera aperta*, that is open works, and from his broader conception of openness in artistic texts. For Eco openness has several meanings. There are certain modern works that are especially open in that they have been created "in a deliberately non-definitive state" so that the reader (or viewer or listener) becomes a collaborator toward a personal completion of the work.[3] More broadly all texts are open: they are subject to a variety of readings. As Roland Barthes was to put it later in "From Work to Text," "the text 'asks the reader for active collaboration.'"[4]

Eco and Barthes focus on stable literary texts, which may change conceptually through response and interpretation but which physically remain fixed. Folklore is by its nature open, in that it is in constant flux in a more literal sense than the constantly reinterpreted literary work. Passed on "by word of mouth," it inevitably changes constantly, develops new forms constantly. When folklore is reinterpreted, its very language and form change. If the John Henry tradition can be called a text, it is a highly "open" one, and the novel demonstrates how collectively we have "interpreted" it into a number of permutations, from local, folk origins to understandings that permeate American society far removed from the contexts in which folksongs and related oral accounts have circulated.

Whitehead accepts the idea that the origin of the John Henry story is in actual events that took place in 1872, accepts it at least in that he has sections that reveal to us the historical John Henry himself as the steel-driving contest approaches, so the starting point for the story and songs is not at issue here. This assumption follows the conclusions reached by the two folklorists who investigated the John Henry tradition in the twenties and thirties, Johnson and Louis Chappell, though Johnson is much more tentative in this conclusion, preferring, he says, to believe in the historicity of the legendary steel driver and the contest despite conflicting evidence, but in fact ending his book by noting: "Maybe there was no John Henry. One can easily doubt it."[5] And their conclusions have been largely accepted by researchers and commentators since, as has been their connecting John Henry with the Big Bend Tunnel (officially the Great Bend Tunnel and named after a nearby bend in the course of the Greenbrier River), because though the folklore of John Henry and the oral testimony Johnson and Chappell themselves recorded locate his contest at various places, the Big Bend was mentioned with overwhelming frequency (and a few informants claimed eyewitness knowledge of John Henry's presence at Big Bend).[6]

But if the ultimate origin of the John Henry tradition is in events, the oral tradition had to be created out of them as the songs took shape (and the tradition is largely a song tradition, comparatively little in the way of prose narrative ever having made an appearance in the folk context itself[7]). Whitehead imagines for us the evolution of the tradition in various episodes through the novel. At one point Pamela, infused with knowledge of the tradition through her father, tells J that originally John Henry appeared in work songs. These were the "hammer songs" used by railroad workers and others who pounded spikes or hand drills and which had verses like:

This old hammer
Killed John Henry
But it won't kill me, boys,
It won't kill me.[8]

Perhaps they date back to the actual Big Bend workplace; perhaps they pre-date the ballad that tells the story of John Henry. But the ballad had to come into existence for the story to spread so widely, and Whitehead gives us a look at its composition.

In a short chapter a man who is apparently a tramp entertainer ("He's been following the rails" and "holds out his hat in taverns after he sings" [102]) sits on a stump and "writes" the song (it must be the ballad, for as he makes it up in his head, he thinks: "Verse, verse, verse, taking the *story* of the man farther" [102; emphasis added]). He might be black or white (de-spite the centrality of John Henry in African American tradition, the ballad has had wide popularity in white tradition and, given the relative rarity of ballads generally as an African American form, mountain whites may have played a key role in the composition of "John Henry"[9]). Evidently he has not created the song, for he thinks of "the man who taught him the song," but is nonetheless a creative recomposer making up a version of his own. Whitehead has a clearly developed sense of the folk process of composition ("The last word of the next line came first . . . . That's half a verse right there . . . . He can only go so far before he has to go back to the beginning. Memo-rize it, chase after that lost word in the verse he just thought up, get it, sing it again and again" [101–2]). Whitehead uses this sense of process not merely to get the beginnings of the song into his narrative but also to suggest the joys of the creative process itself, as the tramp composer sits and puts his song together, "charged, attracting this day and life to him" in an endeavor "like the reverse of dynamite: noise and fire, white light, these elements fly-ing not apart but together into a compact thing" (101). But the folk process also includes a communal aspect, as the composer realizes not only that he is infusing some of his own life experience into the song but that others also have or will have "their own John Henry" (103) and that the song will change as it circulates. Thus Whitehead acknowledges at the beginnings of the tradition the possibilities for the many meanings for John Henry that will appear as the novel progresses and that have infused American culture.

The ballad slowly began to come to the attention of people beyond folk communities through the efforts of folklore collectors who published vari-ant texts in journals and books. The ballad was first noticed in print in the

Journal of American Folklore in 1909, though the first full text did not appear until 1913, in the same journal.[10] A little later such noted collectors as John Lomax and John Harrington Cox published texts and began to comment on the song. The first sound recording of it was made in 1924, sung by Fiddling John Carson, though a black singer, Stovepipe No. 1 (Sam Jones), also recorded it that year (this latter recording never being issued, however, by Columbia, for whom it was made). The books of Johnson and Chappell were a kind of early culmination of interest in "John Henry" and they stimulated further interest.[11]

Whitehead's novel has several collector characters, including the historical Guy Johnson (Whitehead—whether for artistic reasons or because he was mistaken about the racial identity of the historical Johnson, who was white—has him as a black character); Pamela's father, who collected John Henry artifacts but also made field trips to record the song and information about it; and Alphonse Miggs. Miggs is a stamp collector, not a folklore collector, but his centrality in the novel—as a character who initially seems peripheral but who brings the first John Henry Days to a violent conclusion by pulling a gun at the stamp inauguration ceremony—puts collecting into a much broader context and thus calls attention to the significance of collecting as a widespread human activity. Whitehead is suggesting collecting as an important medium of communication in itself and one influential in laying out the meanings of John Henry.[12]

The novel imagines Guy Johnson's difficulties as a fieldworker and its attendant anxieties; his position as a black man trying to interview West Virginia whites; the problems of informants' evasions and quirky memory; the intensity of his competition with Louis Chappell (who would later criticize Johnson and even accuse him of plagiarism, charges that the real Johnson never completely refuted); the complexities of interpreting the material he has with its contradictions and inherent possibilities for error. Yet his collecting and other field research is an obsession; Whitehead has obvious insight into the psychology of fieldwork, though that it is Johnson's obsession is also indicative of the importance Johnson wants to accord the John Henry story, even if the obsessive nature of his quest is not something Johnson as character directly acknowledges.

Despite his problems and anxieties, despite the fact that he feels unable to pull together the John Henry materials as he would like, Whitehead's Guy Johnson assembles meanings for John Henry. (And of course the historical Guy Johnson, it might be argued, did put together our first understandings of John Henry as folk hero, so that Whitehead is in a sense merely acknowledging him as a key actor in the development of our cultural understandings.) Weighted under a "mountain of contradictory evidence" he gains insight, he thinks, "into John Henry's dilemma," that the further he goes into the tunnel, the darker it becomes. Increasing darkness does seem to surround his scholarly endeavor, for John Henry's significance is still hard to comprehend. His ballad has "picked up freight from every work camp, wharf and saloon" (155) providing not merely the usual folkloric variation but a range of half-expressed meanings. Thus Johnson acknowledges the story's multivalent nature, though he realizes that it has become in particular "a reality, a living functioning thing in the folk life of the Negro" (161). Indeed, Johnson's desire to prove the historical reality of the steel driver is because he wants to solidify the very reality of John Henry, something which would make him a more powerful figure in the larger American context. He carries in his billfold the words "*we make our own machines and devise our own contests in which to engage them*" (163; emphasis in original), sentiments that not only call attention to John Henry's symbolic place in the conflict between man and machine but also extend the meaning of his particular conflict to other situations.

The historical Johnson wondered that the John Henry story had not been picked up by "the 'new' Negroes with an artistic bent"[13] to create an epic or a symphony, and perhaps he hoped that his book would bring it to their attention. (Indeed, Brett Williams regards Johnson's study, of the two early books, as the more readable and "more useful to the artist."[14]) That what he envisioned would be written by a white man, the New Orleans journalist Roark Bradford, who not only greatly altered the story as it had been known but also cast it in a manner that today strikes us as racist, might have disquieted Johnson, both the fictitious and the real (the real one did in fact review Bradford's novel for the *Nation* and expressed dismay as well as some praise[15]). Yet Bradford's *John Henry*, published in 1931, proved to be popular and a link moving John Henry from folklore to popular culture.[16] Williams recognizes Bradford's novel as "by far the most influential in shaping John Henry's popular career."[17]

Bradford earlier had enjoyed great success with a book, *Old Man Adam and His Chillun*,[18] which had rendered biblical stories into the dialect in which whites stereotypically put black speech in writing (which has been called "stage," "Amos 'n Andy," and most recently "Remus" dialect[19]), a dialect which enjoyed literary popularity for decades and still charmed whites in the 1930s. He uses the dialect also in his *John Henry* and because *Old Man Adam* had been turned into a Broadway smash hit, sought to make a musical play out of *John Henry*. It is the play, the production of which turned out to be "disastrous,"[20] that Whitehead focuses on in *John Henry Days*.

The play starred the celebrated black actor Paul Robeson, whose accepting the part is certainly puzzling given the racist overtones of the novel and musical and his own outspoken views in defense of African American rights and dignity. Whatever the actor's motives may have been, Whitehead assigns him motives and makes his playing John Henry an obvious focus for criticism of this manifestation of the John Henry story through contrasting Robeson's ideas and great achievements with Bradford's regrettable work. To do so he adopts the breezy style of entertainment journalism (the patent unsuitability of which for the telling of Robeson's heroic and tragic life story adds to the satirical force of the section) to sketch out both Bradford's work and Robeson's career. He quotes from the dust jacket of the novel *John Henry* to satirize Bradford's racist presumptions:

> "*Roark Bradford is amply qualified to write about the Negro,*" *it read. "He had a Negro for a nurse and Negroes for playmates when he was growing up. He has seen them at work in the fields, in the levee camps, and on the river. He knows them in their homes, in church, at their picnics and their funerals." Very impressive credentials indeed. Especially that bit about the picnics. He might as well have a Ph.D. in Negroes. His mastery of the Negro idiom is quite startling. (226)*

As Robeson waits to go on for the final performance of the play, his life is flashed before us, his struggles and difficult triumphs, his growing political awareness. Yet though his life stands in vivid contrast to Roark Bradford's John Henry, we come to an understanding of why (the fictional) Robeson took the part, and in his having done so we see new meanings for John Henry. For Robeson, John Henry is the embodiment of the common man, the laboring masses, people who are closely attached to the land: "Out of this folktale, even if diverted down ruined streams, flows the truth of men and women" (229). This fits with Robeson's views of the significance of folksongs; he is quoted as having said:

> *Folk music is as much a creation of a mass of people as a language. One person throws in a phrase. Then another—and when, as a singer, I walk from among the people, onto the platform, to sing back to the people the songs they have created, I can feel a great unity. (229)[21]*

This perspective fits with an idée fixe Robeson held in his later years that the "ubiquity and universality of the pentatonic scale in folk music around the globe proved the brotherhood of man" and opened up our ability to "peer into human truths" (230). So John Henry becomes a universal figure of the worker with his struggles and his power, the potent man of the people, representative of the dignity of labor, the songs expression of a universal human bond. It is a meaning that would appeal to others, particularly to those who shared Robeson's politics.

But if Robeson's meaning for John Henry comes out of his vision of the steel driver as a figure from folklore, by the 1930s John Henry was becoming firmly fixed in popular culture. Richard M. Dorson saw commercial recordings as producing "the greatest impact of John Henry on American culture"[22] in making the story widely known, though he fixes on the 1960s, a period of folksong revival, and certainly there were commercial versions of the ballad—both recorded and produced as sheet music—before that.

In Whitehead's novel, commercial song publishing makes an appearance as a Jewish Tin Pan Alley songsmith wannabe some time in the early twentieth century[23] tries to get the words and tune for "John Henry" on to paper. This character, Jake Rose, is a song plugger for a music publisher trying to make his way up the ladder to "contract man," a composer or lyricist who gets a "decent salary plus royalties" (203). He remembers how he learned the business of song plugging—making nightly rounds of the New York saloons and dance halls, bribing the musicians to play his firm's latest songs, passing out printed "chorus slips" to the customers so they can sing along, belting out the chorus himself to get them started. And he remembers where and when he heard "John Henry"—just after being mugged and robbed coming home in a snowstorm, his face battered and pushed into horse manure, his pockets with their few dollars cut right out of his trousers. As he lay on the ground a man passed by him, not stopping to help, but "singing that John Henry song."

Jake knows it's an old ballad, has "looked it up," found no version of the song ever published, and now tries to get it down on paper, sitting in his Lower East Side flat amid all the distracting din of the tenement building. He sees it as a song that could be a breakthrough for him ("This John Henry isn't going to be a million-seller, but . . . a fellow's got to start somewhere. This is the twentieth century and you got to make your own luck" (205). It could help him to move his family further along in the American success quest (they have managed to make it from rooms on the air shaft to rooms at the front of the building ["They got air now but it costs money."]).

Ironically, he works in a world where novelty is king and a constant stream of new songs is its reason for existence. By publishing and plugging this old, traditional song Jake would in effect make it the latest thing, turning tradition into novelty ("he's trying to do something unexpected" [199]). He realizes its drawbacks as a pop song—no syncopation, no orphan girls escaping a life of sin—but also sees that "it has a power" (205).

He never articulates the meaning of that power but does associate it with his pain, the pain of being mugged, knocked to the pavement, and robbed, the pain of being poor and victimized, as the Big Bend Tunnel workers were poor and exploited. So the song may express for him—and presumably to those others he seeks to market it to—some of the pain of the struggles of Americans as they labor to get by and get on in life. Certainly Jake Rose works hard to get "John Henry" down on paper and sees the song as a possible ticket to success. As he himself rejects the old world of his own background (he has changed his name, has moved from singing in the synagogue to plugging songs in saloons, reminds his conservative parents that "this is the twentieth century" [202]), he reaches back to a nineteenth-century ballad. In doing so he is transforming it, turning it from folklore into popular culture, performing an important step in the ongoing cultural journey of the John Henry "legend."

We later learn that Jake Rose succeeded at getting his "John Henry" on to paper and out there, because—though we never again see him as a character—sheet music for his song is discovered later by another character, young Jennifer Sutter (whose possible relationship to J is not spelled out), living in Harlem, evidently in the 1940s. She lives in the area called Strivers Row, her father a medical doctor, her mother an active member of the Sepia Ladies Club, facts all indicative of the family's well-to-do, bourgeois status. Mrs. Sutter is highly focused on social position and respectability, and indeed Jennifer suffers her piano lessons largely because of her mother's concern with being "cultured." Jennifer gets a dime to buy candy but when her favorite sweets are out of stock finds her way to a seedy music store with "shiftless-looking clientele" (274) where all she can buy for ten cents is a moldy copy of the sheet music for Jake Rose's "The Ballad of John Henry."

Her mother out of the house, Jennifer plays the song and it is a revelation, music in which she does not hear "any of the usual voices" of the more "cultured" pieces she usually plays. This new kind of music "doesn't go to church and cusses, wears what it wants." She finds that "what she feels most is pushed. This music pushes her" and on repeating it, "this time she decides she'll sing the words. She's in a heat right now. . . . She sings it again and is so pushed that she doesn't hear her mother come in the front door" (278). Her mother is outraged that Jennifer should be playing "gutter music" (278), music "of such low social standing" (279). For Mrs. Sutter the music represents a condition of African American life that she and her husband have rejected and are trying to distance themselves from. The music is associated with "good-for-nothing niggers ... who don't want to take their place in America" (279–80). Ironically the adult Sutters share an ethic of striving with Jake Rose, though he "created" the music and saw it as a means of advancement and Americanization, and they abhor it and see it as something which has held them back in their own "Americanization." Mrs. Sutter's rejection of the song mirrors what Brett Williams sees in John Henry's having become "more an embarrassment than a hero to urban blacks,"[24] indicative of a putting behind of a painful history that kept blacks as manual laborers and back from success in America. Jennifer decides that the song "wasn't candy, but it sure was sweet," acknowledging not only the power and liberating, forbidden appeal of the song but also a new generation's willingness to look at and find a new appreciation for forgotten or rejected roots.

Brett Williams notes how certain qualities of "John Henry" have "inspired a number of blues singers to include it in their repertoires,"[25] and no doubt Mrs. Sutter's negative reaction to the song is in part a reaction to its association with the "disreputable" blues (though we are given little sense of how Jennifer sings it). One blues performer who sings "John Henry" pops up in the novel, and his thoughts on the song add other dimensions to its meaning. He is James Moses, itinerant musician but performing in a Chicago bar seemingly in the early 1930s[26] where a white music scout named Goodman "discovers" him. Moses muses on his life and the women he beds and also upon "John Henry," which Goodman asks him to record. For Moses the song is part of a blues repertoire that helps the blacks who have come to Chicago in the great migration north to "remember the country," that helps to "draw these folks back home" (250) to the rural South. Sometimes he also manipulates the song in his performance strategy and places it in a set to get the audience "thinking about the grave" (260) only to follow it up with something "which really gets them stomping." And when he sings it on his second night in the Chicago bar it's because "he wanted to beat the machine" (259), not the steam drill but Goodman's recording apparatus, beat it in the sense of recording something that will please the record company and maybe bring him a measure of fame.

Moses and Jake Rose and Jennifer Sutter are all indicative of stages in the progress of John Henry into American culture at large, of the progress of John Henry into non-folk contexts and non-folk meanings, and indeed by the 1960s the "legend" of the man was widely known. The folklore collectors found song texts and oral commentary; Johnson and Chappell created a focus and sketched in a historical reality. Roark Bradford moved the story into literary and theatrical contexts, and the world of commercial music gave it a place in popular culture. Of course, there were other influences as well. In the wake of Bradford's work, others wrote plays about John Henry.[27] As early as 1942 books for adolescents were featuring John Henry, and there was what Williams calls a "spurt" of books for young readers between 1965 and 1971;[28] in 1975 the noted African American author John Oliver Killens published his John Henry novel for teenagers, *A Man Ain't Nothin' but a Man*, the title taken from a line of the ballad.[29] Beginning in the 1930s John Henry appeared in a number of popular folklore anthologies, mostly of the sort Richard Dorson would deride as purveying fakelore, and he made his way into school curricula, beginning in 1940 with a Florida program and including radio programs for schoolchildren and school readers. Archie Green, who published a number of articles on the "graphics" of country and traditional music, discusses illustrations of John Henry,[30] and several sculptural renderings appear in Whitehead's novel, including the 1972 statue made by Charles O. Cooper and placed near the mouth of the Big Bend Tunnel and a commemorative bottle made to hold Jim Beam whiskey.[31] There is a John Henry Festival, held in different Appalachian locations to honor the African American contribution to the culture of the mountains, and John Henry Days is a real event held annually in Talcott every July.

Thus it is hardly surprising that several characters in *John Henry Days* who have only indifferent interest in the West Virginia festivities nonetheless recollect some vague, generalized knowledge of John Henry. J. Sutter remembers a cartoon version of the story he was shown in school, as well as the street hustler who sang him the song one night. Lucien, the p.r. chief, recalls having known the story after his assistant brings him a children's book that recounts it. Tiny, one of the flacks covering the festival and stamp ceremony, recalls reading the story in kindergarten where it was used to replace less politically correct stories about black people. Clearly the John Henry story is an open text that has been "interpreted" into and through numerous American communicative media, being infused with a variety of meanings in the process (including now those meanings Colson Whitehead works upon it for his novel). It is the story of humans contending with the machines that might replace them, the story of black people both beating and being destroyed by white, capitalist machinations. It is for Jake Rose a memory of suffering and his means for finding an American dream of material success; for Jennifer Sutter's mother an expression of being retarded in her progress toward a similar dream and a symbol of black people's failures and social inferiority; for Jennifer herself some kind of sweet liberation and a hint of roots to be rediscovered. For James Moses something to remind blacks in the North of their homes in the South; for Goodman the talent scout a commercial property that may sell to blacks but also appeal to whites who might also be willing to buy "race records." For Paul Robeson, John Henry is a type of struggling, working humanity and expressive of some human universality. For Guy Johnson the story is an intellectual puzzle central to the role of black people in America. For the writers attending the first John Henry Days the story is something to wonder about, be cynical about, to further manipulate; two of them make up a parody of the ballad about being defeated by a washer's rinse cycles and one thinks that the steel-driving contest part of the festival might appeal to *GQ* magazine as a "mano-à-mano" piece. The folklore, whatever its meanings and functions to the folk, has gotten recycled into a whole range of new meanings and uses—commercial, intellectual, artistic, personal, and social.

. . .

For the novel the newly created festival is one great culmination of the open text's possibilities with its layers of accreted usage and meaning. The other great culmination is Pamela's father, the grandest John Henry collector of them all, and he and the town that has produced the festival promise to be inextricably connected in days to come.

Pamela's father stumbles on to John Henry collecting in an antique store during a family trip in Delaware when he discovers a statue of the steel driver. As the years go by he amasses a vast assortment of objects, not only numerous recordings but railroad equipment, a jar of soil from West Virginia, drill bits alleged to have been used by John Henry himself, "mawkish pictures" of the man, sheet music, piano rolls (though he has no piano to even be certain what these rolls actually play), playbills from the Bradford/Robeson musical, first editions, hammers, a whole room of statuary. All of which, plus Mr. Street's consuming obsession itself, drives Pamela and her mother from their Harlem apartment. Her father sells his business and maintains the apartment as a John Henry museum where he awaits the great crowds who never come. For Pamela the collection is a painful legacy, John Henry someone who became virtually a rival sibling—that first Delaware purchase rode home wrapped in her own blanket—someone who made her father into a person physically resembling a homeless man, his family displaced by his obsession. For the novel the great variety of objects in the collection is a further statement of the manifestations the John Henry story could assume; the power the story holds over Mr. Street a statement of its power to appeal to many as its meanings are shaped and reshaped. Pamela's father himself conceives meanings for John Henry and those are perhaps the ultimate ones, for he comes to see John Henry as almost a messianic, redemption-bringing figure.

We only know Mr. Street from Pamela's memories, as she recalls his apartment/museum, with its small, easily unnoticed sign, where every day he played versions of the song in a sort of chronological order, matching the history of the music with that of the devices used to record and play it. Although the very existence of the museum suggests something of the meaning of John Henry to him, where the meaning really becomes expressed is in a speech that "slept in his mouth" (382), which he thinks about giving and which Pamela imagines him giving at the stamp dedication ceremony, a speech in reality never delivered. For Mr. Street, John Henry represents "elemental forces flowing through the aperture of this room" (382), as people come "ready to receive John Henry . . . alone or leading friends by the hand to share revelation" (383). Those who come to share include

> children with round faces and wide eyes who were hearing of the legendary steeldriver for the first time and learning possibility, teenagers slouching and cracking jokes to hide what they see in the man but cannot admit, adults, men and women pushed here for so many reasons, getting reacquainted with the story they first heard as children and now connecting to it every one of their hard mornings, these strivers, and the old ones, old as him, who had seen the same things he had . . . understanding the legend as he did now, as a lesson that had finally been learned at great cost, moving from room to room in recognition and resignation, all of them a family he had lost at last returned to him. (383)

These religious overtones of John Henry as salvation-bringer, perhaps even as martyred Christ-figure, begin to seem delusional (and indeed the father Pamela remembers in his later years does seem madly obsessive at best, an eccentric local character holed up with his hoarded artifacts and recordings). Yet Mr. Street's strange vision is one more proof of John Henry's shape-shifting appeal, of the fact that he can take on even religious and mystical meanings as one further modern reincarnation.

Ironically, the collection that accompanied (and in part must have induced) Mr. Street's journey to this John Henry of the spirit may wind up in a more prosaic reincarnation. That is, it seems destined for the projected local museum. And though that museum may have intellectual and educational dimensions in the detailing of local history and the presentation of an important American icon who came out of the folk tradition, the museum founders are much more interested in it as a locus for tourists, who need "sites" to visit; it is to be a generator of cold cash for a small town's economy. Apart from this mundane purpose, there are also our suspicions that museums, whatever their aesthetic and educational value, entomb culture in a kind of stasis, put cultural realities into the dead space of glass cases, so that a museum marks a confining institutionalization of traditions otherwise more vital. Though Pamela's reluctance to part with her father's collection stems in part from deep personal emotions, she may also hesitate to "museumize" these things that were her father's breathing reality and that came through the real lives of many others. However, Mr. Street himself resorted to the context of a (private) museum for communicating his message, seeing museums' transcendent possibilities, not their limitations.

The community that is planning the museum has also created the festival, and the festival seems a complex thing, as real festivals are wont to be. On one level the event in the novel exhibits the familiar characteristics of any local fair. What is described is a virtual catalog of what is ordinary at many rural fairs in America and it seems unselfconsciously assembled by local folk. On another level, however, the celebration also has been a matter of careful marketing, calculated by a local elite and the public relations people who have been hired to do the job, and they observe the event rather differently. Lucien the p.r. chief thinks of himself as "doing a town" (something he has never undertaken before) and as "establish[ing] the brand superiority of Talcott" (195). He has consulted "the Quality boys," taught the locals what to put in a press release, organized the junketeers of the press, and wants to see the event as a consciously constructed "slice of Americana" (294). The attendees are, he thinks, "a herd to be shepherded by those of his elite" (292). "Truth be told, Lucien had no idea who John Henry was when [the mayor] contacted him" (296) but by now he has, he thinks, put it all together and "throw in the museum and this is almost an artsy-type gig. He always felt good after an artsy-type gig" (298). The festival, then, is also in part contrived by outsiders for reasons that are political and economic.

This is to say that John Henry Days is both a prosaic celebration, even tinged by the tacky (if also charming and of communal importance), and one that has been manipulated into existence by persons who are not even of the community and who traffic in artificial creations.³² Yet the festival nonetheless has power. Clearly it brings the town together *as* a community, droves of people attending the event with obvious gusto. And although the event is called with some irony "authentic local culture" (249), and we are asked with some of the same irony "what kind of cold heart despises the sincerity of a county fair on a summer day," we are meant to understand that there *is* authenticity here and something that genuinely warms the heart.

Certainly Pamela Street feels this; as she makes a circuit of the event with J she exclaims: "'My father would have loved this. . . . Not all this junk they're selling, but the idea behind it.' She finally looks at J. 'He would have loved it'" (315). She reiterates how much she hated listening to her father's John Henry stories. "But being here now," she implies, evokes a very different reaction. The event has brought together a mass of people, just like in the dream expressed in her father's hypothetical speech, people who if not assembled for the spiritual meanings he envisioned are nonetheless pulled into a kind of one-ness "by interconnected gears set in motion by the idea of John Henry" (295). The celebration, with all its bad food, tacky souvenirs, and cheap carnival atmosphere, takes on powerful meanings and even manages to succeed as a more elemental ritual of transformation and reconciliation.

It is even a ritual that has actual reenactments of the original mythic act it commemorates. There is an official steel-driving contest pitting (presumably white) contestants from Hinton and Talcott, and J is himself drawn into a hammering contest against a machine when a carnival barker challenges him to try out a strength-testing contraption; the barker's spiel and the machine's scoring are keyed to the John Henry story. And as several characters wander through the festival event they notice a storyteller who recounts the story of John Henry to children, so that there is a literal recitation of the "myth" that the ritual reenacts as the ritual public event itself proceeds.

And the community may indeed be transformed socially and perhaps economically by the ritual. Benny, the motel owner, muses on what he has seen at the festival, seeing it almost as if it has called the community into being, or reassembled it:

People he hadn't seen in years had rallied themselves from whatever side road cranny they called home and said hello, ten years older but still wearing the same clothes. Children clutched the legs of men and

*women he recognized from here and there and suddenly these people
had whole histories, families, descendants. Some of them had booths,
so he could see, finally, what they were all about . . . . It was a success
all around . . . and they'll do it again next year for sure, and the year
after that. (362–63)*

More darkly, his wife, Josie, who is aware of a ghost that dwells in the
motel, has a different reaction: "It is a new beginning but by her sights, it
hasn't been paid for yet. There's some blood to be paid. John Henry spilled
his, for the railroad, for his fellow workers, for Talcott and Hinton" (363). She
wonders: "Where will this weekend's come from?" She senses the ghost in
the room occupied by Alphonse Miggs—who for reasons of his own pulls
a gun at the stamp dedication ceremony and starts shooting, a policeman
does the same, and unnamed journalists are killed. Miggs's final violent act
is the culmination of the ritual, a culmination of an ancient kind: blood
that must be shed to bring about or pay for the important transformations
that are taking place, transformations that include the manipulation of folk
tradition, the reshaping of it into its roles in a postmodern context.

Miggs's action and its aftermath may lay a communal ghost, but certainly Pamela lays her own ghost by burying her father's ashes at the holy
shrine of John Henry, placing those ashes in the burial place where John
Henry may have been laid to rest, deciding finally to part with his burden-
some collection. J, whose actual name is evidently unknown to any other
characters, tells her what J stands for. (Is it for John, as in John Henry? Readers never find out, nor do we know whether J saves himself by leaving with
Pamela and abandoning his mad pursuit of the record, escaping a literal
death when Alphonse Miggs pulls his gun. We hope and suspect that he
has.) His giving of his name suggests a personal realization of identity, and
we understand that personal transformations have taken place for Pamela
and for J, John Henry's meaning for them assuming new forms. As it will
assume new forms for the town for whom John Henry becomes a more
prosperous future with a heightened sense of community identity (unless
the shooting incident itself comes to haunt the place, frightening away the
very tourists the place hopes to attract, an ironic outcome for the carefully
planned, widely publicized first John Henry Days).

• • •

John Henry Days, then, envisions many interests, over a long period of time,
converging upon a folk tradition, making and remaking it. Indeed the John
Henry tradition—and by implication folklore generally—is to be seen as

something constructed by many for a variety of reasons both within folkloric contexts and outside them, though perhaps the dividing lines between contexts are not to be sharply drawn, both contributing somehow to the creation and recreation of the "tradition" in a wider sense. This tradition and its permutations are constructed in several senses, with conscious thought and considerable manipulation and artifice by public relations practitioners, post office bureaucrats, and small-town politicians. Yet the tradition is also constructed in another way, through the cultural processes that come into play as folklore moves from person to person, from group to group, constantly being recomposed, reinterpreted, revalued, reassigned form and meaning, an open text being collaborated upon: recycled. Such is the folklore process, but what is created and originally transmitted by folkloric means expands and the process becomes a larger one, the folklore being appropriated by non-folk forms, modes of communicating, and environments. John Henry is work song and ballad; novel and play; drawn image and statue; festival and ritual; U.S. stamp and commemorative whiskey bottle; collected artifact and collected vinyl. He embodies the black experience; the unity of humanity; the heroism of the oppressed worker; humans in the modern world who contend with dehumanizing machines; the striving to get ahead in America; the forces that retard such striving; memories of a faraway home; interesting, liberating roots; a force for community solidarity. People tell stories about him, reenact his famous deed, work him into jokes, sales pitches, and dreams of prosperity. At the dawn of the twenty-first century he is eminently marketable tourist icon and, indeed, central to this novel that embraces folklore for its author's own purposes but which in doing so embraces the whole process of appropriation and transformation that has gone before.

Jake Rose knows that his commercial-song version of "John Henry" is not likely to become a "million seller." Apparently his expectations are warranted. Though we never learn of the success of his sheet music, we presume that it was limited. Yet John Henry really has become that "million seller," the folk figure having become widely known in American culture, whether through oral tradition or folksong revival or field recording, cartoon or Broadway musical, "fakelore" collection, or some more amorphous process by which a combination of media create for us what might be called a folk idea of John Henry. Whitehead's novel fictionalizes the historical and cultural processes of John Henry's total creation and creates fictional manifestations of John Henry. Not only does the novel work with the tradition itself for Whitehead's own artistic purposes; it also illuminates the possibilities of an open text and the relationships between the media that "complete" the text, taking it from folk form to other forms that resonate in modern and postmodern worlds, illustrating imaginatively the recycling process that appropriates and reuses the power of folk materials for new purposes in new contexts.

Chapter 2

"IN THIS FOLK-LORE LAND"

Establishing Race, Class, and Identity through Folklore Studies

◇◇◇

John Henry Days, then, lays out some of the motives for recycling folklore: commercial, intellectual, personal, aesthetic, communal. Folklore may somehow satisfy the needs of an entrepreneurial individual or group or the requirements of an ideological perspective. Certainly folklore may appeal to the ideas and needs of a variety of individuals who satisfy their personal quests, whether individual or collective, through the study or collecting or presentation or representation of folk materials.

This may be no less true of scholars, or those with a scholarly bent, than it is of artists or businessmen, though scholars may see themselves as wanting only to present an unbiased picture of the nature and significance of lore in its own social context. This chapter and the next look at the endeavors of a group of folklore collectors and of a journalist with scholarly perspectives. In both cases their interest in folklore came to fulfill personal needs and deal with personal issues, being recycled in publications and presentations as part of intellectual strategies that reused folklore in personally meaningful ways.

While folklorists have in recent years become increasingly interested in the role played by folklore in establishing identity (whether personal or sociocultural) for the *performers* of folklore,[1] Elliott Oring in his 1993 American Folklore Society Fellows plenary address[2] argued that establishing identity has played a key role in the development of the *study* of folklore, that it has served as a paradigm of sorts for *scholars* working at various stages in the development of our discipline, that identity has always been a central issue in folklore studies, even when the term was not specifically used. He thus noted the obvious example of Herder's attempt to establish folklore as the repository of German national identity, but also suggested, as a less obvious example, that Richard Dorson's interest in the transformation of European tradition in America was part of a concern with establishing American identity. One might go even further, however, and say that folklore scholarship has sometimes been intimately tied up with identity concerns present in the scholar's culture and even in his or her own life. Indeed, this seems obvious when folklore study has been stimulated by nationalism. Folklorists have already begun to reexamine the nature of the relationship between folklorists/ ethnographers and their informants, increasing our awareness of the extent to which the supposedly authoritative and objective researcher selects and shapes data for publication. This move toward reflexiveness further underscores the need to examine the attitudes, including especially identity issues, which inform and shape the fieldworker's observations and interpretations, and which may lead less to intellectual understanding of the folklore than to a recycling of the lore to fit personal motives.[3]

These questions about the nature of fieldwork, as well as the related question of how folklorists' personal concerns about identity have influenced the history of interest in folklore, take us beyond the purely intellectual aspects of the development of folklore study into a realm where the scholarly intellect mixes with complex emotions, with individual personalities, and with political and economic trends. Rosemary Lévy Zumwalt has cast the development of folklore studies in America in terms of a "dialogue of dissent" between anthropologists and literary scholars, but a broader comprehension of the history of intellectual interest in folklore requires a coming to terms with a great variety of ideas (good and bad), organizations (well-run and haphazard), personalities (incisive and eccentric), and motives (pure and less than admirable).[4] This chapter looks at how concerns with identity are part of that involved history, having combined in complex ways to affect folklore study, especially field collecting and the selection, presentation, and interpretation of collectanea.

Here, we look at two phases in the development of folklore studies in one particular American place, Louisiana, in which a concern with racial and class identity is an important factor: the activities of the branch of the American Folklore Society that functioned in New Orleans in the 1890s, and the work of Lyle Saxon (who directed the Louisiana part of the Federal Writers' Project folklore collecting program) in the 1920s and 1930s. Though Louisiana is but one segment of the American whole, its rich melange of cultures has stimulated a tradition of continuous interest in the folklore of the state. Moreover, regional collecting in itself has been an important aspect of American folkloristics. The complex blend of intellectual issues, personalities, and politics that emerge brings into focus aspects of the

American interest in folklore. Although those intellectually interested in folklore may have seen themselves in line with a "scientific" paradigm or at least as concerned with "authenticity" and intellectual understanding, in fact their methods may have led to a kind of recycling in the context of which they used their relationship to folklore to provide themselves with social status and a sense of class identity.

"FOLKLORE PEOPLE ARE ALWAYS OLD"
The Louisiana Association, Race, Class, and Folklore on the Old Plantation

The women and men who participated in the Louisiana Association of the American Folklore Society (AFS)—which was one of several AFS branches at the end of the nineteenth century—did so for a number of obvious reasons. The organization allowed Louisianians to participate in a developing national intellectual interest, gave literary members material for their writings, and gave women in particular a focus for their intellectual energies. But a less obvious need to establish their identities in terms of race, class, and ethnicity was also one of their purposes, and an important one despite its unstated and perhaps unconscious nature. This need stemmed from place and from time. For a hundred and fifty years Louisiana had been dominated by the institution of slavery. Less than thirty years before it had been devastated by the Civil War, which had destroyed its economic and social base. Additional factors included a huge African American population (the former slaves, although there was also a substantial population of African Americans who had been free and even slaveholders themselves), the urban character of New Orleans (which allowed for a population of artists and intellectuals who could meet together, as well as a substantial tourist business), and a significant sector of the population to whom French ethnicity was important. All of these circumstances combined to create a situation in which people were to use folklore and its study to establish who they were.

AFS IN NEW ORLEANS
Its Members and Their Activities

The Louisiana Association of the American Folk-Lore Society was founded over a century ago, on February 8, 1892, in New Orleans, largely through the efforts of Alcée Fortier, Tulane University scholar of Romance languages and a potent force in Louisiana intellectual affairs. Officially a branch of the American Folklore Society, the New Orleans group promoted an interest in folklore among the flourishing community of intellectuals, writers, and artists that had emerged in New Orleans during the previous decade. A national revival of interest in the South (which was conceptualized in romantic and exotic terms) had helped create a national market for southern "local color" writing, and Louisiana provided its growing community of writers an especially rich source of material to satisfy that market. The literary careers of writers like George Washington Cable and Lafcadio Hearn, whose writing incorporated dialect and quaint local customs, flourished. Cable and Hearn, in their turn, helped create and publicize a romantic image of New Orleans, with its lush semitropical climate and its culturally distinctive inhabitants, notably the white Creoles and Afro-French Creoles of color.[5] By the time the folklore society was founded in 1892 the French Quarter settings of Cable's stories were so familiar to American readers that various sites depicted in them had become tourist attractions. Thus an interest in folklore study in New Orleans in the 1890s in part grew out of both national and regional trends that created a market for southern literary endeavors and stimulated the growth of intellectual life in New Orleans, and some of the appeal of the association for its many literary members no doubt lay in its focus on cultural materials that could be incorporated into their writing.

From 1892 to 1896 the association met monthly to discuss folklore and to encourage its collection and preservation. Besides a predominance of literary figures, the membership included a number of artists, and volunteer activists in service organizations. The membership was all white, but both the Creole and the American (that is, "Anglo-Saxon") communities were represented. In addition, the members were mostly from "society" (but not necessarily from families with money); many had connections with (white) plantation families; their names appeared often in the society columns of the local newspapers. Some were the wives of prominent businessmen, particularly cotton brokers and bankers. Most of the men were educators like Alcée Fortier, the association's founder and primary mover. Along with his Tulane colleagues William Preston Johnston (president of the university) and J. Hanno Deiler (professor of German), Fortier had been an active member of the American Folk-Lore Society even before the New Orleans group formed. He had read papers on the topic of Louisiana folklore at meetings of the Modern Language Association (in 1887) and of the American Folk-Lore Society (in 1888) and had published in the annals of both societies. In 1894 he served as president of the American Folk-Lore Society, and in 1895 published, as part of its new monograph series, *Louisiana Folk-Tales.*[6] In 1898 Fortier was elected president of the Modern Language Association of America.

Fortier used his position as a member of a prominent Creole family, his academic contacts, and his reputation as a respected scholar to recruit members for the local folklore association. The association's roster included two of his nieces, Amelie and Desiree Roman; his cousin's widow, Louise Augustin Fortier, referred to in the minutes as Mrs. Augustin Fortier; and the latter's two sisters, Aimee Beugnot and Marie Augustin. Fortier also recruited several of his colleagues at Tulane and prominent New Orleans writers and artists.

Among the best-known writers, Mollie Moore Davis published a number of volumes of short stories and poetry, but was equally well known in New Orleans society as a hostess. She had moved to New Orleans in 1879 with her husband, a journalist. Lacking funds for impressive living quarters, the Davises took up residence on Royal Street in the French Quarter, taking advantage of cheap rents in what was then a rather shabby residential area. But Mrs. Davis had the vision to recognize in the French Quarter houses, with their brick-paved carriageways and wrought-iron balconies, the potential for creating an interesting and romantic environment for living and entertaining. Her parties were the social center for the city's intellectual and artistic elite, the closest thing New Orleans had to a literary salon. Ruth McEnery Stuart and Cecilia Viets Jamison were also well-known writers. Stuart was prolific and much in demand for public readings of her own work, as dialect stories such as she wrote were very popular in the 1880s and 1890s. Jamison was the author of a number of novels, the most successful of which were for children and featured Louisiana settings, local character types, and other local color.

Also well known was Elizabeth Lyle Saxon, who had a distinguished career as a writer/lecturer and activist, "one of the first women in the South to speak and write on work reforms for women and children."[7] Grandmother of Lyle Saxon, discussed later in this chapter, she initiated the women's movement in Louisiana and traveled widely on speaking tours, working for women's suffrage and organizing for the Women's Christian Temperance Union.

The objects of the Louisiana Association are stated in the minutes to be "to hold during the proper season, monthly meetings at which papers may be read or addresses delivered and by means of which may be promoted the collection of American and other folklore, and also to further by every suitable means the objects and purposes of the American Folklore Society."[8] Alcée Fortier and William Preston Johnston were the primary advocates of "scientific" folklore study. Chiefly this meant reminding the association to heed the exact words of informants or to collect the music along with the words of folksongs, or discoursing on the latest theories about origins or the aims of comparative studies. The association's minutes make the emphasis on collecting texts quite clear. Members were frequently admonished to help accomplish the goal of "the accumulation and collection" of folktales. And members apparently did literally hand in texts, as is made explicit when the minutes note that "Mrs. Johnston's and Mrs. Jamison's stories of folk-lore were put on file, and Professor Dillard was requested to write out his valuable information in that line for the benefit of the Society."[9] The minutes do preserve a record of frequent presentations of folklore (though what happened to the bulk of the written texts is uncertain).

The Louisiana Association, then, functioned in a fairly simple manner. It had arisen under the influence of several hands and served its members in several ways. The establishment of the national folklore society was a key factor and in part the association fulfilled the purposes of a learned society. Its members were also members of other local organizations with intellectual purposes, and the association in part added to the civic life of New Orleans by providing another outlet for the intellectual talents of those who participated. The American Folklore Society was rather more receptive to women than most learned societies of the late nineteenth century, and, indeed, the membership of the Louisiana Association was predominantly female. Hence it provided a forum for women's intellectual aspirations. It was also a response to the local color movement in southern literature and art, appealing to writers' interest in the quaintness of dialect and local lore, giving them an additional impetus to actually collect such lore.

THE PRIMACY OF AFRICAN AMERICAN FOLKLORE

There is, however, an especially striking aspect of the activities of the members of the Louisiana Association, which points to another motive for their work, one less obvious than those noted above but quite fundamental. This is the fact that the folklore collected and discussed by association members was heavily African American. The minutes of the association during its first year and a half record numerous instances of members reading or reporting on "Negro stories" and Louisiana stories "of African origin." The minutes for April 14, 1992, for example, record:

> *Miss M. J. Augustin read a story, "How the negro became black, Flat-nosed and Thick-lipped." This was a story of a contest between the persons of good and evil to obtain the mastery of the human race. The messenger of heaven was a white bird. The devil was so dissatisfied with his creation that he dashed him to the ground, causing the thick lips and nose.*
>
> . . . .
>
> *At the unanimous request of the meeting Miss Augustin repeated the story in the original words of the Negro and also gave some account of him. Panot claimed to be a Housaa prince. His tribe living on the Niger was at war with the Ashantis and Dahomeys. His father was killed in a battle in which Panot was taken prisoner, sold to the Congos and by them to Dutch traders who brought him with other slaves to America where he was first sold to W. Labranche, then given to Mme. Augustin, in whose employ he was taught to cook. His wife Therese was a Voodoo. After the emancipation she wanted Panot to leave his master. She prophesied evil and he died shortly after either from indigestion or from the effect of his wifes witcheries. (April 4, 1892)[10]*

At the same meeting, we are told, Fortier discussed "a negro dancing song or ronde," and on another occasion he "favored the assembly with a quaint negro folk-lore . . . tale of an old Louisiana plantation." On May 8 several African American tales were read to the group and special mention is made of the presenter's connection to plantation life:

> *Mrs. William Preston Johnston then read a picturesque folk-lore story that seemed to come from the heart of the woodland. It was entitled "The Rabbit's Riding Horse," and would have delighted the ear of the little children of to-day as it did its compiler when she heard it at the knee of her old negro nurse in her plantation home. This delicious scrap of memory was followed by another from Mrs. Johnston, entitled "Trouble, trouble, trouble Alligator." The stories were received by the president, who thanked Mrs. Johnston for her kindness in devoting so much time to the interest of the society.*
>
> *Mr. Fortier then favored the assembly with a quaint negro folk-lore story from the pen of Mrs. Jamison. The subject of her sketch was "Aunt*

Cindy's Story," a true tale of an old Louisiana plantation *and the ghostly terrors with which* negro superstitions *and custom enveloped it in the olden days. The story was rich in local coloring, and the* native dialect of the negroes *was given with a fidelity to truth that was immediately recognized. Mrs. Jamison's story was much applauded.*

The next story in order was read by Mrs. Augustin Fortier and embodied her reminiscences of childish lore and the peculiar faculties of an old negro slave *for rehearsing the stories of* African folk-lore, *mingled with the Creole traditions of the island of St. Domingo and early Louisiana.*[11] *(emphasis added)*

Other entries record that stories read or recited were credited to sources such as "a Martinique Negro" (Mrs. Mason Cook, June 14, 1892), or blacks encountered during a visit to Alabama (Mollie Moore Davis, June 14, 1892). On November 14, 1892, pictures of street criers—in the New Orleans context almost certainly black—were mentioned, and on December 12, 1892, "Mme LeJeune sang some Negro melodies and played Bambrula [Bamboula]," said by its composer Louis Moreau Gottschalk to be based upon the music of the African American "slave" dance of the same name.

Theoretical discussions focused on the same subject matter, as when Mr. Beer discussed French Guiana parallels to the lore of black Louisiana. Or when Marie Augustin "drew attention to the savage conception amongst the Bushmen . . . of the transmigration of souls. She pointed out that this people believed . . . the souls of the dead passed into the Gorilla" (May 8, 1893).[12]

The publications of members indicate the same interest in African and African American folklore. Fortier's own *Louisiana Folk-Tales in French Dialect and English Translation*, published in 1895 as the second volume of the AFS Memoirs series, is a collection of narratives taken down from black speakers of French Creole ("not merely a corruption of French . . . [but] a real idiom with a morphology and grammar of its own" [x]) who are variously identified in the notes, sometimes also by name, as "colored man," "little negress," "colored nurse," or "Old negro from *la Vacherie.*" Fortier's contributions to the *Journal of American Folklore*'s first volume had the same focus on the folklore of French-speaking blacks.[13]

Cecilia Viets Jamison, Mollie Evelyn Moore Davis, and Mrs. William Preston Johnston (Margaret Avery Johnston) all contributed to the *Journal of American Folklore,* also, in each case one or more texts of folk narratives reproduced in "Negro dialect." It seems probable, based on descriptions of activities recorded in the minutes, that these tales were earlier among the many tales "presented" at the association's monthly meetings, read or recited in dialect. Mrs. Jamison contributed "A Louisiana Legend Concerning Will o' the Wisp," "obtained . . . from Aunt Cindy, a very old negress."[14] The story explains the appearance of a mysterious light in a certain swamp as the restless ghost of a planter, Mr. Ivey, searching for the bones of his brother, Mr. Jakey, whom he had wronged in order to obtain the family plantation. A second story "by the same narrator" (although the *Journal* provides a confusing indication as to whether this was submitted by Jamison or Mollie Moore Davis) is subtitled "Louisiana Superstition" and is an account of why cottonwood trees seem to tremble and shake (because they were used in Christ's crucifixion). A third story in the same group, this one more clearly a submission by Davis, does not identify a narrator but appears in similar dialect.[15] Entitled "De Witch-'ooman and de Spinnin' Wheel. The Witch Prevented from Reentering Her Skin: A Tale from Louisiana," it is a legendary account that uses the widespread complex of motifs (G252; H57; D702.1.1) of a witch who transforms herself into a cat to go abroad, though here she does so by spinning off her human skin. A man staying in her house destroys her by salting and peppering her removed skin. In Volume 9 of the *Journal* Johnston published two tales featuring the trickster Mr. Rabbit, a figure well known from Joel Chandler Harris's Uncle Remus stories and seen as perhaps the epitome of African American storytelling.[16] These Johnston reconstructed from her own childhood, having heard them from "our young nurse, the daughter of Mammy Harriet," and retold in print in "the language of a house servant, widely different from that of the field hands."[17] One is the story of how Rabbit tricks Mr. Deer into seeming to be his riding horse so as to blunt Deer's powers as a rival for Miss Fox's affections. In the other Rabbit uses Mr. Alligator to escape from both dogs and a fire set by hunters.

Many years later, in 1933, another member of the association, Sara Avery McIlhenny, a niece of Margaret Avery Johnston, published three dialect stories in the *Atlantic Monthly* under the title "Stories Mammy Told Me," noting that these were bedtime stories "related by her old Negro mammy."[18] In one Mr. Rabbit tricks Mr. Dog into having his mouth enlarged; the second is about friendship between Mr. Alligator and Mr. Rooster that becomes enmity; the third tells how Mr. Squirrel escapes the fate of being slaughtered by a man who puts him up for the night and thus now always lives safely in trees, and the trio of tales is followed by a concluding text, of a spiritual used as a lullaby.

Thus the published texts referred to above and the descriptions of presentations and discussions quoted or summarized or referred to in the minutes, all document a definite idea of what interested Fortier and his colleagues. Why they were interested in these particular folk materials is another question. William Wells Newell, as editor of the *Journal of American Folklore*, had set out in his first issue the parameters of folklore and had, in his enumeration of those groups from whom folklore might be collected, included the southern Negro.[19] Thus the members of the local association were picking up on his suggestion when they collected from this folk group that was readily accessible to them. Yet their motives seem to be more complicated than that.

In looking at the collectanea produced by the members of the association, one finds much that is "condescending" or even "racist," especially from our present-day perspective. The "reproduction" of someone else's "dialect" and the patronizing descriptions of informants lead to such a conclusion. To reach a fuller understanding of the group's activities, however, we must first look at aspects of the historical context in which the Louisiana Association flourished.

SOCIAL TENSION, RACE, AND FOLKLORE

The last decade—indeed, the last several decades—of the nineteenth century in Louisiana was a period of social tension and uncertainty. The Civil War and Reconstruction destroyed a social order, not merely undermining but virtually standing on its head the relations that prevailed between whites and blacks and other people of color. The period was punctuated by racial and ethnic violence and, indeed, "virulent negrophobia."[20] In 1874, the efforts of the White League to reestablish white supremacy politically led to the race riot generally known as the Battle of Liberty Place or the Battle of Canal Street in which the state's black militia and the New Orleans metropolitan police were defeated, resulting in temporary control of the city by the league. In 1900 an event less well remembered but at the time receiving almost frenzied attention in the New Orleans newspapers was another race riot, that which resulted in the death of Robert Charles, a black propagandist for African American migration movements. After he shot twenty-seven whites, including seven police officers, Charles was shot down "and stomped into the mud of the street" following "one of the bloodiest, most anarchic weeks in New Orleans history,"[21] when blacks were beaten and killed in the streets and two schools for African American children were put to the torch.

In 1890, the New Orleans chief of police, David C. Hennessy, had been shot down, allegedly by Sicilian gangsters and in 1891, just a year before the association was founded, eleven of the Italians who had been implicated in the murder but who had been acquitted or had their legal proceedings declared mistrials were lynched at the parish prison by a mob. Nine were shot to death, one was hanged from a lamp post, another from a tree. In 1880, and again in 1887, strikes by black workers hit the sugar-growing river parishes (to which several members of the association had strong ties), that of 1887 marked by a number of shootings and by a bloody massacre at Thibodaux in which at least thirty blacks were killed. Between 1882 and 1903, 232 blacks were lynched throughout the state.[22]

To some degree race relations were better in New Orleans than in the rest of the South in the years immediately following the Civil War, probably because of its urban character, in which it differed from most of the rest of the larger region. Although many public facilities, such as theaters, restaurants, and saloons, discouraged black business or segregated black customers, there was also flexibility in accommodating African Americans in some situations. Amusement areas such as Spanish Fort were used by both races, streetcars were not segregated, and the French Opera House allowed blacks in all parts of the theater until the mid-1870s. There was also cooperation between the races in the labor movement. "Race relations in New Orleans," however, writes one historian of the period, "for all the city's reputation for liberality, had never really been much better than in other Southern communities,"[23] and as the nineteenth century drew to a close racial divisions hardened, as "heightened tensions between whites and Negroes" developed particularly in the 1890s.[24] As the federal power of Reconstruction waned, "the color line became increasingly visible and rigid in the 1880s, primarily because a majority of the whites in New Orleans and elsewhere became committed to white supremacy and a caste system identified with the southern way of life."[25] Though in 1888 there were 128,150 registered black voters in Louisiana, by 1900 there were only 5,320, and segregation had become virtually complete.[26]

It was precisely during this period of time that the Louisiana Association was most active, a period when New Orleans whites had blacks very much upon their minds. Hence another reason for the members' intense interest in things African American. In one sense their interest in black culture must be seen as benign, given the extremely negative forms "interest" in blacks was taking in the larger society. Nonetheless, it would seem that these folklorists may also have been using folklore, however unconsciously, to mark their own sense of white identity at a time when their (white) society was very much in the process of drawing "differential identity"—to use Bauman's term[27]—along racial lines as it grappled with temporary loss of power and with the social uncertainty of their situation and the temporary challenges posed by "niggers" and other marginal outsiders, such as "dagos." The very act of "collecting folklore" set up the collectors as socially superior. But beyond that the folk material itself could serve to reinforce identity by seeming to stress by its very nature the otherness of those who possessed it. The heavy dialect of the tales the members published stressed that, as did the sense that the possessors of this lore, unlike its collectors, were superstitious—believing in ghosts and jack-o-lanterns and witches who shed their skin to become cats—or religious in a childlike way—believing fanciful stories about how trees came by their characteristics.

In the "Customs and Dialects" section of his *Louisiana Studies*, Fortier makes the point even more directly:

> *The negroes, as all ignorant people, are very superstitious. The celebrated sect of the Voudoux, of which so much has been said, was the best proof of the credulity and superstition of the blacks, as well as of the barbarity of their nature . . . .*
>
> *The religion of the Voudoux was based on sorcery, and, being practised by very ignorant people, was, of course, most immoral and hideous. It is, fortunately, fast disappearing, the negroes becoming more civilized. The dances of the Voudoux have often been described, and were, according to the accounts, perfect bacchanalia. They usually took place at some retired spot on the banks of Lake Pontchartrain or of Bayou St. John.*
>
> *Although the sect is nearly extinct, the negroes are still very much afraid of their witchcraft. The Voudoux, however, do not always succeed in their enchantments, as is evidenced by the following amusing incident. One of my friends, returning home from his work quite late one evening, saw on a doorstep two little candles lit, and between them four nickels, placed as a cross. Feeling quite anxious as to the dreadful fate which was to befall the residents of the house, the gentleman blew out the candles, threw them in the gutter, put the nickels in his pocket, and walked off with the proud satisfaction of having saved a whole family from great calamities. This is how the Creoles fear the Voudoux!*
>
> *The negroes are also very much afraid of the will-o'-the-wisp, or ignis fatuus. They believe that on a dark night it leads its victim, who is obliged to follow, wither in the river, where he is drowned, or in the bush*

of thorns, which tear him to pieces, the Jack-a-lantern exclaiming all the time, "Aie, aie, mo gagnin toi,"—*"Aie, aie, I have you."*

The old negro who was speaking to me of the ignis fatuus *told me that he was born with a caul, and that he saw ghosts on All Saints Day. He also added he often saw a woman without a head, and he had the gift of prophecy.*[28]

The contrast specifically drawn between the behavior of Fortier's dismissive white Creole friend and the beliefs and practices of "negroes" sharply underscores racial difference.[29] The folklore studied by the members of the Louisiana Association was being used in part to delineate by contrast racial identity at a time when to do so was politically and psychologically important for southern whites, continuing to recover from the loss of their "dead civilization."[30] Thus one of the stories read at an association meeting, for example, called attention to the putative physical characteristics of the "negro race" ("How the negro became black, Flat-nosed and Thick-lipped") and another drew (unconsciously?) on the comparison sometimes made between blacks and apes or monkeys—in this instance describing African beliefs that dead souls passed into gorillas.[31]

It may be that white Creoles in the association felt a particular need to establish their racial and ethnic identity. With his first book, *Old Creole Days* (1879), George Washington Cable had begun to write about Louisiana Creoles and their society.[32] Not only did he give his Creole characters a "quaint lacerated dialect"[33] to speak when they spoke English, but he also wrote for the first time in southern literature about African Americans as other than stereotypes, and he wrote of the Creoles "of color" as well as about white Creoles. Though Cable was to continue to write sympathetically about African Americans and meet increasing hostility from southerners in general for his stand (eventually he resettled in New England in the 1880s), early on he met particular hostility from the Creoles, who feared that he was causing their proud ethnic group to be badly misunderstood. In particular, "they feared that people . . . who might read his stories would get the impression that Creoles were not of unsullied white descent."[34] In 1880 Adrienne Rouquette, Creole writer and missionary to the Choctaws, attacked Cable in an anonymously published pamphlet, comparing Cable to "a foul buzzard" and a "hideous jackal." That he also accused Cable—though perhaps not literally—of "having children by Negroes"[35] suggests that Rouquette was trying to turn back upon Cable the horrifying "truth" that Cable had supposedly imputed to the Creoles, one that hit at the heart of the group's sense of identity. There was also a move at the end of the nineteenth century by such people as writer Grace King ("an arch-foe of Cable's"[36]) to limit use of the word Creole to refer to the white descendants of the original French and Spanish settlers of Louisiana—whereas it had traditionally had several meanings, including an interracial one.

Interestingly, Rouquette also resorted to a "folkloric" accusation against Cable—again one that was probably not meant to be taken literally—that he had joined "in voodoo dances with Marie Laveau, the black voodoo queen."[37] Later, as we have seen, Fortier was to write of the barbarity of the voodoos. Racial identities were being drawn according to folk practices participated in!

Creole anxiety may have been more broadly based in feelings that their ethnic culture was under siege. The challenge to French ethnic hegemony had begun much earlier, virtually with the coming of *les américains* after 1803, the resulting ethnic strife of the 1820s, and the waves of Irish and German immigrants who flooded New Orleans between 1830 and 1860. But by the end of the nineteenth century, assimilationist forces were strong in American society, and in New Orleans "French was fast being discarded by the end of the 1890's by many younger people, both white and colored."[38] Creoles may have felt that they could only lose their culture or become a marginalized group associated with, despite their high social status, the Italians and other immigrants of low prestige who were flooding the country. By including them with those who spoke funny English, Cable was casting the group precisely into that marginal place. The emphasis upon the otherness of African American culture by the Louisiana Association may have been intensified by a need to find distance from the most marginal ethnic group of all, the African Americans, especially those members of it who spoke a form of French. The Creole members of the association may have been drawn to French-speaking blacks because of an affinity of language. But because the blacks spoke a particular form ("a real idiom with a morphology and grammar of its own," Fortier pointed out[39]), having collections of tales in French Creole, a language distinguished from the fairly standard French spoken by the white Creoles, could draw yet another boundary between the two groups.

FOLKLORE, THE PLANTATION, AND CLASS

There is yet another facet of the members' focus on African American folklore—the repeated connection made between folklore and plantation life and servants. The stories reported in the minutes and in publications are frequently said to have been recorded not just from African American informants but more specifically from blacks on plantations with which the collectors had personal connections. A tale was "heard . . . at the knee of her old negro nurse in her plantation home" (May 8, 1892), or was told to a collector "by her mother, who got it from her black 'mammy'" (April 2, 1894). A story was taken down from "a very old negress . . . who had at her tongue's end the history of every [white] family and plantation," or was originally heard at "our plantation home in southwestern Louisiana." In the will-o'-the-wisp legend, the protagonist does evil to his brother specifically in order to obtain the family plantation.[40]

Fortier himself sets his remarks on Louisiana customs and beliefs in the plantation context. Though he notes the "barbarity" of African Americans, he also presents an idyllic vision of plantation life in his account:

> In order to understand fully the customs of a past age and of plantation life before the war, we must bear in mind that the planters lived in the greatest opulence and possessed many slaves. These were, as a rule, well treated by their masters, and, in spite of their slavery, they were contented and happy . . . .
>
> New Year's Day on the plantations was an occasion of great merriment and pleasure for the slaves. Its observance gave rise to scenes so characteristic of old times that I shall endeavor to describe them.
>
> At daylight, on the 1st of January, the rejoicing began on the plantation; everything was in an uproar, and all the negroes, young and old, were running about, shaking hands and exchanging wishes for the new year. The servants employed at the house came to awaken the master and mistress and the children. The nurses came to our beds to present their souhaits. To the boys it was always, "Mo souhaite ke vou bon garcon, fe plein l'argent e ke vou bienhereux;" to the girls, "Mo souhaite ke vou bon fie, ke vou gagnin ein mari riche e plein piti."
>
> Even the very old and infirm, who had not left the hospital for months, came to the house with the rest of l'atelier for their gifts. These they were sure to get, each person receiving a piece of an ox killed expressly for them, several pounds of flour, and a new tin pan and spoon. The men received, besides, a new jean or cottonade suit of clothes, and the women a dress and a most gaudy headkerchief or tignon, the redder the better. Each woman that had had a child during the year received two dresses instead of one. After the souhaits were presented to the masters, and the gifts were made, the dancing and singing began. The scene

was indeed striking, interesting and weird. Two or three hundred men and women were there in front of the house, wild with joy and most boisterous, although always respectful.[41]

He goes on to describe musical instruments and music ("most strange and savage ... but, withal, not disagreeable" [127]) as well as dancing and the customs associated with cutting the last stalk of sugar cane during the harvest ("the procession went to the house of the master, who gave a drink to every negro, and the day ended with a ball, amid general rejoicing" [129]), before going on to discuss superstitions and voodoo.

The plantation connection is clearly drawn also in setting the context for a folk story related by "Pa Medard" to Marguerite Rogers, whose husband, W. O. Rogers, presented it for her at an association meeting in 1893:

Here is a little story that I picked on my plantation home. I do not know if it ought to have been written—it is so simple but the inspiration came . . . when I found myself in this folk-lore land all teeming with folk-lore people my imagination was stirred I say so one bright day I went to sit under the shade of our old oak tree—a monument of folk-lore in itself where I knew I would find the old gardener busy with his hoe—He was there of course the faithful old soul. A Dutch clock could not be more regular. Pa Medard is his name—Pa Medard is old . . . old . . . . All folk-lore people are old—I do not mean the members [of the folklore association]—Pa Medard sees spirits—Pa Medard is an orator and what Pa Medard has not seen nor heard in the matter of strange things is not worth putting in your pipe—I mean thimble—After much urging for a story—Pa Medard was tickled, for of all things he likes after eating is to talk—so he began not the story but guess . . . to rub his nose so violently that you would have wondered if his stories were not going to shower from his nasal regions. I have noticed that about negroes—negroes of the oratory kind—whenever they [are] going to say or do something which calls [for] the powers of memory they always begin by rubbing their nose with that biggest finger next to the thumb. They make it very crooked—like a big black hook—They make it very crooked I say so as to have a good long hold and they rub it as if they wanted to dig it out of its—fortunately flat foundation—It means that something is coming. . . . After this prelude or rather thus collecting his thoughts Pa Medard began.[42]

Extraordinary in several ways, this excerpt is very revealing about the connection being made between folklore and plantation society. For Rogers,
the plantation *is* "folk-lore land" and its (black) residents are the "folk-lore
people" who teem there. The plantation is where folklore exists. These "folklore people" are "old . . . old" not coincidentally but because they must be old
precisely to insure a connection to bygone plantation days, a time period
that came to an abrupt end thirty years earlier. The folklore is an emblem
of those times, when white folks could sit down and partake of the lore of
their black folks.

If we look at some of the literary creations at the heart of the interest
some association members took in folklore in the first place, we again find
the plantation connection. In a story by Ruth McEnery Stuart, "Christmas
Gifts," first published in 1893, for example, the action begins with precisely
the kind of holiday gathering Fortier describes, with the slaves excitedly
coming up to the big house for their gifts, and dancing over to their master,
Colonel Slack, to receive them as he calls out their names. Two of them
sing a spiritual to give the gathering a more religious tone, but the "youthful
antics" of others "soon restored hilarity"[43] and the plot proceeds. Folklore
has been profusely used in this part of the story to establish the antebellum
plantation world at its benign best. The narrative goes on to tell how the
master then sends Lucinda to the house of his married daughter to deliver
messages and Chritmas gifts but also *as a gift* herself, she to become the
daughter's maid (something he has not told her). She becomes wild with
grief upon learning this truth, because she will have to leave her husband,
but harmony is restored when Colonel Slack arrives himself and explains
he has been "the clumsiest old blunderer," but of course meant that Lucinda
and husband Dave were both to come. They are receiving a "promotion" to
house servants and at the end Lucinda happily proclaims: "I's a house-gal
now."[44] It is an amazing story of plantation life, clearly evoking in Lucinda's
predicament the horrors and miseries of slavery, but using the details of
the folk celebration to distract the reader from dwelling on unpleasantness,
finally resolving the conflict within the frame of simple misunderstanding
and the slave owner's essential goodness.

Mollie Moore Davis's more or less narrative poem "Throwing the Wanga
(St. John's Eve)" appeared in 1894 in *The Louisiana Book*, edited by Thomas
M'Caleb, and—as Stuart's story focused on the plantation Christmas season
festivities—it picks up on the other aspect of Fortier's discussion, "superstition" and voodoo. The speaker in the poem is an older black woman who

initially enumerates the charms of a younger woman, Zizi. It turns out, however, that Zizi is stealing away the speaker's husband and thus the speaker is casting a spell ("throwing the wanga") upon her rival, a spell intended to make "red-hot beetles crawl"[45] under Zizi's *tignon*, to cause her head to bleed and Zizi to scratch until death takes her. A setting on the shores of Lake Pontchartrain and the St. John's Eve time frame evoke the voodoo gatherings that were held there and then (though it is not clear whether the speaker is supposed to be at such a gathering or alone).

The poem could have simply been one that uses the voodoo background to evoke an eeriness and an intensity of personal feelings. However, in the middle of the poem there is a sudden change in the stanzaic and metrical patterns, and the speaker begins to evoke the joys of "de cabin at de quarters in de old plantation days"[46] when both the young and old mistresses gave her a lavish wedding and flowers bloomed. But by now the master and his son are dead, killed at Shiloh and the Battle of the Wilderness; her own children are dead; and the speaker wonders:

> *Ole Miss, where is de glory o' de freedom I is foun'?*
> *De ole man he is lef' me fer de young eyes o Zizi!*[47]

So the folklore is here too a kind of entree into the plantation world, in that it is evoked in a situation which also evokes fond memories of a better time before "de war came."

Both the scholarly and the creative writings discussed above served to draw lines between racial identities, to distinguish between the observer and the observed, and they allowed for indulgence in a nostalgia for an older South (even attributing that nostalgia to the former slaves, as in the Davis poem), while making a statement about the essential goodness of the "peculiar institution." But if the interest in folklore enabled the drawing of boundaries, it was also doing something paradoxical. Rather than emphasize division, these pieces which focus attention upon the plantation context suggest a harmony, drawing master and slave, white and black, into a vision of happy coexistence, so that the folklore which is "theirs" also becomes "ours," giving a sense of completeness to a world of the past. Mammies and nurses narrate and white children listen; masters and mistresses give out gifts while slaves gaily dance and sing; evil magic is held in check by the happy world of the antebellum plantation. There is a sense of wholeness here gained by co-optation.

This sense of wholeness fuels nostalgia and apologia and is part of that "romantic falsification of the past" which "transfigure[d] the former existence of black bondage."[48] But it also relates to identity. "Sharing" the folklore of African Americans puts one into the revered world of the plantation, and collecting or recollecting it confers the status of an aristocratic identity. Being there, being privileged to hear the stories of a mammy, puts one into the landowning classes and, in retrospect, into a world romantically conceived of as feudal, courtly, and socially elite. The interest in folklore was one way of solidifying this connection, whether real (in the case of the Fortiers and their relations, who owned several important plantations in St. James Parish, including the fabled Petit Versailles of Valcour Aime, Alcée's grandfather) or fictive (Mollie Moore Davis seems to have implied a Texas plantation childhood that had not really been), and thus a way of claiming an upper-class identity in a world of war-devastated wealth and uncertainty about social position.

MAINTAINING IDENTITY THROUGH THE STUDY OF FOLKLORE

The members of the Louisiana Association of the American Folk-Lore Society were people who, by and large, enjoyed high social status. They and their families had undergone the trauma of the Civil War and its aftermath, had seen their property disappear and their wealth and power dwindle. The social system of which they had been a part, a system based on slavery and a peculiar relationship between the black and white races, had been uprooted, and a new racial relationship had come into being. For the Creoles, their ethnic sense was being threatened by the powerful assimilationist forces of the larger American culture. Economic hard times still prevailed, for a national recession in the 1890s interrupted the returning prosperity of the 1880s. There was much uncertainty in the lives of Louisiana people generally, and it is not surprising that they should wonder who they were and how they could establish a firm sense of themselves. Identity, after all, often becomes an important issue for people who feel that they are threatened by marginalization or by the erosion of their social position.

In the South in general, certainly in Louisiana, political moves in the 1890s were increasingly directed toward reestablishing white power and the superiority of a white racial identity that had been challenged by traumatic

defeat. The Louisiana Association worked in the midst of these developments and this atmosphere. The members by no means constituted a mono-
lithic group, and they had varying motives and perspectives. For example,
so far as race is concerned, Elizabeth Lyle Saxon expressed antislavery sentiments in her writings and Mrs. Augustin Fortier, at one meeting of the
association (March 6, 1894), expressed the idea that the study of folklore
leads to a realization of the equality of all people. Some members were after
local color, others sought intellectual stimulation. Those whose heritage was
French were interested in preserving materials in French Creole. But the
records of the group do indicate that the establishing of identity was clearly
a concern. By concentrating upon African American folklore, the folklorists
could express their sense of difference, their sense that white racial identity
was indeed distinct. Yet by also embracing African American folklore and
folklife, by emphasizing and perhaps creating fictive "shared understandings"[49] of a plantation culture of the past in which both blacks and whites
played mutually satisfactory roles, the folklorists could make a statement
about their "aristocratic" position, their identities as persons of upper-class
status. Thus they kept their distance from the culture of the "other," yet appropriated that culture when it was convenient, to make statements about
both their racial apartness and a togetherness that established class status.

"INTERNATIONALLY FAMOUS LOCALLY"
Lyle Saxon and His Quest into Folklore

The underlying need to establish their social position through expressing
their white, high-status identity arose from a historical situation in which
the members of the Louisiana Association found themselves as a group.
Though Lyle Saxon came to folklore collecting as a means to identity out of
more personal concerns, he too concentrated on African American folklore,
was obsessed by the plantation as a symbol, and worried about his place and
image in society. Because he left not only a partially finished memoir but
also diaries and a copious collection of letters, it is possible to have considerable insight into his personality and its relation to his interest in folklore,
which he would use as a key element in his search for identity.

As a folklorist, Saxon is not particularly well remembered. Richard Dorson did not know quite what to make of him, and Saxon's name does not
even appear in Zumwalt's or Bronner's histories of American folklore scholarship.[50] He was not, of course, an academic and, though an able scholar of

local history, his vision of folklore was neither a scholarly nor a sophisticated one.[51] Yet his was an important interest in southern folklore in the 1920s and 1930s and, as director of the Louisiana Writers' Project and its folklore collecting, he was a figure of some significance in the public sector folklore activities of the New Deal era, producing one of the few early books to come out of the Federal Writers' Project folklore collecting, *Gumbo Ya-Ya*.[52]

In his own day Saxon was well known as a literary figure who moved in some of the same circles as William Faulkner, Julia Peterkin, Sherwood Anderson, Edmund Wilson, and Doris Ulmann. His books were praised by Bennett Cerf and Henry Steele Commager, and, if tourists to New Orleans clutched volumes by Cable in their hands in the nineteenth century, it was said they gripped one by Saxon in the twentieth.[53] John Steinbeck was to write Saxon, "You are bigger than your myth."[54] That he had something of a "myth" about him seems undoubted—he had the charm and charisma to create one—but, inevitably, it was a "myth" that in part obscured his reality, as a personal "myth" is likely to do. To understand Saxon and his interest in folklore and his use of it in forging his sense of self, we must look at some of his personal reality.

LYLE SAXON THE MAN
"Myth" and Marginality

Saxon was a man of considerable charm, a quality attested by various sources. Edward Dreyer speaks of Saxon as a "skilled raconteur who was also possessed of an extraordinary personal charm."[55] The letters of Russell Lee, the Farm Security Administration photographer who came on assignment to New Orleans in 1938, imply the power of Saxon's ability to make Louisiana seem an intriguing place.[56] He was generous and encouraged other writers, and Dreyer tells how over a period of time Saxon regularly bought shoes for a black nun whose order operated a school for African American children in the French Quarter (though the fact that their convent was located in the same building in which the infamous quadroon balls had been held in the nineteenth century may have added to the appeal of his helping to "keep" her). During one of Saxon's illnesses, masses were said for him at St. Louis Cathedral, one friend sneaked a saint's relic into the hospital room, while others had rabbis and Christian Science practitioners at work and perhaps even employed *gris-gris*. In all, Saxon presented the larger-than-life image of a "charming raconteur,"[57] of a man full of vital energy engaged in gracious living and a social whirl, surrounded by friends and acquaintances, able to charm virtually all with his personality and his stories. Edmund Wilson even alludes to a Saxon story in his diaries, making it sound very jolly despite the brevity of the reference.[58]

Certainly his conviviality is reflected in his unfinished informal memoir, which he called "The Friends of Joe Gilmore," in effect completed after Saxon's death by *Gumbo Ya-Ya* coauthor Edward Dreyer and published as *The Friends of Joe Gilmore and the Friends of Lyle Saxon*. In it Saxon provides various accounts of his own intense socializing, of dinners with Roark Bradford, of trips to visit Weeks Hall, the eccentric artist/photographer scion of a noted plantation family, of rambles with illustrator Eddie Suydam, and of trips to Melrose Plantation on Cane River, whose famed chatelaine, Cammie Garrett Henry, had made it into a sort of writers' and artists' colony where Saxon had been given his own cabin. He writes also of his lavish Mardi Gras parties at the St. Charles Hotel (where he lived for many of his later years) and of a visit from Lucius Beebe, who later wrote of Saxon as "living in New Orleans surrounded by seedy splendor and the services of stylish and snobbish Negro servants."[59] Many others called on him at his various residences; John Steinbeck and his wife were married at Saxon's Madison Street house, and apparently some local guides even brought tourists by the hotel to meet Saxon, as though he were a sort of living artifact on the regular tour. By then, he had become known as the foremost journalistic/literary interpreter of Louisiana of his own day, the "literary lion of New Orleans." He liked to joke that he was "internationally famous locally."[60]

Yet despite his gracious living, his charm, his good humor, and his social position, Saxon was—his biographer Cathy Chance Harvey has perceptively noted—an unhappy and even tortured man, who certainly in his later years drank heavily to ease his pain. Part of his unhappiness stemmed no doubt from the fact that he never produced much fiction, though being able to write fiction was his great desire. But the more fundamental cause of this unhappiness seems to have been some sense he had of himself as a liminal figure, a man lacking a clearly established grasp of his self-identity. These conditions of his soul, in turn, probably stemmed from the circumstances of his birth and his bisexual orientation.

Saxon's mother's family were the Chambers, who had roots in the Baton Rouge area. His father was Hugh Allan Saxon, son of Elizabeth Lyle Saxon. Saxon's two principal biographers give alternate interpretations of the circumstances surrounding his birth. Cathy Chance Harvey unearthed his parents' marriage license and implies that Saxon's difficulties stemmed from their early divorce. After their marriage, Harvey notes, Saxon's parents had gone to the West and Lyle was born in Bellingham, Washington, in 1893. Lyle and his mother soon moved to Louisiana, though Hugh Saxon did not come with them, remaining in California, for the marriage seems to have quickly failed. From an early age Saxon was living with his mother and her family in Baton Rouge. Divorce was not widely accepted at the time, certainly not in the small, provincial state capital, and in the 1905–06 city directory, his mother listed herself as "widow of Hugh A.," though Saxon's father lived until the 1950s. Saxon grew up with great antipathy toward his father and well "aware of the irregularity of his family situation and, therefore, of the difficulty of maintaining a normal social life within a small Southern community of the early 1900s."[61]

James Thomas, however, is of the opinion that Saxon's parents never actually married, basing his conclusion on the apparent nonexistence of documents recording either an actual marriage ceremony or a divorce. Illegitimacy, of course, would have carried far greater social stigma than being the child of divorced parents and might even better account for Saxon's intense feelings about his father. Whichever account of his birth we prefer to accept, we can see that the circumstances surrounding it could have had a powerful negative impact on his self-perception.

When he grew older, Saxon entered Louisiana State University. Just three credits short of graduation, however, he left because of his involvement in a sex scandal with his closest friend, George Favrot. Information on the incident is scanty, but the two were evidently discovered drunk and dressed in women's clothing, not because of undergraduate high spirits but because of a fondness on their part for transvestitism. The news spread quickly and Saxon felt impelled to leave town. The incident was the first indication of Saxon's homosexual interests. For the remainder of his life he had sexual and romantic relationships with both men and women.

Thus from the beginning of his life Saxon was a nonsoutherner—at least in literal terms of his birth outside Dixie, in an era when such details counted for more than they do today—though he lived in the Deep South, with its strong feelings about regional identity, and who did and did not belong within its social boundaries. He even let it be widely believed that he had been born in Baton Rouge, to the extent that this "fact" appears in much of the earlier biographical material about him. Any sense of outsiderness he had would have been reinforced by his home situation, at best atypical and less than fully respectable in his middle-class, southern social environment, at worst potentially scandalous. As he grew older, his bisexuality made him another kind of outsider. Though he moved in somewhat bohemian circles, Saxon was aware that his sexuality would not be accepted by many of his friends and acquaintances. As a bisexual he may have felt especially liminal. Whatever his precise feelings may have been, there is ample reason to think that he saw himself as in some ways a marginal person whose sense of identity was compromised.

It seems no coincidence that he often wrote of African Americans, themselves marginal to southern society in terms of how they were commonly perceived by many whites, or that his only novel, *Children of Strangers* (1937),[62] focuses upon an even more marginal group, the Cane River Creoles of color, who existed between the black and white worlds, not accepted by either and whose marginality might be said to be the very subject of the novel. While in New York establishing his reputation as a writer, Saxon referred to himself as "a poor but honest nigger"[63] and in writing his memoirs, he assumed the pose of writing not about himself but about his black manservant, Joe Gilmore. He also referred to Gilmore as Black Saxon, noting with delight how the man sometimes passed himself off as Saxon on the telephone. On some level Gilmore was certainly an alter ego who allowed Saxon to express his sense of marginality.

It is significant that Saxon's first book that concentrated solely on Louisiana, *Fabulous New Orleans* (1928),[64] opens by calling attention to race, while it also plunges into a folkloric context. The relevant section of the book is presented as autobiographical. On Mardi Gras Day young Lyle is brought to New Orleans by his grandfather to experience the great, pre-Lenten festival. They visit an old Creole gentleman of the grandfather's acquaintance, and, because the children of the family have already left, the old gentlemen decide to send the boy out with Robert, the black servant who has been giving them coffee, to see the day's traditional festivities. Robert is able to show us and the boy things that no white man could. They go to a costume shop where Robert rents the boy a red devil costume and the same in a much larger size for "this chile's brother."[65] This nonexistent brother puzzles Lyle until they reach Robert's room. Here the servant puts on the second costume himself, explaining that the white shopkeeper would never have rented it for a black man to use. But now, in matching outfits, masked, Robert's hands encased in white gloves, they have erased their race and can move freely in many of the worlds of Mardi Gras.

So they go to Canal Street, where they blend with other maskers. They set out to watch the arrival of the Zulu king and find themselves in a part of town where there are no white maskers and "negro men picked banjos."

At the edge of the Mississippi they watch the king's approach by barge and the boy notes that "the king and his followers had improved upon Nature's handiwork by blackening their faces." Eventually Robert and Lyle find their way back to Canal Street, seeing the African American Mardi Gras Indians en route, to watch Rex, white, socially prominent King of Carnival, greet his queen, and then his parade too passes on.[66]

They head through an area that is obviously Storyville and wind up at a black saloon where Robert joins in the wild dancing. A fight breaks out, police raid the saloon, they escape, visit the rough Irish Channel, where only Robert's temporary lack of racial identity keeps him safe, for working-class white Carnival. They rest up at Robert's room for the Comus parade at night, accompanied by "prancing negroes ... holding ... flambeaux,"[67] before the day ends.

Saxon's device—black mentor, white pupil, both obscuring their physical racial identities—is a brilliant one, finding in particular a way to cross the racial divide that separates black and white Mardi Gras. Through it, he manages to present his readers with a broad overview of Mardi Gras, describing far more than any single individual would possibly encounter on one Mardi Gras occasion, such that we must view the account as to some degree a fiction.[68]

However, Saxon's device is of interest as more than a literary trick. White Americans have had a fondness for disguising themselves as African Americans, for reasons that are psychologically complex. Blackface minstrelsy is the most obvious example, but Mardi Gras—emphasizing a wide variety of masquerading anyway—traditionally provided an accepted occasion in New Orleans for whites to "mask" as black. Though Saxon does not call our attention to whites costumed as blacks in his account of the Carnival escapades with Robert, he does call attention to two other forms of racial masking: the Mardi Gras Indians, organized gangs of African Americans who have, since the end of the nineteenth century, dressed in elaborate costumes loosely based on those of Plains Indians; and the Zulu Carnival organization, whose African American members blacken their faces and otherwise accentuate features associated with white stereotypes of blacks and of Africa, to satirize those stereotypes. By calling attention to these different performances of racial identity—by which African Americans in the first instance assume a Native American identity and in the second play with their own and with others' conceptions of their own racial identity—and to the tense racial division which forces Robert to hide his and young Lyle's literal racial identities, Saxon establishes folklore—here a festival—as an arena in which race plays an important role. This was to be a key factor in his other approaches to folk materials. For Saxon, as for the earlier members of the Louisiana Association of the AFS, folklore was very much a part of African American culture, or, as with the Mardi Gras festival complex, folklore had a key African American component.

Saxon's approach to the South's great festival complex further calls our attention to his interest in, perhaps even fascination for, persons between socially defined identities. Because he perceived himself to be in such a position, biographer Harvey has said, "He was ... confronted with the need to *create an identity* which would win the approval of the community in which he lived and would therefore assure him a stable connection with that community."[69] She suggests that the identity he created was that of convivial "urban sophisticate" and of a man of aristocratic southern descent. Though Saxon did establish such personas, his search for an identity operated on another, more intellectual level, and he sought to formulate his personal identity in his books.

In part he did so by delineating a sense of place. In fact he did so almost obsessively in that every one of his books deals wholly or in significant part with Louisiana. He wrote several of them while he was living in New York, trying to establish himself as a writer. While there he experienced loneliness and alienation, and the books may have served to provide him with a connection to home, to a place to which he felt a strong attachment. More than that, however, they served to solidify an attachment that the circumstances of his birth had rendered tenuous, reinforced his sense of being truly a southerner, compensated for the somewhat ambiguous status of his childhood situation by giving him the opportunity to assert and repeatedly reassert his sense of regional and social identity. Saxon led many friends and acquaintances to believe that he had been born in Baton Rouge, and his books, though none literally make that claim to birthplace, were another means of declaring his undiluted southern-ness, an absolute sense of self in one arena at least. But Saxon's books deal with more than place and sense of place; they deal with status within the social landscape of place, and this concern was of even greater centrality to Saxon's need to create an identity.

The folk idea of the plantation as a controlling image in popular conceptions of the American South was well established by Saxon's day. This image had been shaped by various forces, including literary and artistic ones. It had been an important factor, as we have seen, in the work of the Louisiana Association of the American Folk-Lore Society. Whatever forces shaped Saxon's own conception, including the reverance for plantation life that prevailed in the world in which he grew up, his books give much attention to the plantation as a place, and they establish at length his existence, even suggest his genesis, in plantation society. Saxon's mother's Baton Rouge family, the Chambers, had a mercantile background. The Saxons do not seem to have been planters. Indeed, Saxon's biographer Cathy Chance Harvey was able to find no family plantation in the days of Saxon's childhood or youth. Yet in his books he provides a number of supposedly autobiographical accounts that link him to one or more family plantations and which in general evoke a childhood world of the big house with its fields, levees, and Negro servants.

The focus of *Fabulous New Orleans*, of course, is on that urban center, but young Lyle's journey into the whirl of Mardi Gras begins from and returns to the plantation home; as the day proceeds, he thinks intermittently of home as though to remind the reader that the plantation world is never far off. Saxon had likewise begun his first book, *Father Mississippi* (1927),[70] with a journey. Here, too, it is a childhood journey, and an older man guides young Lyle to knowledge and understanding. This guide may or may not be the same grandfather who in the later book takes the boy to New Orleans to find Robert and Mardi Gras, but the journey of *Father Mississippi* is one that hardly takes the boy out of his own house. In *Father Mississippi* young Saxon is led through the moonlight, past the "dripping streams of Spanish moss into the dark pools formed by their shadows" on his family's own plantation. The man who leads him tells him that he wants to show the boy "something you will never forget as long as you live."[71] They cross a road and mount the levee of the Mississippi River, but this "familiar ground" becomes unfamiliar when the boy sees the moonlit river itself. In flood stage, the river seems to the boy to have become an exotic ocean. Instead of speaking, he gasps, and then asks what has happened to "my river." He looks back at the plantation house from which they have come and realizes that it and the land surrounding it are below the level of the water, which practically laps their feet. The boy realizes that this is something he indeed will never forget.

This little journey with a mentor and the subsequent early chapters of the book are meant to introduce us to the river, in and beyond Louisiana, which is the book's grand subject, but they also take us into the plantation world as one of its subtexts. In that first, short chapter the boy surveys that world from the vantage point of the levee—one of the few faintly high places in flat south Louisiana plantation country—as though to provide an overview of the place the next chapters take us into. In those chapters, we have more childhood recollections, of life at the big house and in its kitchen, of a wedding of distant "relations" at the house, and of the arrival of a showboat with its calliope and its entertainers. Another chapter tells of the boyhood trips from the plantation to Baton Rouge via the river mailboat. In another he writes of the "aunts" and "uncles" of the plantation; that is, of the older blacks who were accorded these honorifics.

While *Father Mississippi* is about the entire region of the Mississippi Valley and thus only partly about the world of the plantation, and *Fabulous New Orleans* focuses upon Louisiana's metropolis, Saxon's third book, *Old Louisiana* (1929), takes us into a broader area of the state and focuses upon the plantation as a place more than upon any other topic. Though essentially a work of popular history, *Old Louisiana*—like its two predecessors—begins with a personal incursion—here into the plantation milieu.

In the first chapter he reconstructs a conversation he says he recalls from his childhood in which two old gentlemen on the plantation speak of olden times and of plantation families now gone, and this prompts Saxon into three chapters of anecdotal accounts of three such families he himself remembered. One is the Dangerfields, whose "house was overrun with servants,"[72] whose eccentric matriarch has many mishaps with horses, laughs at her flea-infested mansion, and attacks a wildcat in her hen house. Another is the Meadows, whose head, Wild Tim, manages to lose his family fortune through luxurious living and the pitfalls of Wall Street until he winds up an old man full of wild schemes, sued by others for paltry sums he cannot pay. The third is the Blakes, "aristocratic, romantic, and poverty-stricken,"[73] who live on a plantation overgrown by weeds. A son was Lyle's friend and schoolmate, and Saxon writes amusingly and intimately of the family's foibles, including a lesson given by an aunt to the children in dramatic recitation. The Blakes' plantation home was swept away by the river, his friend died in France, shot out of the skies in 1917. The Meadows go to pieces in their poverty. The Dangerfields simply move away and Saxon's letter to the matriarch comes back unclaimed. These are the romantic, faintly doomed plantation whites with their charming if self-destructive foibles and their air of having already passed from the earth even before they really do.

Though rather eclectic creations, *Father Mississippi*, *Fabulous New Orleans*, and *Old Louisiana* are primarily works of history. In addition to including those chapters of supposed memoir already discussed, Saxon deals with the development of Louisiana and New Orleans through the French and Spanish colonial and American periods, though often in a somewhat anecdotal manner, and in *Old Louisiana* he provides, for example, considerable information based on a diary kept by the resident of a plantation near Natchotoches in order to illuminate the everyday life of the nineteenth century. What the chapters of memoir do is to fit Saxon as an individual into the larger historical context. The larger context in a sense vouches for the veracity of the books and lends that air to the memoir chapters, which in fact are at least partly fictional. By describing his childhood and youth on a family plantation that apparently did not exist, Saxon reinvented his own past and invented a personal identity as a scion of plantation society, inserting himself into history and into a more romantic personal "history" than reality provided. He used his books to establish and project an identity fixed in known historical patterns and in a secure social position.

FOLKLORE AND THE OLD PLANTATION, AGAIN

Saxon ends *Old Louisiana* with a section that takes the reader on a step-by-step driving tour of Louisiana plantation country, noting in great detail the antebellum houses that could be seen along certain routes. This section serves to reiterate the centrality of the plantation to Saxon's vision of Louisiana. It also restates his own position as an insider to this world—his knowledge seems both encyclopedic and intimate—while the hypothetical reader/user of the guide is by definition cast as outsider. Interspersed with the tour information are several chapters that relate to African American folklore, and these (along with his Mardi Gras chapters in *Fabulous New Orleans*) represent Saxon's fullest commitment to his interest in folklore prior to the Louisiana Writers' Project.

The first of these involves Christmas-season customs ("for, on a plantation, Christmas is the most important day in the year"). Though Saxon does not hark back to the ritualized gift-giving noted by Fortier and Stuart, he does affectionately describe the custom by which plantation blacks, by saying "Christmas gif'" to a white person before that person can say the phrase, have a right to a gift on Christmas. Later in the day the blacks may "hunt down" Santa Claus—that is, follow a trail, some pretending to be hunting dogs hot on the scent, laid down with bits of mistletoe. In the "hunt" described by Saxon, the "pack" is led by the trail back toward the rear of the plantation house and a member of the white family playing Santa hands out stockings full of gifts. This is followed by singing: "Not the 'blues,' but their own plantation songs . . . and other ballads originated among themselves." Then "the negroes trudge homeward to their cabins, to sing at their own celebrations, and the white folks come indoors."[74]

In this final section of the book there are also two back-to-back chapters containing folklore collectanea. One is a chapter called "Superstitions," comprising a list of African American folk beliefs. The other chapter is "Some Negro Proverbs," which includes over sixty proverbs and proverbial expressions "characteristic of the Louisiana plantation negro." The books ends with an account of New Year's Eve celebrations and traditions beginning with a "singer . . . twanging upon a guitar,"[75] moving on to accordion music, which was likely some early relative of zydeco and which accompanies spirited dancing that scandalizes churchgoing blacks, and finally ending in some minor violence as the white folks ruefully smile and head back to their rooms in the frosty night air.

Though Saxon may in part have intended his folklore collectanea and his descriptions of folk performances as adding local color to his treatment of place, it is significant that—as in *Fabulous New Orleans*—folklore again marks racial division. It is the black folk who have the folklore. As for Mrs. Rogers in 1894, for Saxon in the 1920s the revered plantation *was* "folk-lore land," though it is African Americans who have the lore and whites who share it only indirectly. Whites may observe it, even collect it, but they encounter it strictly as observers or rather peripheral facilitators. Saxon emphasizes the distinction between the folklore-bearing blacks and the whites, who do not have folklore, in other ways. In introducing the chapter called "Superstitions," he writes:

> *The plantation negro is ever alert for omens.* He reads meanings into things which the white man ignores or refuses to see. *The negro has superstitions concerning the sun, the wind, the moon, and the stars; superstitions pertaining to weddings and funerals, eating and drinking; superstitions regarding the men and animals around him, the rats and mice, cats and dogs.* He lives in a world apart from the white man's world, *and in a world infinitely more interesting and terrible; for every breeze brings an omen for good or bad luck and the sunlight itself must be watched for shadows of passing birds.*
>
> . . . *It is not easy to collect them, for the negro fears ridicule and becomes self-conscious when questioned. Fearful of your laughter, he may reply that he does not believe in signs; yet a moment later, the same negro may reprove you for turning a shoe upside down, or for killing a spider.*[76] *(emphases added)*

In *Father Mississippi*, also, he had called attention to superstitions as part of the black world, not the white, noting that the first one he ever learned came from the black boy who was assigned to be his personal servant on the plantation (in addition of course again laying claim to high social status by establishing the existence of a servant). In Saxon's novel *Children of Strangers,* planter Guy Randolph even disparages the interest his brother's writer friends take in folklore, implying that black lore belongs to a realm beyond white interest.

In the course of describing the world of his childhood in *Father Mississippi,* Saxon at one point quotes some lines from the work songs of the black crewmen on the riverboats, two of which are

> *White gal smell like Castile soap;*
> *Yellow gal tries to do de same.*
> *Black gal smell like a ole billy-goat,*
> *But she git dere jus' de same!*
> . . . .
> *White man live in a big brick house;*
> *Yellow man try to do de same.*
> *Nigger lay up in de county jail,*
> *But it's a brick house, jus' de same!*[77]

These words quite specifically call attention to matters of racial difference, as does a verse sung by the guitar strummer during the plantation New Year festivities in *Old Louisiana:*

> *White folks in de parlor, eatin' cake an' cream . . . .*
> *Nigger in de kitchen, eatin' pork and beans!*[78]

This couplet divides the plantation world into two spatial spheres. It is noteworthy that in this book, in treating both the Christmas and New Year rituals, Saxon feels the need to establish—not once but twice—a literal separation of the spheres at the end of each section. At the conclusion of Christmas night "the negroes trudge homeward to their cabins, to sing at their own celebrations, and the white folks come indoors." After calm has been restored after the New Year's Eve fight, Saxon says of the white observers, especially himself, "you go back to your cabin, sneezing as you go"[79] in the chill night. The denizens of the black and white worlds split and go to their respective domains.

Saxon played with the consequences of racelessness in dealing with Mardi Gras. And he may have sometimes seen himself as, in some way, a "poor but honest nigger"; that is, on some level he may have identified with

African Americans as fellow "marginals" because of his own, deep-seated concerns about what seemed to him an ill-defined personal identity. Yet he literally lived in the white, upper-middle-class world and had to find his sense of identity there. He had, ultimately, to reject the "racelessness" of any in-between position in which his sexual orientation or the circumstances of his birth put him. He had, ultimately, to reject any sense of being a "nigger," of being in any way the counterpart of "Black Saxon," in order to put aside that symbolically dark side of himself to more fully integrate with his more fitting place as a high-status member of white society.

Folklore was what he used to make that integration on the intellectual level. As is probably the case with most folklore collectors, his interest in collecting folklore may have stemmed from a variety of motives. But in his books he took folklore and established it as the area of culture where two racial groups clearly interacted while remaining distinctly apart. As he used his books to write himself into a partially invented background, so by establishing himself vis-à-vis folklore as collector and observer, as one who went to the white domain when a black performance was over, as one who sat in the parlor rather than the kitchen (as the folksong had it), he was able to make a statement about his social position and about the identity he finally chose to assert, to "collect" himself, so to speak, out of the feeling of marginality. That is, he recycled his folklore collecting, using the folklore to make a statement about his position in society.

It is difficult to say what effect Saxon's attitudes and motives had on *Gumbo Ya-Ya*, in many ways his most important published contribution to folklore studies. This book was very much a group effort and how much of it was Saxon's work or what part of it was his is difficult to determine. It is interesting to note, however, that whereas virtually every chapter of the book contains something relating to folklore or at least to what Horace Beck has termed "popular lore,"[80] one chapter does not. That on white plantation life contains only social history. It is as though it is there because the plantation itself was so central to Saxon's conception of Louisiana and its folklore, it had to be discussed. Yet the actual folklore was relegated to other chapters dealing with African Americans, where it marked them as the more marginal part of the plantation equation.

• • •

Certainly many folklore collectors have been aware of the class divisions inherent in the very act of collecting, which traditionally involved educated, upper- or middle-class collectors approaching folk collectees who were likely unlettered, working class, perhaps poverty stricken, who certainly embodied some form of otherness—sometimes racial—in the view of the collectors.

Such an awareness might, of course, interrelate with an activist desire to uplift the folk other, a romantic desire to adulate them, or even a revolutionary impulse to expunge the differences that separated. In the case of the members of the Louisiana Association and of Lyle Saxon, however, the awareness worked itself out in other ways, in ways at least tending toward what Kirshenblatt-Gimblett has called "the reactionary potential in the affirmation of difference."[81] Folklore became in part a tool with which to, if not exactly fix, mark and emphasize difference so as to reinforce a sense of race and class divisions and feelings of belonging to an established, high-status group, separate from the lower-status other whose recent changes in status—in the case of the association—proved threatening. Henry Glassie suggests that "identity is a latent dimension . . . made manifest by stress."[82] Indeed, it was the stress of the war and the social dislocation of its aftermath—for the association—and the stress of strong personal feelings of marginality and not belonging—for Saxon—which caused these collectors of folklore to reach toward establishing identity and to use folklore in doing so, recycling their collectanea as personal, if indirect, statements about identity and social position. Their contributions to folkloristics have many positive aspects but certainly some of their motivation was such as would justify Kirshenblatt-Gimblett's call to ask questions about the politics "of the preoccupation with identity."[83] Such questions may reveal less attractive features of the history of intellectual interest in folklore, but may indeed provide deeper understanding of why folklore has been often of such intense interest. Though the work of the Louisiana Association and of Lyle Saxon represent folklore interests in only one American place (at two different times), their work suggests broader possibilities, of how intellectual interest in folklore may not be simply aimed at educational understandings of culture but can constitute a recycling of the lore to express personal and group needs and ideologies.

Chapter 3

"UNRIVALLED CHARMS"

Folklore, Nonfiction, and Lafcadio Hearn

◇◇◇

If Lyle Saxon saw himself inwardly as marginalized, his outward life showed few signs of this, and he was in his lifetime lionized as not only Louisiana's great interpreter but also as a gentleman who came from a genteel background and who lived a life of sophistication in a convivial, upscale environment. Lafcadio Hearn (figure 3.1), however, actually lived consciously and clearly on the margins, a wanderer often beset by economic need, someone who moved in the midst of the louche and the grim, a man with few possessions and few connections (at least until late in life) to a social scene. Yet Hearn, like Saxon, would come to folklore to provide himself with connections to place and, as a result, with a sense of identity, in effect recycling the folklore he wrote about to establish an image of himself as a cultural insider.

In 1877 Hearn, already well on his way to becoming one of the most prolific and interesting writers of the late nineteenth century, journeyed from Cincinnati to New Orleans. In the first newspaper column he dispatched from New Orleans to the *Cincinnati Commercial*, he announces (rather portentously making the statement its own paragraph): "So I saw the sun rise over the cane fields of Louisiana."[1]

The "kind captain" of the steamboat on which Hearn had embarked at Memphis had suggested that he come up on deck early in the morning when they entered "Sugar Country." It was for the writer, who was actually picking up stakes and moving from the Queen City to the Crescent City, a sublime moment, and he goes on with several paragraphs of lyrical reactions. The sun, he says:

> rose with a splendor that recalled the manner of its setting, but of another color;—an auroral flush of pale gold and pale green bloomed over the long fringe of cottonwood and cypress trees, and broadened and

Figure 3.1: Portrait of Lafcadio Hearn in the 1880s; Lafcadio Hearn Papers, Louisiana Research Collection, Tulane University.

lengthened half way round the brightening world. The glow seemed tropical . . . and one naturally looked for the feathery crests of cocoa-nut palms. Then the day broke gently and slowly . . . a day that seemed deep as Space. I thought our Northern sky narrow and cramped as a vaulted church roof beside that sky. . . .

And the giant river broadened to a mile. . . . Between the vastness of the sky and the vastness of the stream, we seemed moving suspended in the midst of day. . . . The green-golden glow lived there all day; and it was brightest in the south. It was so tropical, that glow;—it seemed of the Pacific, a glow that forms a background to the sight of lagoons and coral reefs and "lands where it is always afternoon."[2]

Hearn's move to New Orleans was part of his life's pattern of long but temporary sojourns in places that intrigued him. Then he would move on because he was, in a sense, always looking for a home, having been displaced from the balmy Greek island of his birth when his parents took him to live with his father's family in chilly, northern Dublin; then again when he fell from favor with his Irish relations and they engineered his emigration to America. And he kept moving because the places he sojourned eventually failed him and he found them wanting, even oppressive. He had wound up in Cincinnati as his first American home by force of circumstance, and Cincinnati had given young Paddy Hearn—who would not become Lafcadio until he reached elegant, French New Orleans—his start as a writer and his initiation as a journalist. It had also scorned him for his "marriage" to an African American and it had altogether come to seem entirely too much the cold, bustling, commercial, "beastly," northern city. Exhausted by the pace of his journalistic work there, he was attracted south by a story his editor told of experiences in Alabama, and the "tropics" gleamed with the promise of a languid life removed from the increasingly distasteful modern, industrial world and redolent of a milder climate like the Mediterranean lands of his birth. When he beheld the sunrise over the Sugar Country, the moment must have seemed portentous indeed, and he must have felt that he personally was moving into a more congenial day, that the river of his life was broadening before him like the Mississippi, and he was entering in his imagination a land of lagoons and coral reefs.

In his second *Commercial* dispatch from New Orleans, called "At the Gate of the Tropics," Hearn writes his various impressions of the Crescent City and ends the piece by telling about Père Antoine's date palm, at the time a notable local sight, his discussion ranging from Thomas Bailey Aldrich's "charming little story" about it to the "many legends concerning it"[3] and the people who told them. Hearn's most recent biographer, Paul Murray, finds this piece's mix of "descriptions of architecture, commerce and ancient folklore" typical of Hearn's work.[4] Indeed Hearn's interest in folklore certainly is a constant throughout his career as a writer, a major element in the work of this important literary figure who, if he is of interest today primarily because of his very influential writings on Japan, made a variety of contributions to nineteenth-century letters.

W. K. McNeil has examined Hearn as an "American" folklorist and found him somewhat wanting, despite the value of some of his work:

Despite his numerous publications Lafcadio Hearn has left little mark on folklore studies . . . Intent on finding the odd, he often overlooked the usual. His books on Japanese folklore were written in the mood of the mysterious east and totally missed much of the repertoire of rural

*storytellers. Texts were not sacred to him and he was intent on making
the material he heard palatable to western ears unaccustomed to reading untouched oral data.[5]*

That is, he was a romantic who chose to ignore much and he tampered with
texts. McNeil is right to say so and his looking at Hearn *as* a folklorist is not
an unreasonable approach to Hearn (one I have used myself elsewhere).[6]
However, McNeil notes that in his folklore interests, Hearn was also a literary artist looking for material and, though McNeil implies this compromis-
es his value as a folklorist, this aspect of his work offers us other possibilities
for looking at Hearn and folklore. Hearn offers us a very interesting example
of a writer who re-situates folklore for literary reasons, though perhaps not
the usual reasons writers have had. Indeed, Hearn's use of folklore recycles
it as a means of establishing his personal identity, with motives not unlike
those of the members of the Louisiana Association of AFS and Lyle Saxon
discussed in the previous chapter. He recycles folklore, manipulating it in
his presentation to put himself in a particular light.

Hearn's literary reputation is a somewhat curious one. Though nearly a
hundred years after his death he has his admirers, even his devotees, and
though he is the subject of no fewer than five "major" biographies,[7] his
work has seldom entered the major anthologies of the conventional literary
canon. This may be due in part to his personal multiethnicity and our own
difficulty in placing him easily in a particular national literary tradition,
for though he began writing in the United States and has been seen as an
American writer, he was born on a Greek island under British political control of an Anglo-Irish father and a Greek mother, grew up mostly in Ireland,
and retained his British nationality until he became a Japanese citizen late
in life. Another important factor is that he wrote primarily nonfiction, not
the novels, poetry, or drama that have been of greatest interest to critics;
much of what he wrote is "journalistic."

There is, of course, a long tradition of studying folklore in literature, of
examining how writers "use"—that is, re-situate—folklore in written works,
recycling folklore for various effects. However, the great majority of interest has been in fictive genres. Little attention has been paid to folklore in
nonfiction writing, and such may be the case for several reasons. Folklorists themselves write nonfiction, and it may be difficult for them to think
in terms of writing strategies beyond nonfiction's function in simply presenting, annotating, or discussing the characteristics and social meanings
of folklore. Furthermore, since Alan Dundes[8] exhorted those discussing

folklore in literature to go beyond mere identification of folklore to consider the meaning of the folklore in the literary text, such critics, most commonly folklorists, have indeed sought to look at the folklore positioned in literature in terms of thematic or symbolic import. We are simply more used to doing that for fictive genres. Yet nonfiction may have its own complexities and writers of nonfiction their own subtle strategies for presenting the world. As a particularly talented writer of nonfiction, Hearn produced work the examination of which offers important insights into those strategies. We tend to think that any nonfiction discussion of folklore will be solely a straightforward explication of the folklore concerned, whether providing texts, describing a folk context, or offering explanatory ideas. However, Hearn's work makes clear the fact that writers of nonfiction may have their own motives for writing about folklore and may in effect be recycling it through their discussions of it for personal reasons.

Of course, Hearn developed his talents over many years, and his work came to particular fruition after he had gone to Japan. His years in Ohio, New Orleans, and Martinique, however, served both to satisfy his passion for folklore collecting and to develop his techniques for incorporating folklore into writing. The book which is the culmination of the American part of his life is *Two Years in the French West Indies*, and it is an important focus of this chapter in that it is a unified—though indeed loosely unified—work, which uses folklore in the larger context of presenting place. It is also a minor classic of nineteenth-century travel writing and a book that prefigures Hearn's most mature period in Japan. One finds in it "a reaching toward the simplicity which characterized . . . later work" and it can be seen as a "prototype for his Japanese books."[9] S. Frederick Starr has suggested that Hearn's very residence in the Creole societies of Louisiana and the West Indies was vastly important in shaping his vision of Japan itself and that "Louisiana, not Japan, was the laboratory in which he worked out his understanding of the interaction of tradition and modernity,"[10] an issue that became increasingly central to Hearn's perspectives. Martinique played a similar role.

Where Hearn's interest in folklore had its genesis is difficult to precisely say. Hearn had access to the Dublin library of his great-aunt and unofficial guardian, Sarah Brenane, and he wrote later of its importance in his development, for obviously it provided young Hearn with an escape from his rather gloomy surroundings. He speaks in particular of his discovery of books of mythology, of "all the charming monsters . . . of Greek mythology," and of "stories of the infernal magic that informed the work of the pagan statuaries."[11] The illustrations in these books were later censored, perhaps by the puritanical Mrs. Brenane or perhaps by a hired tutor, the deities and heroes having certain offending body parts excised by penknife. But Hearn had his introduction to myth, nonetheless. Paul Murray further suggests that no one of Hearn's class and inclinations living in Dublin when he did could have escaped noticing the upper-class "enthusiasm for the folk culture of the ordinary people" that would also influence Irish intellectuals like Yeats and Lady Gregory.[12] While he lived in New Orleans Hearn published *Stray Leaves from Strange Literature* (1884) and *Some Chinese Ghosts* (1887), both of which retell folk narratives and other narratives with folkloric connections.[13] Both books are indicative of his interest in mythic and legendary tales, and to produce them he relied upon printed sources. However, it was his newspaper work in Cincinnati that led him to his first real encounter with folklore in the cultural reality of local life and that produced the first writings in which he shows himself to be ethnographer and collector.

THE CINCINNATI LEVEE

Hearn's life in Cincinnati was not a conventional one. He spent his early days there in considerable poverty and desperation, and even when he had established himself as a journalist he tended toward the peripheries of respectable society, partly by inclination, partly because his journalist's existence drew him to the demimonde to cover the seedier realities of life for his paper. Cincinnati was struggling toward prosperous respectability but remained in many ways a raucous river town. Hearn had a reputation for prowling the less respectable quarters, sometimes roaming through the night, by himself or in the company of such bohemian companions as the painter Henry Farny. They might rove through the loud beer halls of the bustling German section or into such riverside neighborhoods as Bucktown, where the mostly African American levee workers had settled. It was in Bucktown and elsewhere along the levees that Hearn found folklore and folk performances that he recorded in some of the dozen articles on levee life that he penned for the *Cincinnati Enquirer* and *Cincinnati Commercial* between 1875 and 1877.

These dozen pieces are collectively impressionistic, dealing very selectively with Cincinnati levee life, yet they are remarkable in preserving valuable details at least of the lives of American working-class people little noticed by other writers of the time (as Simon Bronner has recently noted[14]) and they show Hearn's keen eye for social and cultural observation. In one of the earliest of these pieces, "Pariah People," Hearn dwells on the grim side of the levee district as "a haunt of crime" where "hideous huts" are "often rotten with the moisture of a thousand petty inundations" and "inhabited only by the poorest poor or the vilest of the vicious."[15] The fascination with the grim that permeates "Pariah People" is similar to that in other of Hearn's Cincinnati newspaper articles, showing his taste for the sensationally morbid that gained him local notoriety for his series on the grisly Tanyard murders; and demonstrating his technique of taking respectable newspaper readers to places they would normally never go, as when he wrote of ascending the beetling spire of the city's Catholic cathedral with a team of steeplejacks.

As time went on Hearn obviously became better acquainted with the levee and its denizens, and, though he continued to be attracted by the area's grittiness, he came to write affectionately of those levee people who took in orphans, of the charitable saloon tenders and of various other likable if lost souls. He was soon noting the musical and dance traditions of the place ("three musicians sawing and picking away, the leader yelling off changes in a low guttural tone, twenty or thirty dancers . . . shuffling around" in "Ole Man Pickett"; "furious thrumming of banjos and bass-viols, and the wild thunder of the dancers' feet" in "Dolly"); and in "Levee Life," published in the *Commercial* in March of 1876, he allowed free rein to a penchant for folklore collecting. Here he includes the texts of a number of songs sung by the roustabouts along with description of their performance and other information. Song texts, although not so extensively quoted as here, appear in other of Hearn's levee pieces, and he spends one article detailing a minstrel show put on in a prominent saloon and another in telling about Jot, the levee's voodoo practitioner.[16]

Clearly Hearn was drawn to folklore and folk performance through his being intrigued and charmed by it—as he was ultimately charmed by the rude levee "pariahs" and their marginal milieu. But he was attempting to provide a portrait of a place, a place little known by most who read his articles even though they lived in the same Queen City as the levee people, and he saw in the song and music and dance and folk belief of the people who lived in it something essential to that place, something which defined it and gave it life. When he arrived in New Orleans Hearn set to writing about the new place to which he had come, although his audience for his first New Orleans writings was those same Cincinnatians for whom he had delineated the life of Bucktown, for he still worked for the *Commercial* on a free-lance basis when he arrived in Louisiana. It seems not coincidental that folklore appears in those early New Orleans writings where he mentions voodoo poisons, place-names, and Creole songs, for he saw folklore as inextricably connected to place. Though some of this early use of New Orleans folklore is superficial, in the matter of the legend of Père Antoine's date palm, he does seem to have expended some efforts in doing fieldwork.

In New Orleans Hearn was to go on to write about folklore and folklife in a variety of later works, but it will be useful to look ahead to the major piece of Hearn's writing that was to come out of the period just after he left New Orleans, *Two Years in the French West Indies* (1890),[17] because this book gives us a more unified sense of his interest in folklore before his Japanese period than do his more scattered Louisiana pieces. This book seems related to and might even be seen as the culmination of his Louisiana interests in at least two ways. It continues his intense interest in delineating place, and it continues his interest in Creole cultures. The term Creole meant more than one thing to Hearn. He had a strong interest in French Creole languages. But he was also fascinated by creolization, by the merging of European and African that was so central to both New Orleans and Martinique, and he saw the French West Indies where he went to live not merely as an extension of Louisiana but as a more pure, rarefied version of the Creole.

HEARN'S CARIBBEAN WORLD

Two Years in the French West Indies was published in 1890 by the venerable firm of Harper and Brothers, who had published several of his earlier works. Indeed, he had published parts of the book as articles in *Harper's Monthly* in 1888 and 1889, though he revised those pieces for the book. After living in New Orleans from 1877 to 1887, Hearn had rather wearied of the place and felt impelled to move on—indeed part of a larger pattern of his life according to which he kept on the move, sojourning in very different places for periods of years. He had been moving progressively south, and the West Indies seemed to promise an even warmer climate and a more exotic culture, as well as a less modern, less industrialized society than he had found in the United States—and Hearn was a decided enemy of modernity. He took a midsummer cruise out of New York to the Caribbean in 1887 and, though he speaks of the "unrivalled charms"[18] of the whole region, he was particularly enchanted by Martinique—the account of the cruise itself that forms the first part of the book devotes more attention to that island than to almost any other place—and he returned for a longer stay there and wound up staying even longer than the few months he anticipated.

Indeed, the second part of the book is called "Martinique Sketches" and consists of fourteen individual sketches—that is, informal essays—which are largely independent of each other, though the same people and places reappear. They range across such subjects as the women porters who are key figures in local commerce, the Carnival celebration, his own housemaid, and the great volcanic mountain, La Pelée, which dominates the island. Though he deals with physical landscape both in his general descriptions of the lush tropics that had in part drawn him to the island and in such disquisitions on nature as his several pages on the fer-de-lance, the deadly snake that inhabited even the island's botanical garden, Hearn overwhelmingly favors the cultural landscape and writes primarily of human life.

More than once Hearn refers to taking down dictation and we may assume that he was serious about recording oral data and that he did see himself as a folklore collector is also made clear by the fifteenth part of the "Martinique Sketches," not a sketch at all but an appendix entitled "Some Creole Melodies." He prints here four songs with words and music (the arrangements having been wrought for pianoforte and voice by Henry Edward Krehbiel, the noted musicologist and critic, who was Hearn's friend from Cincinnati, and by a New York composer). This appendix also offers a few introductory comments on Martinique music, such as observations on the improvisational nature of some songs and the creation of *pillard* by which a satirical song is directed at someone "whom it is deemed justifiable and safe to annoy" (424). This section, then, consists of collectanea with notes and thus is not unlike early scholarly contributions to the *Journal of American Folklore*, which was being started during those very years when Hearn was in the West Indies. Yet its conception as an appendix, as a virtual afterthought, is indicative of how Hearn was not primarily intent on presenting collectanea, as were many of the scholars beginning the *Journal*. Various actual sketches in the book are full of folklore, but in every case the folklore is integrated into and subjugated to other literary purposes of the sketch.

In some cases the integration is a simple, almost off-handed one, the folklore being added as a cultural detail, an addendum to the matrix of the local. For example, in writing admiringly of *les porteuses*, the women who carry goods by trekking all over Martinique (thus playing a crucial socio-economic role), Hearn notes that they always try to reach some destination by sunset because "like all her people, she is afraid of meeting *zombis*" (108). In writing about a trip to the remote village of La Grande Anse, he mentions the promontories which form the bay here, including a legend

'TI MARIE.

(On the Route from St. Pierre to Basse-Pointe.)

Figure 3.2: A *porteuse*, one of the female porters who played an important economic and cultural role on Martinique; from Lafcadio Hearn, *Two Years in the French West Indies*.

about an insurgent slave, "shot dead upon the cliff" (126). Or in commenting on the fall of night, he notes that the howling of a dog has no particular superstitious significance, whereas the howling of cats forebodes death in local belief. Or in describing the great mountain, La Pelée, he includes in a footnote information on local weather beliefs, such as that a clear view of the mountain's often clouded top may mean a hurricane, while in writing about the danger of snakes while cutting cane, he incorporates a footnote about local cures for snakebite.

In other instances Hearn provides full texts as well as texts which though partial are fairly long and developed. In his piece on *les porteuses*, for instance, he makes the point that these female porters (figure 3.2) feel free to ask anyone to help them lift their loads and that no one, not even "the proudest planter" (105), ever refuses. Hearn then gives, in a footnote, an excerpt from a folktale in which a woman is unable to find anyone to "help her load" (106) and must resort to asking a passing devil for assistance.

Hearn makes the point that failure to help a *porteuse* can in this society only be imagined (and is, indeed, regarded as a grave breach of conduct). In his sketch of *les blanchisseuses*, the laundry women who wash clothes in the river that flows through the Savane du Fort in St. Pierre (the town where Hearn spent most of his time on Martinique but which was largely destroyed by volcanic eruption in 1902), Hearn provides fairly extensive texts of songs they sang. In his piece about the village of La Grande Anse he includes considerable information on "the old African dances, the *caleinda* and the *bélé*" (143) and on drumming as well as song texts.

Hearn had several purposes in making such inclusions. Though no anthropologist, he sought to include ethnographic information as part of his larger desire to present place. And though he may have felt that folklore provided local color—a function folklore handily filled for many writers of Hearn's era—his presentation of folk materials almost always seems more serious than that, an impression that is certainly reinforced by the fact that much of the material is relegated to notes. In most instances, the folklore, however minor a part of the sketch, amplifies some aspect of the piece. The porters' fear of zombis introduces a general belief of the local cultural system, for example, one which becomes of particular importance in "La Guiablesse," but also explains a detail of the rather extraordinary island system of commercial transport. The lengthy discussion of drumming and dancing reminds the reader of the importance for Martinique of its African heritage, one element in the place's multicultural quality, something which fascinated Hearn, who was particularly interested during these years in multiracial people and creolization.

However, in several sketches folklore emerges as more vitally central, and it is in these that we get particular insight into some of the subtleties of a writer of literary nonfiction using folklore. One of these is a longer piece, "La Vérette," which deals with an attack of chicken pox while Hearn was in residence on Martinique, the other, "Un Revenant," in which Hearn looks at the early history of the island.

In "Un Revenant" Hearn plays with the meanings of the French word *revenant*, meaning both a haunting spirit and someone who returns; this latter meaning ties into Martinique's being called *Le Pays des Revenants*, which Hearn translates as "The Country of Comers-Back," because of its being a "wonderful island . . . where Nature's spell bewitches wandering souls like the caress of a Circe" (148), causing people always to return. Whoever first gave this appellation to Martinique did not, Hearn asserts, ever mean to think of the *other* meaning of *revenants*, did not mean to label it the Land of Ghosts. Yet Hearn himself does precisely that, segueing into legends of the supernatural as his route to talking about a key figure from the island's past.

"Almost every plantation," Hearn writes, "has its familiar spirits" (148). In one legend a body is lifted out of its coffin and taken away by the devil through a window no human can close; in another a ghostly rider roams the hills trying to find the grave of a friend buried many years ago; in a third a planter is mysteriously summoned from a feast only to completely vanish. These narratives do not necessarily involve the ongoing presence of spirits. Hearn means that the legends themselves "haunt" the place with a particular sense of the past. Another legend relates to a "widespread" "legendary expression," which translates as "in the time of the big wind of Monsieur Bon" (149) and which locals use to refer to a time in the distant past. It springs from narratives that make out Monsieur Bon to have been a wicked man and a slave owner so cruel to his slaves that God sent a great wind which blew away him, his house, and all its inhabitants, "so that nothing was ever heard of them again" (150). Hearn thus shifts from folklore of literal haunting to folk narratives that involve mysterious and supernormal happenings and that provide small windows into the folk historical memory. He finally turns up an "informant," a "charming old gentleman," apparently a member of the white upper classes, who provides the "true facts" about Monsieur Bon (150). Bon was, it seems, a Collector of Customs who accepted a captain's invitation to breakfast on board his ship when a hurricane blew in. The ship made for open waters and was never seen again. Monsieur Bon was in fact "a kind old soul. . . . Never had a slave in his life" (151). Thus Hearn puts legend in opposition to "true" history, as others before and since.

Why he should, in order to do so, accept another oral account—one passed down by the old gentleman's grandfather, who claimed to have known Monsieur Bon—this one from an upper-class, white informant, is an interesting question, but what matters is that Hearn has set up the history/legend opposition. "The legend of 'Missie Bon' had prepared me to hear without surprise," he goes on to say, "the details of a still more singular tradition,—that of Father LaBat." He explains that he was coming home "from a mountain ramble" with a native guide in the gathering darkness. He suddenly sees on the side of a nearby ridge, which he had thought an uninhabitable jungle, a moving light. His guide also sees it, crosses himself, and exclaims, "I believe it is the lantern of Père Labat" (151–52). When Hearn naively asks if Père LaBat lives there, the guide further explains that the man has been dead for hundreds of years. Later his neighbor tells him that the light is thought to be a lantern held by LaBat's ghost, carrying it as penance for having introduced slavery to the island.

Hearn speaks of this tradition as "the most impressive legend in all Martinique folk-lore" (152), but the folklore is really his frame for talking about LaBat as historical figure. Just as Monsieur Bon was not an evil slaveholder, so LaBat did not introduce slavery to the island, but he did play an important role in developing the colony, especially the church and the power and wealth of his own Dominican order. He explored the whole region, drove off English corsairs, and wrote extensively about Martinique, producing a source that Hearn himself obviously found valuable. The priest was an odd mixture, not uncharacteristic of his age, of the practical and the credulous, building a little empire for his order but also vouching for the occult powers of the African slaves and who once ordered to be horribly whipped a slave "soothsayer" who correctly predicted the death of a slave owned by the Dominicans, an act of cruelty that perhaps resulted in his reputation as the local founder of the cruel institution. LaBat's position as a powerful cleric enables Hearn to end the sketch with comments about religion on Martinique, including descriptions of home altars and wayside shrines.

Legends of hauntings are particularly tied to locality, to the places ghost-endowed, and thus are particularly expressive of the local. By working with two such narratives, Hearn is able to tie aspects of his book about a particular place more tightly into local context, intimating that he has become privy even to such significant markers of the local, while also suggesting that the evils of slavery remain a strong focal point in the folk memory of the black population and that the Catholic religion has an important, ongoing presence here. The LaBat and Bon legends pose an alternative history that has purely local meaning, providing both literal ghosts who haunt and a sense that the past "haunts" the worldview of the islanders. This allows Hearn to develop information and express himself about verifiable history. That neither historical personage ever actually returned to the island—Bon was blown to sea and never again seen; LaBat died in Paris, prevented from returning by politics—and that neither is a *revenant* in that sense adds a note of irony but also suggests that the need for retaining the past in local tradition is so important that even those who left and in the end did not literally return are nonetheless still always here.

The other sketch in which folklore is so central, "La Vérette," takes the reader through certain events from February 15 to April 13, 1887. February 15 is Ash Wednesday, the final day of Carnival, which in Martinique does not end on Mardi Gras but continues and concludes on the first day of

Lent, an anomalous situation that still prevails today. Of this day of the "last masquerade" Hearn provides an impressionistic but nonetheless detailed description. He observes the descent into the town from the nearby ridge of the two "great dancing societies," "maskers in rose and blue and sulphur-yellow attire" (206) who specialize in satiric songs:

> *Then all the great drums suddenly boom together; all the bands strike up; the mad medley kaleidoscopes into some sort of order; and the immense processional dance begins. From the Mouillage to the Fort there is but one continuous torrent of sound and color: you are dazed by the tossing of peaked caps, the waving of hands, and twinkling of feet;—and all this passes with a huge swing,—a regular swaying to right and left . . . . It will take at least an hour for all to pass; and it is an hour well worth passing. (207)*

And he goes on to provide song texts, describe costumes ("rather disappointing" though "not unpicturesque"; crimson and canary predominate; there are mock religious costumes; most maskers wear white wire masks; the devils and devilesses are striking), and notes the "droll ceremony" (209, 212) during which a dummy representing some unpopular thing is paraded and finally buried or tossed into the sea.

What makes the Carnival Hearn describes so remarkable, however, is that it is taking place while an epidemic of chicken pox rages across the island (because chicken pox was unknown on some Caribbean islands, it could strike with a singular virulence, making it a more serious disease than that with which Americans are familiar, though whether anyone would actually die, as Hearn indicates they did, is doubtful). As the celebrations proceed, victims of the disease assume costumes that mask faces already disfigured by this "hideous malady" and join the madcap festivities in the streets:

> *And in the Rue Ste. Marthe there are three young girls sick with the disease, who hear the blowing of the horns and the pattering of feet and clapping of hands in chorus;—they get up to look through the slats of their window on the masquerade,—and the creole passion of the dance comes upon them. . . . We will have our fill of fun: what matter if we die after! (208–9)*

In the mocking Carnival spirit one masker offers to sell pox sores, though no one laughs at this joke, while plans to make the ceremonially buried dummy represent the "plague" also do not come off because the disease is "too terrible a visitor to be made fun of" (212).

The epidemic allows Hearn to endow his description of a folk festival, then, with a particularly macabre quality, suggestive of the medieval dance of death (and sets the stage for concluding the sketch with an account of death from the pox of Yvette, a pretty dyer of traditional headdresses, despite the ministrations of Manm Robert, a folk healer "always . . . pleased to chat [with Hearn] about creole folk-lore" [225]). The epidemic doubtlessly adds to the drama of the folk event and doubtlessly appealed to Hearn's own love of the grotesque, an aspect of his writing since his early days as a journalist in Cincinnati when he delighted in reporting on the most dreadful murders and such subjects as the practices of slaughter houses. Yet the macabre context of the epidemic also adds to the reader's sense that Hearn is indeed closely involved in the local context—this is no account of Carnival by some casual, passing visitor but clearly by someone so acclimated here that he is involved with the intimacies of disease and death and is able to look behind the flimsy wire masks of celebration to something more fundamental.

Hearn's extended uses of folklore are in part literary strategies designed to convince the reader that he is, yes, a travel writer, but one who has connected to the local context to the extent of having reached significant understandings of local texts. He is not a native but has become cultural insider enough to comprehend not only the local Creole language but also the folk traditions that are not encountered by the passing tourist. True, he once passed through the Caribbean as a sort of tourist, and that trip was recounted in "A Midsummer Trip to the Tropics," the first section of his book. But that section contrasts with the "Martinique Sketches," which prove that he returned, a *revenant*, as a serious sojourner on the island who wrote down local stories, who was privy to the intimacies of folk history, who understood the realities of death behind Carnival masks. Thus he establishes himself as a particularly authoritative voice and as someone who has found a kind of home.

Hearn—who referred to himself as a "wandering ghost," who was early displaced from his own native island, whose Irish family rejected him— particularly sought local connections to mitigate his personal sense of exile, rather as Lyle Saxon did to come to terms with his own sense of being marginal. In every place he lived during his adult life, though he kept moving on, Hearn tried to establish through his writing a connection to local cultural contexts that would rival a native's. His interest in folklore, so often tied to local contexts (at least in the imagination), served him well here, while his longing for a home also added energy to his writing and led him to literary strategies that certainly worked well for his West Indian writings. By writing about folklore, he could manipulate it to imply that he had become a cultural insider, to reassure himself that he had found something of a home.

FOLKLORE AND NEW ORLEANS

Because he spent more time in New Orleans (ten years as opposed to two in the West Indies), because he worked for New Orleans newspapers and had to write on an incredible variety of topics and in a variety of styles and forms, Hearn's use of Louisiana folklore is more scattered. In New Orleans he did, however, produce what is arguably his only full volume of collected folk texts—*Gombo Zhèbes* (1885)—in that his later, well-known collections of Japanese tales consist of literary re-renderings. *Gombo Zhèbes* pulls together 352 proverbs in Creole French dialects, not only from Louisiana but also Martinique, Haiti, Mauritius, and other places where Afro-French cultures had taken root. The non-Louisiana proverbs were taken by him from printed sources which are carefully listed in a bibliography. How he acquired those from Louisiana is not entirely clear, although apparently most if not all came from his friend Professor William Henry, head of the Jefferson Academy in New Orleans, who thus seems to have been the actual collector. Hearn's contribution lay not merely in his bringing the sayings together in one place, but in envisioning a book with a comparativist focus and in providing comparative data and other useful features. It is a scholarly book replete with footnotes on every page. Sometimes an equivalent English proverb is given (in addition to standard French and English translations), and the notes comment on lexicography, aspects of meaning, African retentions, and historical references. Hearn was familiar with the publication of Creole folk texts in French periodicals and obviously had a knowledge of Creole folklore from his own observations. Thus he includes in the notes snippets of folk poetry where the same word as found in a proverb is also used and references the folktales that seem to relate to certain proverbs. Certainly he was attuned to how proverbs have meanings in relation to their actual performance, although he seems to have seen this as especially important to cultures whose people are of African descent. He writes that "a large majority of negro sayings depend altogether upon application" for meaning and "possess a chameleon power of changing hue according to the manner in which they are placed." He goes on to say that "the art of applying one proverb to many different situations is one in which the negro has no rival,"[19] and in the notes provides both fictional dialogue and recollection of actual usage to illustrate proverb meaning in context.

Gombo Zhèbes, certainly a significant contribution to the study of Creole culture, actually is indicative of several things about Hearn. It makes clear that he could be quite scholarly, whereas his interest in folklore often has been seen as purely romantic. His inclusion of comparative data and his awareness of foreign scholarship reminds us also of how cosmopolitan his interests were. Indeed, during his years in New Orleans his writings ranged over a vast array of subjects. His *New Orleans Item* pieces alone range over such subjects as French translation of Poe, communism, discoveries at Pompeii, and Zola, Daudet, and Bismarck. The sheer amount of his work while in New Orleans is staggering, including poetry, translations, reviews, editorials and, as he was a working journalist, countless news articles, most published anonymously and some of which have never been attributed to him. Though these contributions do move over a wide range of subjects, Hearn's writings on New Orleans and Louisiana are many and especially important. Indeed, S. Frederick Starr has called Hearn "the man who invented New Orleans," by which he means that Hearn played the pioneering and key role in pulling together in his writings the "literary construct," the collection of images that are New Orleans in the modern consciousness— images that include the ideas of New Orleans as less modern, less American, more sensual, and culturally more "authentic" than other American cities. Until Hearn, Starr argues, "not one writer had consistently developed every one of the elements of this literary gumbo."[20]

The extent to which Hearn created a certain vision of New Orleans is no doubt very complicated. Surely he did not consciously mean to "invent" New Orleans, and that sort of postmodern terminology would have seemed quite foreign to him. In his writings, however, he does deal with the facets of New Orleans culture that have come to be central to a local imagination and worldview. He doubtlessly sought to bond with his (temporarily) adopted home, and writing about it was his personal method for doing so. For someone of his generation folklore would have seemed closely attached to place, and folklore became an important element in his attempt to bond with the Crescent City as it did later in Martinique. In *Gombo Zhèbes* he says in several notes that "In Louisiana *we* say . . ." (emphasis added), thus positioning himself as part of the local population (and, indeed, the local Creole population he saw as the essential ingredient of the city's culture).

He also, however, speaks of "*our*" (emphasis added again) proverbs in giving English equivalents, thus suggesting his ongoing membership in a culture beyond the world of New Orleans Creoles. It is difficult not to see *Gombo Zhèbes*, Hearn's "little essay in Creole folklore," as a way of dealing with his cultural bifurcation, as a way of slipping into a Creole home, despite his cultural origins elsewhere, by demonstrating his intimate knowledge of things Creole. That is, as he would do later in Martinique, Hearn was using folklore to position himself as a cultural insider, recycling his relationship to folklore to imply something about his identity.

In a critique of Alcée Fortier's Creole grammar Hearn notes that all attempts to preserve "Louisiana traditions, folklore, colonial manners and customs, [and] linguistic peculiarities"[21] should be encouraged. Hearn's interests in language and folklore obviously were closely intertwined, and his associating customs and manners with the colonial period suggests that his interests in all these things was partly an interest in survivals from the past, not an uncommon perspective for those interested in folklore in that day. In *Gombo Zhèbes* he notes that "our cook" speaks the old Creole "patois in its primitive purity,"[22] whereas her daughter's speech is influenced by standard French, revealing a view that sees in Creole something ancient and pure that can only be corrupted. Hearn, despite his intense interests in many contemporary developments, increasingly moved toward a rejection of modern, late-nineteenth-century life and culture, and his being able to see folklore and the Creole "patois" as of a more congenial past stimulated his interest in these elements of culture. Of course, the appeal of New Orleans itself was in its being something of a relic with a culture in opposition to that of modern, industrial American society. To make New Orleans his own was thus in part intertwined with his embrace of the past, so that his folkloric interests were involved not only in bonding with place but with a place that represented a certain by-gone way of life. Eventually he was to leave New Orleans in part because he thought it was being increasingly corrupted by the infusions of modern American life.

Folklore appears in Hearn's work of the New Orleans period in a variety of ways, ranging from the scholarly approach of *Gombo Zhèbes*, to chance translation of folktales that came his way, to the use of street cries and songs in the short newspaper pieces that sought to give brief impressions of the city to local readers and that were eventually collected (in 1924) as *Creole Sketches*.[23] However, by looking at several of his longer, more concentrated pieces we get a fuller idea of the role he assigned to folklore in his literary nonfiction.

In several of his New Orleans essays we certainly see Hearn's skill as an observer and indeed as an ethnographer (Bronner speaks of Hearn's writing "ethnographic journalism"[24]), though not in any literal, scientific sense of that term. We can also see his development as a serious commentator on folk culture if we compare, for example, the piece he published on a noted New Orleans voodoo practitioner with that he penned on Jot, the voodoo man of the Cincinnati riverfront colony. The earlier piece, though it demonstrates Hearn's interest in folk magical practitioners, is vague and less than really informative. It simply speaks of Jot's reputation on the levee and recounts a visit to his residence, which is described in some detail, and suggests that the man deals in charms and the like. Jot seems little more than another levee character. In the New Orleans piece, however, "The Last of the Voudoos," originally published in *Harper's Weekly* in 1885, nine years after the piece on Jot, Hearn provides much more concrete detail, mostly in terms of the life of his subject, Jean Montanet also known as Dr. John, or Voudoo John, but to some extent on how Montanet actually practiced his "Creole medicine"[25] and on his amalgamation of the African and the European; it is far richer culturally and more informative.

"The Last of the Voudoos" is undeniably more sophisticated than the earlier piece and an indication of Hearn's growth as an ethnographer, but it is in "The Creole Doctor" that Hearn gets more deeply into the actual substances and behaviors of folk magic and folk medicine. The Creole doctor referred to in the title is not the trained physician but rather the folk healer, and the essay ranges fairly systematically over what the author has ferreted out about the use of various *tisanes* or about cures for chills and fever, tetanus, or headaches. Hearn admits that some practitioners were reluctant to "either sell or give away the secret"[26] of their cures, but he manages to set out a small wealth of information on such subjects as the power of honeysuckle, how jaundice is treated with melon seed tea, or how cockroach tea for tetanus is widely used also by the non-Creole population of New Orleans. A little later Hearn showed himself to have been a keen observer of folk beliefs and their contexts generally in "New Orleans Superstitions" (originally published in the *New York Tribune* in 1886 and included in *An American Miscellany*), and he acknowledges that the beliefs and related practices he describes may be both African and European in origin.

Then in "St. Malo" and "St. John's Eve—Voudooism," Hearn recounts what could be called field trips, in the first instance to a "Malay" stilt village in the marshes of Lake Borgne northeast of New Orleans, in the second to a voodoo dance on the shores of Lake Pontchartrain. The second of these (recently attributed to Hearn by S. Frederick Starr and Delia Labarre, a rea-sonable attribution[27]) is rather less successful than the first in that Hearn never makes clear how he happened to find the remote spot for the voodoo dance despite being declined information by a number of people and in that he seems to believe—or at least professes to believe—that voodoo celebrants worship the devil, an awfully conventional perspective he might be expected to have transcended. Yet he does provide fairly detailed description of what he saw and provide the text of a song he recorded. "St. Malo" gives us good close observation of the marsh settlement and also provides considerable information on the gambling that takes place in the settlement and texts of the rhymed Spanish verses used in calling out numbers in gambling.

In his New Orleans writings, the inclusion of folklore never becomes the central strategy for writing about place and connecting to place that it would become for Martinique, yet it prefigures his Martinique interests and suggests how he saw folklore as providing him with an entree to a sense of belonging in a particular place and its cultural context.

Hearn was very much a writer about place, and Cincinnati, New Orleans, and Martinique gave him the opportunity to further consider the roles folk-lore and folk culture play in defining a place for its inhabitants or visitors as well as how folklore could serve him in his personal attempt to fit into places as he searched for some location he might call home. Whether he finally found that home in Japan is debatable, but his search through the world produced much interesting writing that calls folklore to the attention of the world. In producing that work, however, Hearn sought to use folklore for personal psychological ends, using his knowledge of it as a statement about his position in the societies to which he came. Rather as the members of the Louisiana Association of AFS and Lyle Saxon used folklore to say something about their respective positions in the plantation world, Hearn used it to situate himself in American and then Creole society, to give him-self the sort of home accorded to the cultural insider that he aspired to present himself as.

Chapter 4

PHOTOGRAPHING FOLKLIFE

Document, Symbol, Propaganda

◇◇◇

Photography has been with us for over a century and a half and has become a commonplace of life, offering virtually anyone who has access to the tools of modernity like cameras the opportunity to produce visual representations of the reality around us. "Average" persons have been able to possess and use picture-taking devices at least since Eastman Kodak began to manufacture cheap, easy-to-use cameras in the late nineteenth century, and in the twenty-first the incorporation of cameras into ubiquitous cell phones has meant that vast numbers of people have constant access to photographic image creation and, indeed, many people seem constantly to be taking snapshots. We have become very used to photographically recording what we encounter, taking for granted our ability to reproduce reality as an image and conceiving the belief that our images do indeed reproduce reality. Those who have taken photography seriously, from its inception in the nineteenth century to its acceptance as a major art form in recent years, have been more aware of how photographic images can manipulate and transform the reality they record, although we tend to see photographs as something "stencilled off the real," as Susan Sontag has put it,[1] as documents representative of realities beyond the image itself. A wedding photograph or a newspaper shot, we think, simply tells us about something which was.

But of course photographers can manipulate their subject matter. A soft-focus lens can produce a dreamy, romantic effect. A particular angle chosen can produce a particular impression. Merely the choice of what to take or what not to take (or what to print or not print or crop or not crop) influences the vision of reality shown to the viewer of the final photographs. The desire to capture the dramatic on film may obscure a vision of normal life. In taking several of his famous Depression-era photos, Arthur Rothstein moved around a cow skull to different positions. In doing so he sought to

capture the fearsome drought of the area in which he was. What he succeeded in doing is debatable (at the time, the discovery of what he had done
created a political furor), but he undoubtedly in part created the reality that
he recorded. Photographic historians and critics have long recognized these
truths, but there is a lesson here also for those who would use photographs
in interpreting folklore and folklife,[2] whether they are photographers, folklorists, and anthropologists, social planners, preparers of cultural impact
statements, or exhibit designers: photographic images are not mere stencil-
lings of reality, but have been shaped by human decisions influenced by
personal visions and social concerns.

Of course, photographers can and do make images of virtually everything and can manipulate virtually anything. However, the camera certainly
has been used to record folk contexts. Many photographs of folk contexts
have been intended to provide visual documentation of realities: a folk
performer, an example of vernacular architecture, some aspect of a process such as quilt making or a ritual practice. Yet the folk is full of inherent
meanings (or what we may presume to be such), and folklife as a subject
matter lends itself to a variety of artistic uses that can appeal as much to the
photographer as to a writer like Hearn or promoters of tourism like some of
Colson Whitehead's characters. Because we like to think of photos as simple
reproductions of what is, we may be inclined to miss at first glance how
photography may recycle folklife for a variety of reasons, ideological and
political, social and personal. This chapter looks at some of those reasons
and at several recyclings of folk realities into images that present folk contexts as symbols and as propaganda, as evocative of ideas and beliefs and
commercial concerns.

The argument can be made that the modern study of folklore and the
practice of photography practically grew up together. The word folklore
was coined by W. J. Thoms in 1846, and photography began its history in
the late 1820s and in the 1830s. Though the earliest photography was not
ethnographic, folklife became an area which photography has consistently
documented and interpreted visually. In England in the 1880s, for example,
Peter Henry Emerson was photographing the rural folklife of the fen country of East Anglia for a series of books and portfolios that wound up giving
a detailed picture of a way of life, and his contemporary Frank Meadows
Sutcliffe was doing something similar for the shoreline folk of the Yorkshire
coast. Somewhat later, Sir Benjamin Stone set about recording the England
of his day with a particular interest in the folk customs and ceremonies of
the countryside, which, like the folklorists of his day, he saw as "survivals"

of ancient culture.[3] In India Samuel Bourne was taking pictures of "native types" by the 1860s; in Cyprus in the 1870s John Thomson was recording local culture. In the mid-1860s the French stereographic firm of Lallemond and Hart even produced series of card stereographs on the ethnic and occupational groups of Europe and North Africa under such titles as "Costumes of the XIX Century."[4]

On the Continent, out of action after wounds suffered during the First World War, Andre Kertesz turned his lens toward the village folklife of his native Hungary, and later in the 1920s he made "several lyrical studies of folk life and traditional labour, in Brittainy and Lorraine."[5] In Finland in 1894, the travel writer I. K. Inha, while collecting information on traditional epic songs, also photographed the folkways of the province of Viena Karelia. In America Edward S. Curtis, between the 1890s and 1920s, produced his famous documentation of North American Indian cultures. Though some might object to the inclusion of native American culture under the folklife rubric, Curtis documented in great detail, not only photographically but also in the texts of his many photogravure-illustrated volumes, those areas such as pottery and basketry and other arts and crafts that have been at the heart of folk studies.[6] A number of other photographers turned their lenses on North American Indians.

In the 1930s the Farm Security Administration photographers, whose work in one American state will be dealt with below, documented those areas of American society which have also been the traditional focus for folk studies, the rural farm community and the "common man" in such communities, and many of their photographs are valuable as folklife documentary. In the city, Photo League members Sid Grossman and Dan Weiner photographed Italian street festivals, while Arthur Leipzig did a whole series based on children's traditional street games. Even Edward Weston, a great photographer not particularly identified with the documentary aesthetic, captured on film the vernacular art of *pulquería* murals, and during those same days in Mexico he and Tina Modotti were the photographers who collaborated with Anita Brenner on her important incursus into Mexican culture, *Idols behind Altars*, work discussed in chapter 6.

Although photographic interest in folklore and folklife falls across time periods and worldwide cultural contexts, the rest of this chapter looks at how photographers working in one American state, Louisiana, sought to use folk materials as their subject matter; this restricted group and place can be taken as representative of larger trends, interests, and possibilities. Though we do tend to think of photographs as merely providing "documentation" (and photographs certainly are documents, whatever else they may be), clearly photographers have sought to draw upon the presumed meanings of folk contexts to in effect recycle folklife in images.

REGIONAL SYMBOL

In the second half of the nineteenth century, the chief impulse in American photography was a commercial one, and portrait photography was the bread and butter of professional photographers. This generally meant photographing clients for personal portraits, but there was also a market for celebrity portraits. In addition, local photographers could produce "views," pictures of architecture, monuments, and topography. These would be sold, often as stereographs (two pictures of the same thing, taken from slightly different perspectives and mounted for use in a viewer to produce a 3D effect). Stereographs were particularly popular in the United States and, indeed, by the 1870s there was a highly competitive tourist trade for photographs.[7]

It is in the context of such views of local scenes that we find the earliest, concerted photographic attention in Louisiana paid to subjects that we would today call folklife. In these images—taken by G. F. Mugnier, Andrew D. Lytle, Theodore Lilienthal, S. T. Blessing, and others—folklife is an element of the local scene, something which, along with landscapes, statuary, public buildings, and notable private houses, could be offered as distinctive to or typical of the area, pictures to be consumed by appreciative locals, visitors to the state, or people elsewhere who collected photographic views. Folklife is not a dominant subject matter, yet it is there, particularly in the photos of Mugnier: street vendors, vernacular houses, festival activities, traditional folk occupations and processes. Mugnier, the best known of Louisiana's nineteenth-century photographers, left the fullest range of folklife documentation. In 1884 he advertised his willingness to take pictures to order and also announced himself as "Publisher of Stereoscopic and Graphoscopic Views of Louisiana Scenery, New Orleans and Vicinity," thus placing himself squarely in the developing tradition of local, commercial, topographical photography.[8]

Mugnier was clearly interested in culture, in human life, and he tried to capture it as effectively as he could, given the limitations of still cumbersome equipment. For example, a picture he titled "From Mulatto to Negro" shows four African American boys and young men posing for the camera against the planked wall of a building, their differing shades of skin color (a factor in racial identity that obsessed southerners) alluded to by the title. It is difficult not to see here a certain fascination with the Louisiana cultural interplay that could particularly produce racial mix, the informal portrait mirroring ethnic history and diversity. Mugnier actively photographed in the cane and cotton fields, on the busy New Orleans levee, on the streets, and along waterways where fish were caught or lumber milled. The folklife of New Orleans streets is represented by, among other images, a Negro bootblack stooped over the shoes of his seated white customer, by the horse-drawn milk wagons that were a popular photographic subject of the day, and by the praline seller (probably Mugnier's most famous image), her torso and tignoned head framed by the irregular shape of the black umbrella that shields her from the sun, her wares, the traditional, sugary southern candy, set out for buyers on a basket in front of her.[9]

In his pictures of the rural countryside Mugnier was even more consistently the documentor of folklife. Though he could not, with the limitations of his equipment, successfully capture movement, he nonetheless attempted to document various traditional processes, especially during the 1890s, by shooting series of pictures that follow the process through stages. Thus we see a worker "bleeding" a tree in a turpentine orchard to collect the sap, are shown the still where the turpentine was processed, then the cooperage where it was infused into barrels. Or we follow sugar cane as it is cut in the fields, loaded by hand on to carts, hauled to the mill and weighed, while other pictures take us inside the cane shed or down to the plantation landing.

There is certainly an abundance of photographs that illustrate Louisiana folklife as it existed at the end of the nineteenth century and at the turn of the twentieth century taken by Mugnier and his contemporaries. Not surprisingly, they often fixed on the obvious. Although we may find something ethnographic in their images, they were not trying to be ethnographers but rather to attempt to reveal what was "around." It is important to consider which aspects of folklife were photographed and which were not. What was photographed was what was most easily accessible: ceremonies and festivals (like the public face of New Orleans Carnival), outdoor labor, vernacular structures (Mugnier photographed a remarkable palmetto house, for example), and street vendors. This was not yet a time when photographers sought out interesting, remote communities, or practitioners of arcane crafts or musical performance styles (though Baton Rougean Andrew D. Lytle took a striking picture of convict musicians and dancers [figure 4.1], and Blessing set foot into the swamps to photograph alligator hunters).

Figure 4.1: Andrew D. Lytle, Convict musician and dancers in prison camp, late nineteenth century. Andrew D. Lytle Collection, Mss. 893, 1254, Louisiana and Lower Mississippi Valley Collection, LSU Libraries, Baton Rouge, LA.

In acting thus they were not really unlike the far fewer persons who had conceived a conscious interest in American folklore. At this early stage, except for a hardy few who sought out American Indians, folklorists were still gleaning their lore mostly from familiar settings and people close at hand. Photographers in Louisiana were taking what was close at hand, and this often included the more obvious aspects of folklife. However, the photographers, probably more than the folklorists, were very much aware of a need to project the local. Their very market depended upon their ability to project images of place and to create identities for place. Locals were looking for images of themselves and what was typical about themselves; those from elsewhere were looking for what could define the places they visited. Though Mugnier and other nineteenth-century photographers were working at a time before identity became a key concept and focus for interest, they were nonetheless looking to express local identity, to find some of the symbols of localness with which people made psychic connections and which indicated some level of regional uniqueness. Many photographs of the era record important buildings, statues of the prominent and the honored, or other landmarks. Though each city would of course have different such landmarks—the national Capitol in Washington, the French Opera House in New Orleans, Admiral Farragut's monument in D.C., the Margaret statue in the Crescent City—there would be a certain static sameness to these large edifices and chiseled or cast likenesses, produced by architects or sculptors trained in the same elite tradition. They would squat monumentally in the photographic frame, usually devoid of real people, accurate but not particularly intriguing images of cultural solidity and uniformity, items not seen elsewhere but very much like items in other places.

Folklife, nevertheless, offered other possibilities, people engaged in doing things and thus providing an element of life and activity, and a certain local flavor that could distinguish a place. Workers making turpentine, costumed revelers parading for Mardi Gras, and a clothes-pole seller delivering his wares provide a focus for interest that goes beyond bricks and mortar, however grand. Certain folk cultural traditions emerge as an integral part of the local scene. The composite "self-portrait" of Louisiana which the pioneer photographers produced includes folklife as part of a regional sense of identity (though it may be a vaguely conceived sense of region; of course Louisiana was not the only place to produce turpentine or have clothes-pole sellers; Lytle's striking image of dancing African American convicts evokes the larger South as much as it does Louisiana per se). Take, for example, Mugnier's iconic praline seller. This large African American woman not only wears a tignon on her head, a garment traditionally associated with free women of color in New Orleans, but escapes the hot sun under an umbrella she holds, suggestive of local weather conditions. Of course, she sells pralines, a folk food item not limited to New Orleans but very much eaten in New Orleans and, even by the time Mugnier photographed, an item sold to visitors as a local treat. By positioning her near some barrels suggesting the levee and with commercial-looking buildings in the near-distance, Mugnier gives her local context. Through this and the positioning of two figures, perhaps local men or boys, just to the right behind her, Mugnier may even be trying to suggest that a praline seller is not simply someone who engages with tourists (as might be suggested had she been posed by the wrought-iron fence of Jackson Square) but someone who belongs in local life and tradition, someone who is clearly emblematic of the folk in New Orleans (although the very appearance of praline sellers in tourist venues may have been meant to indicate that same thing in a different way; even today, when actual street praline sellers are gone, praline shops continue to sell their candies to tourists and may have names or signs evoking the older figure). Thus a local participant in the folk practice of street selling, an African American woman, vending a folk food item becomes symbolic of locality in a photograph intended for several audiences, local and more remote.

Photography did not establish the romantic image of Louisiana in which folklife played a prominent part, but it played an important role in visually representing romantic Louisiana, partly through the creation of folklife images. Although local studio photographers continued to document the folklife around them, from the 1920s other forces became the dominant ones in shaping the photographing of folklife. One such force was the developing use of photographs for book illustration. Charles Alan Watkins has called attention to several photographers, James Edward Rice, Arthur F. Raper, and Bayard Wootten, who were working in other parts of the South at social documentary, and he suggests that their work in part be seen against the background of book publishing, particularly the development at the University of North Carolina Press of a tradition of publishing important books dealing with southern society and the use of photographs in those books.[10] In Louisiana the situation was a different one, but the work of several photographers can also be seen against a background of book publishing and a tradition of writing, although not sociological writing as in the case of the photographers Watkins discusses. Rather they need to be seen in the context of the literary tradition of writing about Louisiana as an exotic, romantic place that stretches back at least to George Washington Cable and Lafcadio Hearn. However, through the twenties, thirties, and forties this vision of the state certainly gained new impetus through the writings of such people as Edward Larocque Tinker, Lyle Saxon, Harnett T. Kane, and Frances Parkinson Keyes. The title of a major article in the *National Geographic* in 1930 makes evident what mythos was being projected: "Louisiana, Land of Perpetual Romance."[11] Certainly one can see many of Mugnier's images, of moss-dripping trees or winding bayous, as romantic, and a romantic impulse strongly influenced several photographers in Louisiana in the period 1920–1960. Though their romanticism included interest in a variety of possibilities, including the natural landscape and the plantation big house, folklife was a significant element in their worldview.

One such photographer was Fonville Winans, a Texan who came to live in the Bayou State and who has articulated how soon he was struck by the romantic feel of the place:

> *It was absolutely fascinating. To me, it was like being in darkest Africa. . . . Alligators, and palmettos and Spanish moss. I tell you, it really*

grabbed a hold of me. To me it was pure adventure. I was like in deepest
Africa and I loved it . . . I just loved the way [the people] talked.

Being interested in photography (he had been a newspaper photographer for a short while in Fort Worth), he decided to capitalize on his own fascination. He outfitted a boat, the *Pintail,* which he bought for twenty-five dollars and fixed up to make seaworthy. With two assistants, who paid fifty dollars each for the privilege of going along on the adventure, he cruised the waters of south Louisiana, filming motion pictures. These he showed in high schools in Fort Worth and Dallas ("sort of a poor boy's 'Bring 'Em Back Alive'—Frank Buck"), lecturing to appropriate phonograph music, a sun helmet completing the props for the performance.[12] From the outset of his motion picture making he was also taking still photographs, recording not only the lush south Louisiana landscape but also the folkways of its people, such as crabbing, festivals, oyster shucking, oyster bars, and the life in swamp stilt villages.

Although his photographs were used in several books, such as Harnett Kane's *Bayous of Louisiana,* Winans never actually collaborated on a book (although his collected photographs would be published in book form years later). Elemore Morgan Sr., however, another major documentor of folklife in this period, worked on a book with one of the most famous of romantic popular novelists of the day, Frances Parkinson Keyes. Morgan's son, painter and photographer Elemore Morgan Jr., has said that his father had "the . . . Southerner's inclination . . . to romanticize . . . certainly . . . a lot of the Southerner's sentimentality . . . which no doubt appealed to Keyes' own inclinations." In working on her novels Keyes came to an area, immersed herself in it, and "just grilled people about local information." She came to Louisiana around 1944, rented an antebellum plantation on the River Road south of Baton Rouge where she created "a romantic ruin" with "servants . . . people pulling fans, [others] sitting on the porch with mint juleps, it was just incredible," and she produced such Louisiana novels as *Dinner at Antoine's* and *Crescent Carnival.*[13] She also decided to collaborate with Morgan on a work of nonfiction for which he would provide the photographs, *All This Is Louisiana*, a book project out of which many of his best folklife images came.

All This Is Louisiana (which turned out to be one of Keyes's lesser successes in terms of reception and sales) tries to present a portrait of the state[14] and it and Morgan's images range over the leprosy hospital at Carville to oil refineries to the murals in a Baton Rouge church to the bird sanctuary on

Figure 4.2: Elemore Morgan Sr., St. Amico procession, 1940s. Courtesy of Mary Morgan.

Avery Island, a noted New Orleans hotel, and a Shreveport museum. But Morgan (who influenced Keyes as to what she covered and who did much of the necessary travel involved) had a penchant for folklife and clearly saw it as a key element in limning the state's identity. His vision of Louisiana was obviously a sophisticated and complex one, and though the romanticism of Keyes was central to the book, Morgan seems to have wanted to include in her conception a wider sense of the romance of the state as encompassing folk culture, particularly those aspects of it that might appeal to outsiders as distinctive and exotic. Morgan's photographs thus include such subjects as curing perique tobacco, blessing of the cane fields, the sewing of Mardi Gras gowns, and a New Orleans snowball cart ringed by street kids hankering after the ice-based local treat.

A Morgan photo of the St. Amico procession along River Road "between Vacherie and Donaldsonville" (figure 4.2) is indicative of the complexity of much of his work and of his sympathy for ordinary people (who may none-theless do and have extraordinary things), as opposed to the elites often associated with southern romanticism with its grand plantation houses and fancy-dress balls. In this image, a statue of the saint (honored particularly by a local Italian American family) is carried on the shoulders of worshipers. An older man and boys precede the statue with a cross and American flags, while a brass band—an ensemble of a type ubiquitous in south Louisiana—follows behind, bass tubas sticking up with particular prominence. Telegraph poles remind us of the everyday reality through which proceeds the sacred, while weather-beaten houses with metal roofs provide a note of local architectural context. The photograph pulls together a vision of solemnity and religious devotion in the midst of the everyday world, of simple but dedicated people who maintain a tradition as they move through a landscape of road, structures, trees, levee. Morgan calls attention to Louisiana's fascination as being multifaceted. If the River Road is commonly associated with the great Mississippi and the remnants of plantation culture, here too are ethnic groups with their singular customs, carrying on an activity that might almost come from another world.

Morgan and Winans were certainly stimulated by a regional romanticism, recognizing that folklife could be emblematic of the vitality of a regional culture that they sought to celebrate. Another, slightly earlier photographer, however, evolved a different romantic approach to folklife as representative of place, and it is in his work that the influence can be seen most strikingly. This was Arnold Genthe, a photographer with a considerable national reputation today, who came to New Orleans twice in the 1920s, already well established from his work in San Francisco, specifically in search of the picturesque.

Genthe had been strongly influenced by the romantic writings of Cable, Hearn, and Tinker, and he sought to capture the city on film as they had done with ink on paper. Though he eventually concluded that "no American city contains as many fascinating picture-motifs in such a small area," he was at first disappointed. It seemed to him that much of the city of Cable and Hearn had disappeared. There were only a few colorful street vendors left, only a few black women who still wore the famous *tignon*: "My first reaction on arrival was one of disappointment . . . the levees, in former days one of the most famous and interesting sights, had lost much of their picturesque character. Prosaic sheds and immense warehouses now look out upon the lazy Mississippi . . . Gaudy signs disfigured fine old buildings."[15] But gradually he came to find "the vanished beauty and charm of the old days," photographing mostly if not exclusively in the French Quarter, although he had to go to more trouble than he had originally expected.

Given his orientation toward finding the picturesque past, plus the fact that he came to feel that he was recording the last vestiges of that past,

Genthe's photographs, especially as they were published in *Impressions of Old New Orleans*[16] (1926), very soft-focus, almost blurry, are exceedingly romantic ones: misty doorways, French Quarter patios, quaint architectural detail. Yet he did not neglect the human aspect of the place and his New Orleans photographs include a number depicting the folklife of the streets, stoop sitters, a praline vendor, a boy selling ice off the back of a cart, women going to market, workers staring at a bale at a cotton press, an organ grinder gazed at by small boys.[17] Although Genthe clearly saw the architectural glories of New Orleans as a backdrop for establishing the identity of the city (they suggest antiquity and echoes of Europe and the Caribbean and the charm of half-hidden gardens), he was well aware that the city's street life, too, was important and that urban folklife had attracted the attention of earlier commentators like Hearn who wrote particularly of African American vendors, roustabouts, and performers as giving this place some of its identity as a multiethnic port city. He was attempting to visually follow up on earlier commentators, and he was looking for *tignons* and busy levees and the urban folk culture those implied. Though, unsurprisingly, much of the city's nineteenth-century ambience had drifted away, Genthe found what he could and used not only enduring architectural monuments but pockets of urban folklife to create his impression of this part of Louisiana, projecting a vision of the place as culturally distinct.

Genthe's praline seller (figure 4.3) is interestingly different from Mugnier's, here a woman who might as easily be resting on a step as perched there to sell, whose umbrella is furled up, whose backdrop is flatter and more restricted. Yet she still wears a *tignon* and is still a fixture on the local scene, suggesting a persistence of tradition through an African American street vendor and her traditional culinary wares. His French Market vendors and customers are more suggestive of the bustle of New Orleans street life, crowded into the frame, whether sitting or standing to sell from baskets or wagons or looking over the offerings. His organ grinder is a reminder of the creative life on the streets, attracting listeners even as the street itself seems empty, as though they have just been waiting for an artistic focus.[18]

The photographers who recorded Louisiana in the later nineteenth century and into the twentieth did not invent the romantic vision of the place, but they certainly took advantage of it in creating their images for public consumption, whether prints sold out of their shops or through books published locally or elsewhere. They sought to represent Louisiana's essence to the world, like other photographers elsewhere were doing for their own regions. In their regionalism, men like Mugnier, Winans, and Morgan looked

Figure 4.3: Arnold Genthe, Praline seller; from Arnold Genthe, *Impressions of Old New Orleans*; copyright 1926 by George H. Doran Company.

to a variety of subject matter, but certainly hit upon folklife as an area that could be exploited to suggest local modes of life and local identity. Tradition suggests continuity, which suggests something ingrained in locality and thus representative of it, something which stands out as being "ours" and to be presented as indicative of who and what we are.

SOCIAL CONCERNS
The Farm Security Administration

Certainly by the early decades of the twentieth century the vision of Louisiana as an exotic place (though one well within the southern stereotype of grand plantations and a code of gentility) had been established, and photographers of Louisiana had played a role in exploiting that vision, using folklife among other subjects to visually present the place and its identity. When, however, the Great Depression, the economic calamity that began with the stock market crash of 1929, hit America, profound cultural changes would result, and photography would turn to other needs and uses. Folklife would continue to interest photographers as a subject that could be used to represent issues and ideas in the midst of new economic realities and new social realizations. Out of the era emerged one of the great attempts to document America photographically, the project created by the Farm Security Administration. And although the FSA photographers were hardly sent out to document folklife alone, they would photograph folklife in abundance and find that it well served the purpose of influencing public attitudes.

The Farm Security Administration was one of a number of federal agencies set up under the umbrella of the New Deal, the program the Roosevelt administration established to deal with the economic and social problems of the Depression. Originally called the Resettlement Administration, the FSA was established under an assistant secretary of agriculture, Rexford Guy Tugwell, to relocate families to planned communities. Because it became highly controversial, the RA was turned into the FSA, whose purpose was to help the rural poor. Still controversial (activities of the agency smacked of collectivization of agriculture to some), Tugwell sought ways of creating positive public relations. He hired Roy Stryker to head up a Historical Section within an Information Division, whose task was to undertake publicity functions.

Stryker, an economist by training, was something of a specialist in the use of visual materials, notably photographs, for educational purposes. In 1924 he had been asked to compile the illustrations for a textbook by Tugwell and Thomas Munro, *American Economic Life*. This was certainly not the first textbook to use photos, but Stryker was particularly committed to finding strong pictures as well as those which showed social consciousness, and those he picked showed his sense "of the photograph as a special and unique ... transmitter of information."[19] In the course of doing the research for the textbook, Stryker began a lifelong fascination with the photograph as a medium of communication. Though initially his section was to be concerned with the history of the agency, the economists, statisticians, and like personnel he had been led to expect failed to materialize. He was able, however, to hire photographers, and the Historical Section took shape as the unit that would provide the agency's photographic needs. He managed to hire exceptionally talented photographers—initially Arthur Rothstein, Walker Evans, and Carl Mydans; later Dorothea Lang, Russell Lee, Marion Post Wolcott, and others—who would create some of the iconic images of the era.

Although the photographers expended considerable energy on agency projects, their mandate was broader, in part because Stryker envisioned an encyclopedic history of American agriculture and he wanted pictures for it. Acting as a very loose-knit sort of team they recorded a great cross-section of America. Although eventually the over 270,000 photographs they took would come to be seen as a composite "portrait of a decade,"[20] as capturing key insight into the nation during this very difficult time, their main objective was to create propaganda that served the publicity needs of the RA/FSA itself. The photographers were not conscious recorders of folk culture, though by the very nature of the places where they worked and the people with whom they came in contact, they wound up photographing it. Given their need to produce propaganda, they found folklife a useful subject matter that lent itself to positions they sought to express.

Stryker maintained a vigorous correspondence with his traveling photographers, and they were influenced toward finding particular subject matter. They were to find pictures to illustrate "that America, particularly rural America, was OK[;] the Depression had caused some trouble but help was on the way."[21] Folklife was perfectly suited to expressing such a message. On the one hand, it would seem to many, particularly urban Americans, as existing in a context of poverty and backwardness. Hence it illustrated the "trouble." On the other hand, traditional folkways could be seen as symbolic of America's positive values, self-sufficiency, a fundamental aesthetic sense, a connection to the land. These values might be temporarily under siege, but the government programs of Roosevelt's New Deal would help to save them. Photographs might depict one or the other or both of these perspectives.

One of the earliest FSA photographs taken in Louisiana, in 1935, by noted artist Ben Shahn is of an "Unemployed Trapper, Placquemine [*sic*] Parish." This man stretches out on what may be the porch of a cabin with a rusty tin can, a cigarette pack, and a box of matches in front of him. His pose might at best be described as a languid one, and his very inactivity suggests the economic and cultural stagnation of the times. We wonder how his traditional occupation, the folk base for a business ultimately dependent on higher-end clientele and the national economy, is doing, and we suspect not well. Yet just a year later Carl Mydans took a delightful photo of nuns in New Orleans's celebrated French Market. Here the nuns, arrayed in habits that seem particularly otherworldly complete with headpieces coming to exaggerated points, make their way with other customers down an aisle piled high with produce with bunches of what appear to be bananas or plantains hanging from above. Though the nuns provide a touch of the sacred in the midst of the profane world of commerce, they also indicate how multifarious is American society, a polyglot mix that stands together in these times. But what the image particularly suggests is abundance. The bins here are not empty, however difficult may be the times, when hunger is not unknown and some of us may want for food. It is a reminder of better days in the past and an announcement of better days to come, all symbolized by the every-day activity of market going, the availability of local foods, the confluence of folk productivity and the popular appeal of the great market. If Shahn's trapper may seem down on his luck, Mydans's market goers bustle with the promise of new possibilities.

Folklife, with its connections to local food products and cuisine, offered many opportunities for photographically presenting abundance, for repre-senting America as still a land of abundance, despite the soup kitchens and bread lines that characterized the era. Though a number of FSA photogra-phers passed through Louisiana, Russell Lee and Marion Post Wolcott were the principal ones who recorded the state. Lee was especially intrigued by Louisiana folk cultures, perhaps because he met up in New Orleans with Lyle Saxon, author and director of the Louisiana Writers' Project, the state branch of another New Deal program that did considerable folklore field research, eventually producing *Gumbo Ya-Ya*, the now well-known book on the folklore of the state.[22] In 1938 Lee undertook a trip down the Mississippi on a small cargo vessel, a trip which resulted in pictures "of great interest," including some good interior shots of "stores, bar rooms, dance halls, slot machines."[23] One image that came out of Lee's trip is "Crab-Boil, Raceland, La." Here (figure 4.4) four individuals, perhaps a family, sit at a table, prob-ably in a barroom or restaurant, eating crabs. The crabs, however, literally pile up on the long table, which is covered by newspaper. At one end of the table a woman sips from a bottle of Jax beer, and two other, mostly full bottles sit in front of other diners. These people are not merely eating crabs, they are engaging in a veritable feast, in devouring mounds of food and washing it down with locally made brew, which also seems to be available in large supply. Here, too, is abundance, expressed in terms of traditional food and a traditional activity, a crab boil, a part of local folk culture being used to suggest that Americans can still eat well and, indeed, consume what they have always consumed, that Americans are still resourceful in exploiting their resources and taking care of their needs. Placing newspaper on tables while eating seafood is a regular practice in Louisiana and elsewhere, and this newspaper was no doubt placed there for the usual reasons of neatness and cleanliness. Nonetheless, one might wonder whether Lee meant to sug-gest that perhaps elsewhere were widely trumpeted stories of bad times; here, however, is a counter to any such stories, as Americans literally pour their abundance over news that might say otherwise. Lee's photo made on

Figure 4.4: Russell Lee, *Crab-Boil, Raceland, La.* 1938. Courtesy of the Library of Congress, FSA neg. no. 11653-M1.

the same 1938 trip, "Unloading Oysters from Fisherman's Boat, Olga, La.," which shows two African American workers working with burlap sacks as they tote them from boat to dock, is similarly a presentation of the abundance of America, another vast pile, this time of sacks containing another traditional Louisiana food.[24]

Lee was also much taken with showing folk creativity and artistic sense, in effect using folklife to suggest a positive vision of America in the midst of the difficult times of the FSA years. That is, Lee was suggesting that on the fundamental folk level, in the lives of people who might be most stressed by those difficult times, beauty could be found, a concern with beauty might even flourish. On his Mississippi River trip, for example, Lee took a photograph of a woman (figure 4.5), cigarette dangling from her mouth, pumping the arm of a slot machine in a barroom in the town of Raceland. We might wonder about the meaning of the slot machine (although such gambling devices were common in south Louisiana at the time), but what probably interested Lee most was the decoration on the wall behind the machine, a sailboat and flowers painted on the shiplap-style surface. These paintings call attention to the existence of a concern for beauty in even the plebeian confines of a barroom; their freshness suggests an up to the moment interest in maintaining beauty even in the face of the difficult times. The many flashes of creativity Lee and others recorded in their images defy those

Figure 4.5: Russell Lee,
*Girl Playing Slot Machine
in Decorated Bar Room,
Raceland, La.* 1938.
Courtesy of the Library of
Congress, FSA neg. no.
31411.

difficult times, suggesting that the spirit of the American people, far from being done in by the Depression, continue to create and to produce objects of aesthetic interest. This can be seen in several of the Louisiana images Lee produced in which people ply their traditional crafts. For example, in "Migrant Cane Chair Maker on U.S. 90 Near Jeanerette, La.," the craftsman, though he may be a migrant, fashions what will no doubt be a beautiful chair by the side of the road, though in the image he has only gotten to the stage of shaping one piece of cane; however, its lovely arc is indicative of something fine to come. In a camp for migrant workers in the strawberry fields around the town of Hammond, Lee captured an almost scholarly looking man (figure 4.6), his denim work clothes looking worn and dusty. He sits on a wooden chest in the midst of obviously humble quarters, yet he's working to make nothing less than an ornament from horn, giving his careful attention to scraping or polishing his work. He may be in the middle of a migrant labor camp, but his interest is in creating folk art, in making something that surpasses his environment. In another picture from

Figure 4.6: Russell Lee, *Migrant Worker Who Makes Ornaments from Horns, He Is Filing Down a Wooden Block to Be Used as a Base for Horns, Hammond, La*. 1939. Courtesy of the Library of Congress, FSA neg. no. 32803.

this Hammond series, Lee shows a child in the living quarters of the camp (figure 4.7), peering out from a doorway where a quilt has been hung as a divider. Again, clearly the circumstances of the place are humble, no doubt poverty stricken. But the fan-pattern quilt, in fact in good condition, hangs as a once-resplendent example of something in temporarily reduced circumstances, a beautiful token of something that can rise again.

Lee also liked to photograph ritual occasions, such as the *fais do-do* during the Crowley Rice Festival in 1938. ("This really sounds like something," he excitedly wrote Stryker before going. "Cajun bands, balls and all sorts of ceremonies."[25]) He took one pleasant picture of the band at the occasion, young men gathered around a microphone on break, their instruments held by them. They sip away at beer, not unlike the woman in the Raceland barroom, suggesting a joyful ambience whatever the tenor of the times. And Lee liked musicians in other contexts. In New Iberia he photographed two African American musicians in the back seat of a car, both with accordions. One has his dangling cigarette, his eyes soulfully closed behind his glasses

Figure 4.7: Russell Lee, *Quilt Hung Across Doorway Which Separates Living Quarters of Two Families of White Migrants. Berry Pickers near Hammond, La.* 1939. Courtesy of the Library of Congress, FSA neg. no. 32881-D.

as he fingers his keyboard. It is a marvelous image, the music we almost hear transcending anything outside the vehicle, the sound of people making beauty in the possible face of hardship. This, like many of the FSA images that capture folklife and folklore, offers hope, suggesting that basic American values and aesthetic performances offer the possibility for transcendence of the current difficult moment.

SOCIAL CONSCIOUSNESS
The Standard Oil Project

With the coming of World War II, Roosevelt's New Deal shifted focus and many of the projects devised to deal with the Depression were dropped or changed. The Historical Section of the FSA was canceled in 1942, though in effect its operations were transferred to the Office of War Information and some of its photographers continued to do virtually the same work if only for a short time. Stryker found the new agency with its different needs less sympathetic to his interests, his position reduced to that of a virtual librarian giving out photographs that could be used as war propaganda. Fortunately for him, he was soon offered a new position heading up yet another great group photography project, that created by the Standard Oil Company of New Jersey (SONJ). He was even able to employ some of the same photographers he had worked with at the FSA.

This new project was in many ways similar to the FSA project, though its goal was also radically different. Like the FSA project, it was created for reasons of public relations; its intended message, however, was quite a new one. At the start of the Second World War, Standard Oil had received extremely negative publicity because of charges that agreements the company had entered into with a German firm had created a cartel threatening America's supply of rubber, a vital war material. Standard was eventually exonerated, but a negative public image lingered; a poll indicated much negative feeling toward the company, especially on the part of "thought leaders," those people like journalists who were influential in shaping opinion. In 1943 Standard's public relations firm recommended a project rather like that of the FSA, which would use photographs to show a human, more positive face of Standard. An employee of the public relations firm knew Stryker, who, though hesitant at first, agreed to head up such a project, and he soon realized that indeed a giant corporation like Standard could put more money at his disposal than the federal government ever had. He bought supplies, hired photographers, and set about documenting the petroleum industry in a way that would put it in a positive light. In the mid-1940s these photographers were turned loose on Standard's operations and the oil business, working in a way not unlike that of their FSA predecessors (who, in some cases, they were). Stryker felt that his mandate was a broad one and that his people might photograph people and things only loosely related to the oil business or affected by the oil company. The things oil employees did off the job, the communities where oil was important, even aspects of community life that had little directly to do with petroleum could all be photographed.

The SONJ project would come to produce fewer pictures than had the FSA (fewer that 70,000 images would result as opposed to over 270,000 for the FSA) and the scope of the project was more geographically restricted, to states where Standard had a presence. Nonetheless, its photographers produced a wealth of pictures, and, again, folklife proved to be a significant subject matter, though the social consciousness behind the project had a commercial basis and stemmed from an awareness of the social impact of a particular industry. Traditional culture could seem the epitome of old-fashioned, could provide a world that seemed not only good and in keeping with older American norms and values but also a world supposedly far removed from the modernity of the oil economy. If it could be shown to coexist with oil or to actually participate with oil modernity, that would create a positive impression of oil's lack of intrusiveness, its helpfulness, and its adaptability.

Photographers could show how oil, even oil production, coexisted with society. One photograph, for example, shows oil drilling rigs sprinkled throughout a Louisiana bayou community, doing their work while, presumably, normal human life goes on.[26] But folklife could seem particularly apt for its supposed simplicity and continuity with the ways of the past. Thus Arnold Eagle photographed a woman "Making French Coffee" in 1946. Her dress is modestly traditional; behind her the background is not sharply defined but suggests an old homestead, perhaps a farm. She has just poured coffee beans into a pan for roasting; her implements seem well worn, homey, old-fashioned. All this suggests working by hand and time-honored folkways, yet she will toast her beans using kerosene, a petroleum product, thus tying her traditional world to that of oil. In 1945 Edwin and Louise Rosskam took a picture of the annual blessing of the shrimp fleet in Barataria (figure 4.8).[27] Here we see, beyond lush Louisiana vegetation in the foreground, boats of the shrimp fleet with numerous flags and pennants flying, with people waiting for the approach of the clergy's procession. The clergy indeed approach, attired in churchly garb, bringing the power of God to the everyday world of the boats. This is all a traditional ritual, full of special actions and costumes, as well as a gaiety of purpose that infuses the scene on what is a beautiful day. But of course the shrimp fleet is powered by gasoline, the ancient ritual and the world of oil coming together.

Other Louisiana SONJ photos depict folklife in settings where the petroleum connection may not be so direct. An Arnold Eagle photograph titled "Cypress Trees on Lake Veret [sic]" indeed depicts this lake (actually Verret) with its expanse of water and with Spanish moss–hung cypress trees, but the image also includes a boat full of moss and a moss gatherer, thus depicting the traditional moss-gathering "folk industry" that once flourished in the area.[28] Possibly the picture calls attention to petroleum in that Spanish moss, at one time used in making a variety of folk items, increasingly had come to be used for stuffing automobile seats. More likely, the image shows us the peacefulness of a lake and of a traditional occupation in an area where lots of oil drilling was taking place. Martha McMillin Roberts took a 1947

Figure 4.8: Edwin and Louise Rosskam, *Barataria, Louisiana. At the Annual Blessing of the Shrimp Fleet. The Procession on Its Way from the Church.* 1945. Standard Oil (New Jersey) Collection, SONJ 28086, Special Collections, University of Louisville (Special.Collections@louisville edu).

photo of "Mrs. Louis Brunet, of the Bayou Cane Community, Plaiting Strips of Bleached Palmetto for a Palmetto Hat" (figure 4.9), thus showing us the practice of a traditional craft, as Mrs. Brunet sits in front of her charming fireplace with its lovely old clock on the mantel, working with her palmetto strands (indeed used locally for hats and other artifacts). Petroleum may be far away, even if this is still a community engaged in the oil industry; but here in Louisiana the old, traditional ways continue, undisrupted, even as the modern world with its oil-based economy exists outside.

. . .

Both the FSA photographs and those done by the SONJ photographers were directed by constrained purposes, and insofar as folklife appears in the resultant images, it is being used to serve those purposes, as a kind

Figure 4.9: Martha McMillin Roberts, *Mrs. Louis Brunet, of the Bayou Cane Community. Plaiting Strips of Bleached Palmetto for a Palmetto Hat.* 1947. Standard Oil (New Jersey) Collection, SONJ 50741, Special Collections, University of Louisville (Special.Collections@louisville edu).

of propaganda. The FSA group meant to depict social wretchedness but wretchedness that could be corrected, especially given the essential values and culture of the American people. Folklife could show those essential values and cultural norms. The SONJ project aimed to show not wretchedness but prosperity and happiness, a state of well-being in a world touched by a giant corporation and its industry. Folklife, imbued with feelings of basic American values and culture, could show how harmoniously those values and their associated ways of life could coexist with the oil industry and one company in particular. Folklife got swept up into ideologies and came to be used to convey ideas and perspectives on American society. The photographs may document folklife, but they are meant to promote certain conceptions, to work with folklife as symbolic, even to use it as propaganda for government programs or the purposes of a vast commercial enterprise.

Earlier photographers had found folklife useful for other reasons, as a subject matter that could be presumed to have a regional uniqueness; its depiction could convey a sense of place that would appeal to those looking for visual representations of place. Of course, photography was not itself unique in being an art form whose practitioners sought to capture place. Yet it became increasingly favored by the public as it became more widely practiced and recognized. As people became more used to having their likenesses snapped, they became more amenable to being captured doing their usual activities, such as occupational crafts. The camera could fairly quickly capture fleeting moments—of a ritual, of craft production, of performance—in a way that other visual art forms could only do only with much greater complication and difficulty. Photography was well suited for producing images of folklife, and the practitioners of photography found reasons for using folklife as a subject, projecting images of it to the public to make various points, aesthetic, political, personal, social. Because we came to think of photographs as primarily documentary in nature, as straightforward representations of the real, the messages they convey might be particularly subtle ones. Folklife was recycled as potent image on paper and meant to evoke various associations and interpretations, as the image was literally sold or intended to "sell" understandings of commerce or culture or social needs through our immediate response to the visual.

Chapter 5

"THE AGE OF FIRE AND GRAVEL"

"Occult" and "Alternative History" Uses of Folklore

◇◇

In 1969 a Swiss writer and former hotel and restaurant employee named Erich von Däniken published a widely noticed, much-discussed book called *Chariots of the Gods?*[1] It had appeared the year before in Germany, where it also garnered attention (and sold several hundred thousand copies), as *Erinnerungen an die Zukunft*. The thesis of the book is that space travelers from other worlds visited earth in ancient times, showing our ancestors some of the ways to civilization, interbreeding with a few earth women to produce advanced humans who skipped some of the stages of regular evolution, and leaving various traces of their having come. Although von Däniken's book stirred up interest and controversy (he would publish several subsequent volumes building on the first, his work would be translated into other languages, and *Chariots of the Gods?* would be adapted as a film), he was hardly the first to offer this hypothesis (he was probably influenced, for example, by the Italian journalist Peter Kolosimo, whose book *Non è terrestre* won the Premio Bancarella in 1969, and perhaps ultimately by H. P. Lovecraft's fiction) or to set himself up as an author who proposed ideas that contradict orthodox, modern understandings of the past.

From the outset of *Chariots of the Gods?* von Däniken writes of "secret libraries" and "knowledge that was hidden,"[2] implying that information about ancient space visitors exists but has been obscured. It is hidden in mysterious phenomena, ancient texts, and, indeed in oral traditions, that is, folklore. In taking this perspective he is again hardly alone, placing himself at the end of a long line of commentators who have sought to illuminate history by delving into "occult" knowledge (occult in its earlier sense of hidden or secret, not in its more common sense of applying to certain aspects of the supernatural[3]). This knowledge is hidden in the sense that it has been misunderstood, misinterpreted, or even deliberately ignored or covered up in the context of more orthodox historical and scientific interpretations and understandings. Some who have written on these subjects also have been involved with mystical organizations or have claimed knowledge from such sources as secret brotherhoods or personal visions, thus involving themselves in occult activities of another sort. Some have been more rationalist in approach, looking for what might best be termed "alternative history," interpretations of the past that radically diverge from those widely accepted. Whichever their approach, such commentators have looked at a number of phenomena—archaeological sites, ancient literature, including the Bible, inexplicable events—and many of them, including von Däniken, have shown an almost touching belief in a sort of euhemerism,[4] arguing that oral tradition is a source for finding obscured knowledge about the past (and certain present realities), that folklore carries on "by word of mouth" accounts of remarkable past events long otherwise forgotten, be it of visiting spacemen or lost worlds and, when properly interpreted, can reveal information about these matters. That is, these "occult" and "alternative" commentators have recycled folklore as a kind of historical document, using it to advance their ideologies and agendas of belief. For them folklore becomes a repository of occult or alternative knowledge, a repository that can be tapped to provide underpinnings for unorthodox theories about the nature of the past and of reality.[5]

Von Däniken himself looks at a wide variety of "evidence" to support what he eventually refers to as his "theory of the Utopian past of mankind." He brings into his discussion, for example, the Piri Reis maps, charts left by a sixteenth-century Turkish admiral that present accurate depictions of geographical features of the earth's surface which could not possibly have been known until recent times (and which, of course, must have been made from spacecraft hovering high enough above the earth to have perceived it accurately). He writes about the Nazca lines found in South America, visible lines scratched in the earth over a large area. Seen from the air (which the ancient inhabitants of the region could hardly have done), they resemble (at least to von Däniken) an airfield and "were undoubtedly meant as signals for a being floating in the air. . . . What other purpose could they serve?"[6] Among other things discussed in the book are a supposed nuclear explosion in Siberia in 1908, carvings from the Mayan ruins at Palenque, which can be interpreted as depicting an astronaut at the controls of a spacecraft, and the biblical Sodom, seen as having been destroyed by a nuclear explosion. Von Däniken sets out his evidence with virtually no references to allow a reader to refer to what his original sources of information actually say, and he relies heavily on a Hollywoodish idea that of course primitive "savages," being suddenly confronted by technologically superior people, would explain such people by considering them "gods."

But certainly important to von Däniken's enumeration of phenomena that support his hypotheses are oral traditions (in some cases filtered through ancient texts, such as the Mahabharata, which are essentially written documents). Legends, he says, are a form of "indirect knowledge" of the past, for "primitive peoples . . . naively hand down from generation to generation in their sagas" their memories of the space visitors. "Ancient legends say" that local women were fertilized by the visitors and then drugged into long periods of unconscious sleep (though what legends indicate this or why this should have been done remain unclear). Many traditions, such as the Icelandic and Norwegian, mention not only sky gods but flying vehicles that could only have been spacecraft. On Easter Island an "orally transmitted legend tells us that flying men descended and lighted fires"[7] in ancient times. The narrators of *The Thousand and One Nights* (as von Däniken calls the classic folktale compendium) obviously got a wealth of ideas from their knowledge of the technological marvels the space visitors brought, such as "a lamp from which a magician spoke when the owner wished"[8] or the "Open, Sesame" formula from the tale of Ali Baba (clearly indicating something akin to a modern department store door operated by photocells). Von Däniken neither defines nor refines his conception of tradition (a term he uses frequently, along with legend and saga, though his ideas of generic differences are at best limited), nor presents actual folk texts or very precise references to what he is referring to in his use of folklore, but certainly he sees folklore as an important source for references to human memories of space visitors.

Von Däniken continues a similar line in *Gods from Outer Space*,[9] his second book, which he saw as in part a response to responses to *Chariots of the Gods?* Again he sees himself as escaping "traditional patterns of thought" and defying taboos about our knowledge.[10] Again he mentions ancient "mysteries" which can be explained by seeing them in the context of visiting spacemen (the giant statues of Easter Island, for example, are from a time when space visitors were stranded on the island; they used their advanced technology to create the famous statues, either so the local natives would remember their visit or perhaps to attract their rescuers); or suggests possible interpretations of human history or theology (the concept of the Fall of Man may refer to a period after the space gods had left earth when the local population reverted to their former practice of having sex with animals). Again he brings in folklore, though not so much as in the earlier book. The motif of Aladdin's lamp must refer to a "materialization machine" whereby someone like Aladdin could cause "supernatural" beings to materialize. Creation myths from many cultures indicate the coming of spacemen to create the world as we know it but also the preponderance of spheres (that is, spherical spacecraft) used in the process (a memory reinforced by the discovery of many spherical carvings and other objects in many parts of the world). Passages in the Cabbalistic book the Zohar (with 1,800 years of oral tradition behind it, von Däniken emphasizes) tell of a conversation between an earthman and someone stranded here from another world.[11] "Are the traditions that have accumulated in myths . . . meant to be far less mysterious and far more practical than was believed for millennia?" von Däniken asks and indeed he himself offers simple, uniform, literalist interpretations of oral traditions. "I am in the habit," he says, "of considering the descriptions in . . . ancient texts [whether written or oral] as real,"[12] that is, as offering us information about real, historical space visitors.

In his first two books von Däniken is silent on the question of what brought ancient space visitors to earth, but in a subsequent volume, *The Gold of the Gods*,[13] he lays out a hypothesis for that. Starting from what he says is the discovery of a vast network of man-made tunnels in the Andes mountains, he calls attention to the many oral traditions that relate the stories of wars among the gods. It was a war on other planets, he concludes, which drove space visitors to earth. The defeated were forced to leave wherever they were and landed on earth, where, afraid of pursuit by the victors, they burrowed underground (thus creating tunnel networks, not only in South America but elsewhere as well), while they also created—to throw off their pursuers—a more visible "decoy" settlement on a planet which no longer exists but which was once between Saturn and Jupiter (it was destroyed by the pursuers; hence the great distance between Saturn and Jupiter and hence many flood legends,[14] for the planetary destruction caused inundations on earth).

If the myths of warfare among the gods seem to be a basis for von Däniken's thesis of interplanetary warfare, he also includes in this book more detailed and specific accounts of and quotations from mythic and legendary material that more generally support his ideas of space visitors' coming and interacting with humans. For example, a Maori legend includes a character who undertakes a countdown "just like they do at a Space Centre." Or the Hopi Kachinas must have been spacemen who helped the Hopi in times of need; for example, when members of the group "were suddenly attacked

from all sides" and the Kachinas built a tunnel that opened "behind the enemy lines" so that the tribespeople were able to escape "without shedding
blood." Or there is a Polynesian story that describes outer space. The story
of a Chinese goddess, drawn from a dictionary of mythology, suggests that
"heavenly birds" that provide a sky bridge for heavenly lovers to meet might
really refer to "spaceships patrolling between the stars." The dragon and flying snakes found in many mythic narratives (and "in traditional popular
art") are also the spaceships in which the visitors traveled.[15] The references
to other worlds "are there in the legends," according to von Däniken, and
he sees "a mythology that is daily acquiring a more tangible and realistic
background." "I prefer to stick to the legends," he writes of one context, "because their contents are more plausible" than those of scientific explanations
offered thus far.[16]

Von Däniken published a number of other books on his subject and
even opened a Swiss theme park where visitors could go to exhibition pa-
vilions devoted to some of the "mysteries" the author calls attention to in
his books, such as the supposed flying machines described in ancient Indian texts. After his initial few books, however, with their rather repetitive
arguments, von Däniken's popularity faded (and the theme park eventually closed). Nonetheless, in the late 1960s and early 1970s a spate of books
about ancient astronauts by other writers, often published as mass-market
paperbacks, appeared on the scene. Some of these gave little attention to
oral tradition as "evidence" but others put considerable emphasis on it.

Joseph F. Blumrich's *The Spaceships of Ezekiel*[17] (a book directly influenced
by *Chariots of the Gods?*) works from biblical materials, notably one book
of which von Däniken also makes much (and it also works from its author's
background as a NASA engineer). Barry Downing's *The Bible and Flying
Saucers*[18] looks to the Bible as a whole for his source material (Downing, for
example, sees the bright light associated with the conversion of Saint Paul
as coming from a UFO and one of his sections is called "The Space Cloud
and the Ascension of Christ"). Jacques Bergier, whose *Les Extra-Terrestres
dans l'Histoire* was translated in 1973 as *Extra-Terrestrial Visitations from
Prehistoric Times to the Present,*[19] looks exclusively at unexplained phenomena such as the Nasca lines and the appearance of green children in Spain
in 1887. And Jean Sendy's abstruse *The Coming of the Gods*, translated from
the French in 1973, posits a sort of unitary Myth and a closely related Tradition which hold that Galaxians or Theosites came from space, "two legged
mammals who came from the sky and departed"[20] after bringing all that
makes up civilization (events Sendy dates as having happened in Paleolithic

times around 22,000 BC). But its author cites no specific mythic or legend-ary texts, relying on learned commentary from various times and the idea that many ancient and medieval thinkers and writers were well aware that their knowledge came from the sky. Andrew Tomas does note that "Legends can be interpreted as fanciful records of actual happenings" and that "folk-lore preserves history in the guise of colorful tales," yet looks briefly at two Greek myths and otherwise considers only other kinds of documents in laying out the case that people in former eras possessed modern scientific ideas and technical skills that must have come from "an unknown outside source" (presumably extraterrestrials).[21]

However, W. Raymond Drake, an admirer of noted investigator of "inex-plicable" phenomena Charles Fort, starts off his *Gods or Spacemen?* (which actually appeared several years before von Däniken's first book) with a lengthy consideration of the place of folklore in his evidence, and he delves into a wide variety of oral traditions in such subsequent books as *Gods and Spacemen in the Ancient East.*

Drake makes such assertions as that "legends from far antiquity evoke ... race-memories" of former times, that memories of "mighty civilizations" founded by space visitors "inevitably become confused into folk-tales," that "ancient myths agree" that transcendent beings came from the skies, or "leg-ends and folklore everywhere agree" that giants formerly lived on the earth. He goes on to say that "legends suggest that hundreds of thousands of years ago, the Uranids, highly civilized Beings from space, landed on earth"[22] and eventually fought with giants already here. And throughout his books he cites a wide variety of specific traditions to make his points about space visitors and their influence. For example, an old Hebridean chant preserves the memory of Britain's earliest inhabitants as having come from the skies:

Not of the seed of Adam are we,
Nor is Abraham our father;
But of the seed of the Proud Angel
Driven forth from heaven.

A Scottish "myth" states that a race of giants inhabited the country. The clas-sical Bellerophon legend indicates a possible conflict between space beings and Britons. "Irish mythology extols the powers of Cuchulain who fought aerial battles in flying chariots and annihilated his enemies with flashing lightning ... all suggestive of Overlords from space." A story in Keightley's *Fairy Mythology* is about a prince in his astral body "borne aloft," perhaps a space being. Stories about fairies and apparitions likewise suggest visitors from other worlds.[23]

In *Gods and Spacemen in the Ancient East* Drake moves on from Britain and devotes chapters to Babylon, Egypt, India, Japan, and other "Eastern" cultures. In Japan, for example, he refers to the eighth-century *Nihongi*, a compilation of material including a variety of traditions and also records of strange happenings not unlike, Drake suggests, the work of our modern Charles Fort, and to other written works containing legends and folklore. Among a number of possibilities, he calls attention to an Ainu legend that tells of an ancient god who descended from heaven in a shining "cradle" and landed at a certain place, while "the only Star God mentioned in Japanese myth"[24] was said to be a conquered rebel, possibly suggesting a conflict in outer space.

These numerous books promoting the idea of ancient visits by space travelers produced a reaction that brought about such oppositional books as Clifford Wilson's *Crash Go the Chariots* and the collection of short essays by a number of Australian writers, some with relevant academic credentials, *Some Trust in Chariots*.[25] Whether such debunking volumes had a major impact, or whether wide public interest simply ran out especially as mainstream thinking largely dismissed or simply ignored von Däniken and the others, after the early 1970s the ancient astronauts hypothesis fell into comparative obscurity. Publications asserting it did continue to appear but got nothing like the attention von Däniken and his contemporaries had. And although a religious group, the Raelians, grew up that included elements of spacemen as gods theories in its belief system, it did not succeed in becoming more than a rather obscure cult occasionally in the news. Nonetheless, these ideas did have their day in the public eye, and some of these writers did rely heavily upon interpretations of folk materials for their "evidence." That is, folklore came to be bizarrely recycled as historical document, as texts indicative of, or at least suggestive of, fantastic new interpretations of mankind's past, an ideological use of folklore quite different from, say, nationalistic ones. Probably von Däniken and these other writers looked to folklore for "evidence" because their elusive hypotheses were so tenuous and any "evidence" was to be appreciated, perhaps because folk texts are often so amenable to a variety of interpretations and folklorists in the past so often eschewed interpretation themselves. Ultimately they may have been influenced by the notion that folklore, coming down by word of mouth through many generations in a way that might seem almost mystical, is supposed to be very ancient and a unique window into some distant past.

LOST WORLDS

The spacemen as gods theorists may have been then but a blip in the continuum of "occult" thinking, but they represent that continuum nonetheless, one strand of thought (and one strand of folklore recycling) influenced by the trends of their day, such as developing possibilities for space travel in the 1960s and 70s. Some of them were also well aware of other strands of occult thinking and tied this into their own ideas. W. R. Drake, for example, suggests that Adam in Genesis represents an early race on earth who opposed the space invaders and who probably came from Atlantis.[26] Thus he draws a connection between the space "gods" and one of the lost worlds which have fascinated many and which have had a special place in the ideas of those occult thinkers, notably Helena Blavatsky and her Theosophists and the American mystic and healer Edgar Cayce, concerned with mystical spirituality and secret knowledge handed down by spiritual "masters" or intuited in visions.

The Atlantis story is traced to the writings of Plato, although the claim made there is that the story derives from old oral tradition. Plato tells the story of Atlantis in two dialogues written around 355 BCE, the *Timaios* and the *Kritias*. One of the characters in the dialogues, Kritias, tells a story which has been in his family for generations, a story they are said to have heard from Solon, the great Athenian statesman and lawgiver who died 558 BCE. Solon had gone to Egypt and was discussing history with some Egyptian priests, telling them how ancient were some Greek traditions. They laughed at this but went on to point out that he was evidently ignorant of some important Athenian history, how there had been a great Athenian empire thousands of years before, contemporaneous with a land called Atlantis, a huge continent beyond the Pillars of Hercules (the Straits of Gibraltar). There was a golden age both in Atlantis and Athens, but the Atlanteans became "decadent and greedy"[27] and sought to conquer the Mediterranean region. The Athenians, however, fought and defeated the Atlanteans, though suddenly there were great earthquakes and floods, the armies were swallowed up, and Atlantis itself sank into the sea.

Whether the Atlantis narrative was meant as history or as some sort of moral fable remained undecided in ancient times, but knowledge of the story continued, and interest in it revived with the discovery of the Americas and "attempts . . . to incorporate the American Indians into Western history."[28] Perhaps the Native Americans were descendants of people who had escaped the deluge that overcame Atlantis. In the 1860s a French scholar named Brasseur "translated" a Mayan codex that supposedly contained an account of a great catastrophe rather similar to that of Atlantis. Central American legends provided similarities as well. The stage was set for a revival of interest in the Atlantis story in this new context, and the American author Ignatius Donnelly would play a central role in doing so; he "came along and tied up the loose ends, at least to his own satisfaction," as Daniel Cohen has said,[29] penning a volume published in 1882, *Atlantis: The Antediluvian World*,[30] which became a mainstay for those interested in the sunken continent.

The Irish-American, Philadelphia-born Donnelly was an interesting man, a populist politician who served as lieutenant governor of Minnesota and a Republican member of Congress for several terms and who was the nominee for vice president in 1900 of the People's Party (also called the Populist Party), as well as a prolific author of books including novels. In his introduction to *Atlantis* Donnelly sets out thirteen numbered points about Atlantis that he is asserting in the book, starting off his work with the first comprehensive modern statement about the existence and nature of the lost continent. According to Donnelly, Atlantis once really existed, "a large island, which was the remnant of an Atlantic continent" near the entrance to the Mediterranean, Plato's account having been a historical one; furthermore, Atlantis was where human civilization arose; from it many parts of the world were populated, the people going to those places bringing their civilization with them (the Greek gods were merely the ancient kings of Atlantis; Egyptian and Peruvian mythology derive from there, ancient Egyptian culture in particular being closely derived from Atlantis, as were Bronze Age implements, the influential Phoenician alphabet, and the Indo-European and Semitic peoples); then there was a great "convulsion of nature" after which the place sank, although a few people escaped, bringing with them the flood legends found in many parts of the world. Atlantis was the Garden of Eden, Mount Olympus, Asgard in the imaginations and memories of such people.[31]

Donnelly goes on to compare a number of world civilizations and much of his argument depends on noting cultural similarities and assuming a common point of origin, namely Atlantis. In particular, he sees similarities between certain cultures on both sides of the Atlantic:

> *If we find on both sides of the Atlantic precisely the same arts, sciences, religious beliefs, habits, customs, and traditions, it is absurd to say that*

the peoples of the two continents arrived separately, by precisely the same ends. When we consider the resemblance of the civilizations of the Mediterranean nations to one another, no man is silly enough to pretend that Rome, Greece, Egypt, Assyria, Phoenicia, each spontaneously and separately invented the arts, sciences, habits, and opinions in which they agreed.[32]

That is, he rejects the idea of polygenesis but as a way of leading up to Atlantean origins for similar customs and beliefs. Some of his cultural comparisons are vague at best, and he notes, for example, only that civilizations on both sides of the Atlantic possessed the art of painting or both developed working with metals. In other instances, however, he is more precise and detailed. Beliefs in confession and penance and sprinkling the dead with water were known to multiple cultures. Belief in ghosts is found on both sides of the Atlantic. Both the Ojibwas and European peasants thought that the barking of a fox was an ill omen. The Kickapoos believed that their ancestors had tails, thus suggesting a kinship with European belief in satyrs and other half man-half animal creatures. The snake hair of the Medusa has a parallel in similar locks possessed by an Iroquois culture hero. In the Mandan buffalo dance the participants wore masks made of buffalo heads and horns, while even in the present-day Hindu priests and Tibetan lamas wear animal masks to "dance . . . demons out, or the new year in." Other parallels appear when we compare an Ojibwa with an Irish oral narrative or an Asian with a Native American one. A motif from a Central American story matches one from a Grimm märchen.[33]

Thus in some ways Donnelly's writing reads not unlike that of the British evolutionary anthropologists and folklorists who made comparisons between cultural traits, perceiving similarities and relationships that in retrospect seem simplistic. Where they sought "survivals" that indicated the evolution of culture, however, Donnelly looked for proof of a common origin in Atlantis. In particular, Donnelly was looking for memories of Atlantis, and it was not surprising that for him myths and legends "should preserve some recollection of events so appalling and destructive"[34] as the inundation of a now-lost world. Hence he devotes several chapters to deluge legends, reasoning that the wide spread of such narratives must indicate an oral record of the catastrophe that overwhelmed the lost continent.

In addition to the widely known biblical flood and its less well-known parallel, the flood in the Gilgamesh story, he notes the Greek Deucalion narrative and a wide variety of not only narratives from other cultures but also salient rituals. The Mayan *Popol Vuh* has a deluge story. In North America the Mandans actually have an ark in their flood story, and even had a sacred object that looked like a large barrel and that represented that ark; they called it the Big Canoe and it contained their most powerful medicines. The Aztecs had a festival to commemorate the wholesale destruction of a people and their artifacts, presumably Atlantis. The Celts had traditions that formerly their country had extended out into the Atlantic but that part was destroyed. Donnelly even suggests that other traditions are indicative of Atlantis and its destruction and can be seen in the same context as the deluge narratives themselves. An earth emergence story includes an underground lake and that lake must represent the ocean that surrounded Atlantis. The Tower of Babel story, in fact known on both sides of the Atlantic, is about building a structure tall enough to escape deluge. Aryan hymns that ask the gods to hold the land firm came about as a response to the Atlantis disaster.[35]

Donnelly's book sold widely (and, indeed, is still in print in the twenty-first century), becoming a basic work in the library of Atlantis literature. His work would become a basic source for later figures like Madame Blavatsky and the Theosophists who were more literally involved in occult approaches to reality in the sense that they claimed to offer access to hidden mystical knowledge.

Helena Blavatsky received much notoriety in her own day (and has been viewed as a grand charlatan by many). She enjoyed a varied career indeed as something of an adventuress. Born into the Russian nobility in 1831, she would later abandon her husband of a few months and embark on a life of wandering. She claimed to have converted to Buddhism in Ceylon and to have spent two years in Tibet studying with the mystic Brothers and where she was initiated into ancient mysteries. She claimed significant psychic powers and worked as a medium, factors that led her in 1873 to the United States, where spiritualism and mediumship were enjoying great vogue. In 1875 she founded, along with the American journalist Henry Steel Olcott and others, the Theosophical Society, which she later moved to India when she migrated there herself, though she later went to England and died in London in 1891. The ideas of Theosophy—belief that every religion holds some truth, in the ability of individuals to evolve spiritually assisted by entities called Monads, in various kinds of spirit matter which humans can access, and in the historical development of a series of earthly races—are largely based on her writings. Blavatsky writes that much of humanity as we know it stemmed from the race called Aryans, who originally came from Atlantis, where modern humans finally developed. Hence Atlantis played an important role in Theosophical conceptions, Blavatsky herself borrowing much of her own conception of the reality of Atlantis and its connections to world cultures from Donnelly.³⁶

In part because of her charismatic personality, in part because she lived in a time of intense interest in certain kinds of spirituality, Blavatsky had a significant influence. Probably her ideas about the Aryan race influenced Hitler and the Nazis in their more mystical moments (although her Aryans included Jews and Arabs), and some trace New Age spirituality and philosophy to her as well. Although Frederick Churchward, another occultist who made significant reference to the power of legends as explanatory of "history," was not a Theosophist, he, too, pursued a lost continent that had like Atlantis preoccupied Blavatsky. He called it Mu, a name that, actually, had originally referred to Atlantis, though she and others knew it as Lemuria. While Atlantis had, as its name implies, perched in the Atlantic Ocean, Mu had once filled much of the Pacific.

Lemuria, Daniel Cohen suggests, came into existence out of "the human longing for symmetry,"³⁷ out of early assumptions of Europeans that most of the earth should be land mass and that roughly half of the earth should be above, half below the Equator. Hence there should be a large southern land mass, and early European explorers of the South Pacific expected to find one. When it was not found, some guessed that it like Atlantis had been "lost." Then in the post-Darwin nineteenth-century, evolutionary biologists sought to explain how lemurs (a genus of primates) happened to exist on several continents and posited the possible existence of a former continent, Lemuria, which had connected the others across the Pacific and had allowed these animals to populate a large part of the world. Thus this hypothetical continent took on prominence in the world of scientific speculation, though before long it had attracted the attention of others who began to see the hypothetical place as another lost world which once had been home to a lost civilization, perhaps remembered in oral traditions such as Middle American legends about Quetzalcoatl. Blavatsky incorporated Lemuria into her book *The Secret Doctrine*, deciding that the continent had been the home of what was in her conception the third race to appear on earth (the Aryans were the fifth, the Atlanteans the fourth), citing an Atlantean book called *The Book of Dzyan* as her source. The Lemurians were, according to her idea of them, psychic visionaries.

Despite Blavatsky's interest in a lost Pacific continent, Churchward had his own sources for Mu. British-born, eventually resident in the United States, he had been at one time a tea planter in Ceylon. He claimed to have encountered, while he was assisting in famine-relief work in India, a wise and learned Indian priest (sometimes referred to as the "old Rishi"; that is, holy man), who was very interested in ancient records. Perceiving that Churchward was interested in deciphering some local inscriptions, this priest called Churchward's attention to both an ancient language (supposedly the original language of mankind) and to stone tablets supposedly inscribed in that language and having their origin with the Naacals, a priestly brotherhood sent out as colonists from Mu. With the collaboration of the priest (in a lecture he delivered to the American Society for Psychical Research in 1931, Churchward identifies the priest and two of his cousins as the last survivors of the Naacal Brotherhood[38]), Churchward was eventually able to read the Naacal tablets, which told the story of Mu, and he later took considerable interest in tablets discovered in Mexico by William Niven. The Scottish-born Niven was a mineralogist who had worked for Thomas Edison and discovered several new minerals in the course of his career, though he had discovered the tablets in 1921 in the Valley of Mexico after taking up archaeology; when Niven sought to stir up interest in the tablets (and possibly sell them) Churchward determined that they had been created by people who had escaped the destruction of Mu (and turned up in both India and Mexico) and that these tablets contained further information about this lost Pacific world. The Indian priest would never let Churchward take possession of the Naacal tablets and Niven's Mexican ones were said to have been lost in transit from Mexico to the United States, so access to these sources was severely limited for anybody but Churchward.[39]

Churchward was primarily a symbologist who seemed to take particular delight in "deciphering" the glyphs on his two sets of tablets (whether any of these tablets ever really existed in any form is difficult to say, though Churchward's books are full of illustrations of the pictographs that supposedly appeared on them and of other "ancient symbols" drawn from various sources). Much of his Mu information comes from his "translations" though he also makes reference to archaeological sites and ancient ruins he associates with Mu. When it comes to folklore, Churchward clearly sees the value of legends and "traditions" as historical accounts. In his second book, *The Children of Mu* (1931), he starts off with a summary of the case he made in his first book, *The Lost Continent of Mu* (also published in 1931) and lays out his sources of information. "The existence of this great continent," he writes, "is confirmed by" a variety of written records and archaeological remains but also by "legends throughout the world."[40] However, Churchward's faith in legends is a rather generalized one and though he states that legends prove this or that, he is, unlike Donnelly, often vague about what legends he actually means or what his sources for these oral traditions are.

Thus he makes such statements as "Legends of the creation are prevalent among the peoples of the world, and . . . I have found so much of the material identical that the only conclusion to be drawn is that . . . their genesis was in Mu." Or that "The Maoris . . . are rich in legends of the dim past." Or "legends point to about 5000 years ago" for the existence of a particular empire. Or that "various Pueblo traditions . . . *prove that the Pueblo Indians originally came to America from Mu*" (emphasis his). Or "legends all through Oriental countries" say that the mountainous parts of Asia were formerly flat. He may get a bit more specific in some instances, as when he says that an Easter Island legend says that the island was once part of a great continent, or that Zuñi "myth" indicates that these people once had contact with dinosaurs.[41]

In a few places Churchward does linger a bit with particular legends or "traditions" and look at them for rather more specific information. He seems, for example, to have a handle on actual texts of the Quetzalcoatl legends (seeing Queztalcoatl's migrations to and from the east as indicative of migrations from Mu). And he seems to believe that a legend actually told to him by the old Indian priest about the existence of a whole Naacal library hidden somewhere might eventually bring him the discovery of more Mu information. In the realm of folklore he also looks at times to beliefs and rituals, such as the Mayan belief in the West (where Mu existed and was destroyed) as a place of darkness but also of the afterworld, and the practice of fire walking (which he views as evidence of the cosmic mysteries that came from Mu). Even the absence of legends may tell him something. The fact that there are no traditions in modern Cambodia about who built the famous Angkor ruins suggests that they are very ancient (and go back to Mu).[42]

Churchward clearly was fascinated by symbols and had a strong desire to interpret the meanings of graphic symbols. The interpretation of such symbols may call for a very imaginative approach and such symbols may be open to a variety of interpretations. Certainly in reading Churchward's writings one comes away with the sense that the man's imagination played a key role in what he says and that he was able to imagine meanings and facts which other, perhaps more sensible people simply would not see. Nonetheless, he does try to give the impression that his case is based on more than his interpretations of symbols from ancient tablets not even available to other potential researchers. He refers to ancient texts; he speaks of famous manuscripts, notably some relating to Middle America and in Aztec or Mayan scripts, never translated (except, evidently, by Churchward himself!); and, of greatest relevance to us here, he expresses his faith in the historical power of oral tradition to back up his theses. The very fact that he seems to know (or at any rate says) very little about specific legends or other folk material is actually indicative of why he and other occultists look to tradition. Of course, they seek to marshal all possible evidence, and legends offer one seemingly significant possibility for them. Additionally, however, legends have a ring of antiquity that must have appealed. Though legends can come into existence at any time, they may seem to go back to distant events and distant times and thus stand as almost eyewitness accounts. They have the appeal of the hoary, a romantic ancientness that in itself gives them authority. Furthermore, though legends may be well known to those who circulate them by word of mouth, to outsiders they may be unknown and seemingly a sort of secret knowledge ("known only to the tribe"). Hence they would appeal to occultists like Churchward with their penchant for hidden secrets. Though Churchward does refer to some particular legends, for him the very idea of legend and the "historical" possibilities of legend may have held the real fascination.

THE HOLLOW EARTH

Probably because of the considerable antiquity of the Atlantis idea and its beginnings in the work of one of the greatest of Western philosophers, the lost continent of the Atlantic has been far better known than its less well established Pacific counterpart, Lemuria/Mu. Both places, however, are conceived by their devotees as having once existed and then disappeared, whereas another "lost world" which has occupied the attention of a number of intellectual speculators, some of whom have cited oral traditions to make their case, might be better described as a never-quite-found world. This is the "hollow earth," or rather whatever worlds, lands, realms, or natural phenomena have been posited to exist within the interior of our planet. That our earth is indeed hollow and contains a landscape, seas, light sources, and beings is an idea with a fairly long history, sometimes presented only through fiction but sometimes in scientific thinking and esoteric theories.

Indeed, the hollow earth idea—if we discount ancient ideas about underworlds—first pops up in the thinking of a noted astronomer, Edmond Halley, best known for the discovery in 1682 of the comet that bears his name. Halley supported the landmark publication of Isaac Newton's *Principia Mathematica* and in an attempt to understand the magnetism of the earth and in part drawing on Newton he posited the idea that the earth contained inner spheres, going on to suggest that the inner earth had light sources and animal populations. Then in the earlier decades of the nineteenth century in the young United States, one John Cleves Symmes created considerable attention by declaring that the earth was hollow, "containing a number of solid concentric spheres"[43]; the earth was also, said Symmes, open at both ends, allowing access to the inner world as well as the intrusion of regular sunlight inside. Possibly influenced by the Puritan divine Cotton Mather, he did this initially in a circular published in 1818, but he also wrote the first American utopian novel, *Symzonia: Voyage of Discovery* (1820), set inside the earth, and took to the lecture circuit to propound his ideas to the public. He argued for an American expedition to the poles, even getting a senator to propose this to Congress, for such an expedition might not only prove his own ideas but be of considerable strategic and economic interest to the United States at a time when polar exploration was enjoying a wave of interest. Symmes was evidently not an inspiring lecturer and so managed to enlist a co-lecturer of greater abilities, Jeremiah Reynolds. They parted ways before very long but the more able Reynolds went on lecturing and then published a book about Symmes's ideas.

It was Reynolds who attracted the attention of one of the greatest of nineteenth-century American writers, Edgar Allen Poe, who would produce several works of fiction tied to Arctic exploration and a hollow earth (and who would draw Reynolds into a literary mystery by crying out Reynolds's name as his dying words). *Symzonia* had not been the first hollow earth novel (Robert Paltock had published "a whimsical sort-of-subterranean English novel, *The Life and Adventures of Peter Wilkins,*"[44] in 1751, and Casanova's multivolume *Icosameron* of 1788 has characters who stumble into the interior of the earth), but if readers are at all familiar with earlier fiction about polar exploration and mysterious lands and people found at the poles it will be with Poe's *The Narrative of Arthur Gordon Pym* (which may have been based on *Symzonia*), although Poe's stories "Ms. Found in a Bottle" and "A Descent into the Maelstrom" also owe something to not only polar exploration but to fantastic notions of what might be found at the poles stemming from the ideas of Symmes (David Standish says of the first story that Poe "owes his ending to Symmes' Hole" [that is, to his theory of polar openings][45]).

For much of the time since Poe, much of the interest in a hollow earth was fiction centered. Jules Verne's *A Journey to the Centre of the Earth* appeared in 1864 and, like much of Verne's fiction, has been widely popular since, having been filmed in 1959 starring James Mason and crooner Pat Boone. Beginning in the 1920s another celebrated writer of science fiction and fantasy adventure, Edgar Rice Burroughs, published his Pellucidar series, novels and stories set in a world inside the earth. In 1929 he even introduced his most famous character, Tarzan of the Apes, into the subterranean world of Pellucidar in *Tarzan at the Earth's Core*, in which Tarzan goes into the earth to rescue the main character of the Pellucidar books. And although Verne and Burroughs may be the most famous authors of hollow earth novels, they were hardly the only ones. Edward Bulwer-Lytton published a hollow earth novel and in one of L. Frank Baum's Oz books his character Dorothy falls into the hollow earth. Verne's was not even the first hollow earth novel in French (Jacques Collin de Plancy published one in 1821), and David Standish's list of hollow earth novels published between 1880 and 1915 has over thirty entries and is only a selective list. "In the 1950s," Standish writes, "the hollow earth began appearing in movies. It was a natural for low-budget science fiction melodramas."[46]

However, the hollow earth idea also has had a life well beyond the day of Symmes and Reynolds as an actual proposition about reality. In the later nineteenth century, the American Cyrus Reed Teed founded a cult, the Koreshans, which developed communes and believed that not only was the earth hollow but that humanity was already living inside it. Although such an idea seems difficult to grasp, that did not prevent Teed from having a number of followers and creating a flourishing community near Fort Myers, Florida (today a state historic site). In the 1930s Adolph Hitler *may* have been interested in the hollow earth idea.[47] Then in the 1940s the idea took on new energy with the publication of work by Richard S. Shaver in a science fiction magazine, *Amazing Stories*, edited by Raymond A. Palmer. Shaver had radical political ideas, thought that a demon had killed his brother, and had a history of mental illness. He conceived ideas according to which an ancient alphabet he had discovered enabled him to understand that the Atlantis legend was true and that ancient legends about the gods stemmed from a super race that once lived inside the earth. Originally this race had come from another planet and settled on Atlantis and the members of this group created a complex web of tunnels and eventually a vast underground civilization. Finally they abandoned the planet, leaving behind humans (a "robot race" they created to work for them) and, underground, the deros, a monstrous "robot race" that stayed underground and used the machines left behind by the super race to cause humans trouble (everything from plane crashes to stubbed toes). Shaver evidently believed in these delusions and Palmer, whose *Amazing Stories* dealt in the sensational and in the space opera preferred by less sophisticated readers, published Shaver's writings as nonfiction. To Palmer's surprise, Shaver's work elicited considerable interest, and he continued to publish it even after Shaver had been committed to an asylum. Palmer himself added the idea that flying saucers, which were beginning to attract attention in the 1940s, came not from outer space but from inside the earth, and he went on to edit a publication devoted to UFOs, continuing to press the idea that their origin was the interior of the earth. Shaver and Palmer, then, pulled together several esoteric theories, the hollow earth, UFOs, ancient alien visitors, and sunken continents (notably Atlantis, though Shaver's best-known piece was called "I Remember Lemuria").

Hard as this may be to conceive, Shaver's strange writings (and Palmer's probably opportunistic promotion of them) gave new impetus to interest in the hollow earth idea. However, there was another strand of hollow earth thinking prevalent in the twentieth century, one stemming in part from theosophy and Madame Blavatsky. Blavatsky's extensive travels supposedly included two years in South America where she heard about fantastic networks of tunnels stretching out under the continent. Later, leaders of the Brazilian Theosophical Society floated the idea that the tunnels were part of the subterranean world of Aghartha, whose capital city was called Shamballah, picking up on Buddhist ideas about a real or symbolic underground world. Aghartha had originally been written about by several occult-minded European explorers of Tibet and Mongolia in the early twentieth century, including Ferdinand Ossendowski and Nicholas Roerich.[48] The Brazilian Theosophists added the notion that flying saucers came from this world and also made a connection with the once-celebrated English explorer Colonel Percy Harrison Fawcett, who had disappeared in the jungles of the Matto Grosso in 1925. According to their perspectives, Fawcett, who did in fact have occult interests, had been searching for the entrance to the underground world and had found it, disappearing within with his two companions; they were still there.[49] Whereas Shaver and Palmer envisioned a frightening hollow earth peopled by the fearsome deros, the Theosophists and Aghartha promoters thought the hollow earth contained an enlightened civilization, derived from origins in Atlantis, of spiritual masters and virtually immortal beings. The flying saucers had, they thought, been sent to the surface by these enlightened people to warn humans about the dangers of nuclear war.

Although the information provided about this version of the hollow earth often seems to come out of thin air (or from mysterious, probably imaginary, documents deciphered from unknown languages, or from visionary experiences), proponents of Aghartha try to offer other kinds of evidence of its existence. They may offer accounts (not unlike alien abductee stories) given by people who claim to have been kidnaped into the inner earth by dero-like beings.[50] They have given considerable attention to some ambiguous statements made by the polar explorer Admiral Richard Byrd, which they interpret to indicate that he flew over polar openings. They have accepted as factual what were almost surely intended as works of fiction, such as Willis George Emerson's 1908 *The Smoky God; or A Voyage to the Inner World*,[51] in which an old Swedish fisherman narrates how he accidentally sailed into a polar opening and into the hollow earth. They cite supposed facts about Arctic regions: animals migrate *north* (that is, toward the polar opening) in winter; in the far north temperatures become not colder but warmer (because of the openings and what lies inside); animal life is more abundant in the Arctic than in the tropics.[52] But, like other occult thinkers, they have certainly placed some reliance on folklore and on oral narratives, again recycling legends, for example, as documents. Like other writers on the occult subjects discussed in this chapter, writers on Aghartha are at best imprecise in citing their sources, and they may speak of oral narratives in the most general terms, displaying faith in its suggestive power but being unable to interpret actual texts.

Raymond Bernard, whose writings have been a central source for contemporary hollow earth believers, even wonders whether Santa Claus is a "race memory" of a "benefactor" of humankind who once came out of the interior of the earth on a flying saucer (remembered as a flying sled with reindeer pulling it).[53] But he also calls attention to the Norse Ultima Thule as a mythic place that could reference the polar opening and the wonderful world within the earth; an ancient Irish legend of "land beyond the sea" (168); and Eskimo "traditions" that these people had originally come from a land of sunshine (the hollow earth believers posit an interior sun) beyond the northern ice (these traditions, Bernard says, "must be given full weight" [168] as sources of information). Eskimo legends "handed down generation after generation" (169) describe an interior land with a sun that shines perpetually. The Atlantean migration to the hollow earth is a subject of Teutonic mythology, and the middle American god/hero Quetzalcoatl, who according to legends visited the Aztecs and Mayas and taught them many things before he "returned back to the Subterranean World from which he came," riding a flying saucer (34), was, of course, an Atlantean.[54]

Bernard touches on supposed Asian traditions of Agharta, but Eric Norman, whose book *This Hollow Earth* presents itself as skeptical but offers much support to hollow earth belief, delves more into these Asiatic folk sources. In general he argues or at least proclaims both the factual basis for much folklore ("many legends have a basis in fact"; the Hollow Earth Society "believes that the legends and myths handed down from ancient times often contain important clues"), and the prevalence of folk traditions about such hidden places as the hollow earth ("Since ancient times there have been . . . legends about other lands, hidden worlds"; "stories of tunnels can be gleaned from the legends, folklore, and myths of almost every country"). And he notes "widespread research into the legends of the Far East" which might reveal the truth of an interior world. There are Buddhist traditions about visitors from other worlds (presumably Agharta) who come in times of "great turmoil" to bring help for humankind.[55] Ossendowski encountered Central Asian legends about Agharta, and "Doc" Anderson, an American occultist living in Georgia when Norman interviewed him, had traveled in Asia as a young man and heard numerous legendary accounts of Agharta. Ossendowski heard an oral narrative about a lama who believed in the reality of Agharta who journeyed to Siam where he met a fisherman who could take him to a mysterious island where he could meet people from the subterranean world.

> . . . *the lama agreed to accompany the fisherman to the mysterious island. Upon his arrival upon a rock and coral-studded isle, the lama was introduced to several tall, robed men who claimed to be from the subterranean world.*
>
> *These strange beings led the old pilgrim to a bird cage. "I saw a bird with sharp, fang-like teeth," related the holy man. "It was a species unknown to the surface world. I was also shown a strange animal with sixteen feet and one eye, like the legendary Cyclops of ancient times. The people assembled there told me they were from the subterranean kingdom of Agharta. They journeyed from the inner land in vehicles unknown to surface men. They said their cars could be driven through subterranean tunnels that connected with all points of the earth."[56]*

This account, which has folktale-like motifs and may indeed be a traditional tale or based on one, leaves the seeker at the virtual entrance to

Agharta, and in other accounts other surface folk *hear* about the interior world (through legends or other sources) and maybe even learn the location of a door which leads inside but seldom do they actually enter. David Standish suggests that the hollow earth became of interest to writers of adventure fiction as the surface of the globe became better and better known; the interior was an unknown whose nature still could be invented. Perhaps those who believe in its reality prefer to have only speculation and hearsay (and legends can be seen as a form of hearsay as well as stories bearing kernels of truth and may be useful "sources" for that reason), to never quite find the hollow earth, for then they can imagine the flying saucers or remnants of Atlantis or super beings or monstrous demons that may reside within.

CATASTROPHISTS

From the middle of the nineteenth century until the latter decades of the twentieth the science of geology worked from the paradigm of *gradualism*; namely, the proposition that the physical earth had developed very slowly over the course of millions of years in a continuous process. Prior to the general acceptance of gradualism, some had suggested that the physical development of the earth had come about through the occurrence of widespread catastrophes, such as floods, which shaped the nature of the physical world. The noted French naturalist Georges Cuvier, for example, was influential in proposing catastrophes as the cause of geological developments, though by the middle of the nineteenth century (Cuvier died in 1832), gradualist ideas had prevailed.

Intermittently, however, counter proposals by catastrophists have been laid out to assert the significance of great disasters in the formation of the earth and in human history. The two most widely known of these catastrophists—the redoubtable Ignatius Donnelly in the last quarter of the nineteenth century and the more recent Immanuel Velikovsky—have relied heavily on the use of folk materials (including ancient myth) to make their points. Given the scientific context of the ideas concerned, catastrophists have worked more on the edges of science than in the occult world of the Theosophists and hollow earth proponents. The noted paleontologist Stephen Jay Gould, for example, notes that Velikovsky, though certainly wrong, was neither a "crank" nor a "charlatan,"[57] categories into which many Atlantis and hollow earth theorists surely would be cast. Nonetheless, catastrophists certainly have been aware of presenting unorthodox ideas and may have

taken pride in their opposition to the world of mainstream scientific thinking; they have looked to unorthodox documentation, such as folk traditions,
for their support. And certainly they propose interpretations of history alternative to those generally accepted by scientists and scholars.

Donnelly published his book *Ragnarok: The Age of Fire and Gravel* in
1883, the year after he published his Atlantis book, in an active literary period during a hiatus in his political life. Its title is, interestingly enough,
drawn from Norse mythology, and it posits the idea that the earth was
greatly affected by an encounter with a comet in ancient times—an idea that
would in fact be echoed over sixty years later by Velikovsky in a much more
sophisticated way. Donnelly's *Atlantis: The Antediluvian World* had been a
considerable commercial success (it had gone though twenty-three American and twenty-six British printings by 1890) and his new book, written in
about two months time, was designed to likewise attract public attention
in a day when history and new scientific discoveries were of wide popular
interest. Despite the interest his books evoked with the reading public,[58] his
ideas would never be taken seriously by scholars or scientists in his own
day or later, yet he did attempt to undertake his work in a semi-scholarly
fashion. When he started his Atlantis volume and *Ragnarok,* he evidently
bought a large number of relevant books and periodicals and surveyed
a wide array of published sources which he cites in numerous footnotes
(though evidently he worked very much alone, not attempting to consult
any experts in the fields about which he was writing[59]) and for both *Atlantis*
and *Ragnarok* he rather argued his case not like a scientist but like a lawyer,
massing a great deal of evidence (but without assessing the value and valid-
ity of his many sources).

In *Ragnarok* Donnelly works from his interest in the *drift*—that is, the
"out of place" geological debris, "a vast deposit of sand, gravel, and clay"[60]
which overlays the solid, fixed, underlying bedrock. Such drift is commonly
geologically variant from the bedrock and has generally been accepted by
geologists as having been shifted by glacial movements during ancient ice
ages and was so explained even in Donnelly's day. He, however, argues that
its origin is not known and goes on to suggest that it is the debris left behind
by the comet that had a close encounter with the earth in ancient times.
Furthermore, he reconstructs the human experience of the comet and the
calamity it caused the earth and the people who were living on the earth
at the time of the experience, the "age of fire and gravel" of his title. These
people "witnessed the appalling and sudden calamity"[61] which unfolded.
Indeed, he is little concerned with the drift itself but rather with the larger

event of the comet's visitation. The record of that catastrophic visitation he finds largely in folklore, mostly legend and myth but also in ritual, to the extent that his book is in a sense an exercise in folklore scholarship, though folklorists would be no more likely to accept it as such than scientists would be to accept it as a legitimate scientific treatise. Indeed, Donnelly repeatedly expresses his faith in folklore as historical record and as providing in particular a picture of the key catastrophic events. "Every detail of the mighty catastrophe has been preserved in the legends of mankind," he writes. "We shall see all this depicted in the legends." Humanity "has preserved recollections of the comet to this day in . . . myths and legend." Myth, especially if it is a "universal" one, "is based on some fact," and the reader "must concede that it describes some event which really happened."[62] He realizes, of course, that the picture passed on by oral tradition is not a literal or entirely consistent one (it agrees about the comet and the ensuing calamity in certain basics—the "monster in the air"—that is, the comet—the terrible heat and fire that the comet generated on the earth, the retreat of human survivors into caves to escape the conflagration, the disappearance of the sun—due to dust from the comet—the eventual reappearance of the light, though obviously the creation of various narrative traditions has meant the cloaking of the events in a variety of forms and guises). Donnelly claims to understand that storytellers modify their creations, thus explaining the variety of traditions he claims as relating to his theory, though he also stresses that humans lack great originality and repeat the same things over and over again, thus reinforcing his point that many cultures retain stories that reflect the far distant past and the particular events of his interest. Folklore collectors, he says, have proven that the same stories have been repeated by "all the nations" of the world.[63]

Donnelly sees a narrative memory of the coming of the comet, for example, in Hesiod's "description of two or three aërial monsters" (the American was aware that Hesiod did not live in the far distant times of the comet but assumes he did transmit very ancient traditions by his writings). For example, Hesiod writes:

> [Night] Brought forth another monster, irresistible nowise like to mortal man or immortal gods, in a hollow cavern; the divine, stubborn-hearted Echidna (half-nymph, with dark eyes and fair cheeks; and half, on the other hand, a serpent, huge and terrible and vast), speckled, and flesh-devouring. . . . But she . . . bare Chimaera, breathing resistless fire.[64]

Donnelly makes much of the fact that the comet, with its long tail, was perceived as a serpent. Of course, the myth of Phaëton, who drives his father's fiery chariot across the sky and cannot control it, is another narrative manifestation of the comet, whereas in Norse mythology the Fenris-wolf (another monstrous animal embodying a conception of the comet) makes great mischief with the earth, eventually causing Ragnarok, the age of darkness.

Other traditions convey memories of the comet or of the terrible destruction that follows its advent, including the obscuring of the sun when comet dust blocks out the normal light. Native Americans living in the vicinity of Lake Tahoe in California have legendary accounts of the cosmic destruction:

> Half a moon had not elapsed . . . before the earth was . . . troubled . . .
> with strong convulsions and thunderings. . . . The poor slaves fled to the
> Humboldt River, and, getting into their canoes, paddled for life from the
> awful sight behind them; for the land was tossing like a troubled sea,
> and casting up fire, smoke, and ashes. The flames went up to the very
> heavens, and melted many stars, SO THAT THEY RAINED DOWN
> IN MOLTEN METAL UPON THE EARTH.[65]

For Donnelly an Aztec account of the destruction of mankind by the sun is a similar record, as is a battle between Rama (the sun) and the demon Ravanna from Hindu sources. Donnelly lived in a time when the intellectual climate was preoccupied by solar mythology, and Manibozho, the Algonquin culture hero is likewise the sun whose "'foe was the glittering prince of serpents'—the Comet." A version of the Earth Diver story from a group in British Columbia which includes a terrible fire sweeping over the earth is also an account of the comet's destructive path, while an Ojibway version of the Sun Snarer tale provides a depiction of the loss of light occasioned by the comet dust.[66] Donnelly provides a list of those cultures whose "traditions . . . tell us that the earth was once swept by a great conflagration."[67]

But because humanity, despite terrible destruction and loss of life, managed to survive, other folklore tells how people stayed alive by retreating into caves and eventually emerged to repopulate the world. At first they faced a terrible darkness (the comet dust), though finally the sun's light returned (as the dust settled and dissipated). The Toltecs, for example, had a legend of escaping a terrible hurricane by taking refuge in caves, while the Navajos have maintained "the most complete account of the cave-life":

The Navajos . . . say that at one time all the nations . . . lived together underground, in the heart of a mountain. . . . Their food was meat, which they had in abundance, for all kinds of game were closed up with them in their cave; but their light was dim, and only endured for a few hours each day. There were, happily, two dumb men among the Navajos, flute-players, who enlivened the darkness with music. One of these, striking by chance the roof of the limbo with his flute, brought out a hollow sound, upon which the elders of the tribe determined to bore in the direction whence the sound came. The flute was then set up against the roof, and the Racoon sent up the tube to dig a way out, but he could not. Then the Moth-worm mounted into the breach, and bored and bored till he found himself suddenly on the outside of the mountain.[68]

Donnelly notes that the digging was necessary because the drift had covered the mouth of the cave. Indeed, emergence stories in general provide Donnelly with accounts of people coming out of caves after the great conflagration (though in fact such stories commonly include no mention of conflagration).

"All cosmogonies begin with an Age of Darkness," Donnelly writes, "the air thick with comet-dust." "In the beginning, *before the light of the sun* had been created, this land was *in obscurity and darkness* and *void* of any created thing," says a legend from Cholula, but light was created (that is, it appeared as the dust cleared), as an Eskimo story has it:

In the beginning were two brothers, one of whom said, "There shall be night and there shall be day, and men shall die, one after another." But the second said, "There shall be no day, but only night all the time, and men shall live for ever." They had a long struggle, but here once more he who loved darkness rather than light was worsted, and the day triumphed.[69]

Donnelly then ends his book with a consideration of the biblical books of Job (which he seems to assume is legend based and ancient) and Genesis. He decides that the legends[70] he has uncovered indicate that pre-comet humankind was quite civilized and, unsurprisingly, traces their history back to Atlantis, subject of his earlier book, and to land bridges that enabled the people of Atlantis to migrate to other parts of the world.

Immanuel Velikovsky, born in Russia in 1895, educated there and in France and Scotland, came to the United States in 1939, not intending to emigrate but only to spend a sabbatical, researching a book both inspired by and intended to counter Freud's *Moses and Monotheism*. Looking into the biblical Book of Exodus, he undertook the exploration of possibly complementary Egyptian documents which might include information on an actual Jewish exodus from ancient Egypt. What he noted, both in Egyptian sources and the Old Testament books, led him to conclude that there had been cataclysmic cosmic events at the time of the exodus, and he proceeded to further develop ideas about catastrophes which had taken place in ancient times and which had been recorded, albeit obliquely, in historical, literary, and folk sources.

Velikovsky had noticed some of the same accounts of turmoil and disaster in legends and other sources as had Donnelly. Indeed, in his introduction to a new edition of Donnelly's *Ragnarok*, sometime folklorist Leslie Shepard suggests that Donnelly had "put forward the same basic concept"[71] as Velikovsky would later, no doubt in part because Velikovsky's more recent writings had attracted so much attention. Velikovsky probably was not actually much influenced by the far less scientific Donnelly, noting his work in one footnote and pointing out Donnelly's evident ignorance of similar ideas expressed in a late-seventeenth-century work by William Whiston,[72] yet he, too, was struck by the power of oral traditions to carry on expression of the human encounter with cosmic catastrophe. Velikovsky is far more scientifically sophisticated (and, given that he was working nearly seventy years later, far more knowledgeable), and, though folklore is an important source for him, he relies heavily on literary and other written materials. Donnelly's books have been popular, but he has been largely simply ignored by scientists and scholars; Velikovsky's work, however, not only attracted hundreds of thousands of readers but also stirred great controversy and attracted much scientific comment.

Unlike Donnelly, whose vision of ancient comet-caused catastrophes was not time-specific, Velikovsky offers dates for the events he discusses, the middle of the second millennium BCE and the eighth and seventh centuries BCE for two different sets of catastrophic events. In the first instance a comet (which in Velikovsky's view eventually became the planet Venus) came extremely close to the earth; in the second, the planet Mars, then on an orbit different from the one we know today, came close to colliding with the earth. As a result of these planetary mishaps, there were virtual "wars in the celestial spheres,"[73] experienced by and noted by ancient humanity.

These "wars" were recorded in written sources and oral tradition, and Velikovsky's first book, *Worlds in Collision*, introduces both cosmic events and the supposed records of them. His later book, originally published in 1955, *Earth in Upheaval*, would develop further the evidence for the events he outlines but deal only with evidence from nature and explicitly ignore any written or folk evidence.[74]

Like Donnelly, Velikovsky expresses considerable faith in the power of oral tradition to transmit memories of past events, and he explicitly includes it in his list of useful sources:

> *The historical-cosmological story of this book is based on the evidence of historical texts of many people around the globe, on classical literature, on epics of northern races, on sacred books . . .* on traditions and folklore of primitive peoples, *on old astronomical inscriptions and charts, on archaeological finds and also on geological and paleontological material.*

"Let us . . . investigate the traditions . . . of ancient man," he writes, for "the great discharges of interplanetary force are commemorated in the traditions, legends, and mythology of all the peoples of the world." He goes on: "World conflagration is a frequent motif in folklore," and "we can assume that the folklore of different peoples deals with one and the same factual event."[75]

In somewhat narrower terms, Velikovsky notes that, for example, the Incas, Aztecs, and Mayas all had traditions of cosmic catastrophes, as did Hawaii. Many cultures had the mythological-cosmological idea of successive ages, each ending in some catastrophe, to be followed by a new age. "The aborigines of British North Borneo, even today, declare that the sky was originally low, and that six suns perished, and the present world is illuminated by the seventh sun." When the Venus comet swept the earth it not only brought prolonged periods of darkness due to comet dust and the retardation of the earth's normal rotation but also abnormally long periods of day and night, red-colored particles from its tail, naphtha from its gaseous composition, rains of meteorites, and terrible storms and inundations. The red "hail" is recorded not only in the Old Testament but also in the *Kalevala*, which has the world sprinkled by red milk during "the days of the cosmic upheaval," and in Mexican chronicles and oral tradition where the motif of "a hail of stones . . . is repeated again and again."[76]

The naphtha is remembered as "descent of a sticky fluid which came earthward and blazed with heavy smoke . . . recalled in the oral . . . traditions of the inhabitants of both hemispheres." In the East, in Siberia, "the Voguls carried down . . . this memory: 'God sent a sea of fire upon the earth,'" while further south, "in the East Indies, the aboriginal tribes relate that in the remote past *Sengle-Das* or 'water of fire' rained from the sky." Peoples to the west, south, and north of Egypt "have old traditions about a cosmic catastrophe during which the sun did not shine," "the Peruvians describe a time when the sun did not appear for five days," and the Polynesians speak of a great chief who wandered in utter darkness. In Japanese mythology the sun goddess hides in a cave from the devastations of the storm god, and "traditions of many people persist that seas were torn apart." Velikovsky also sees tradition as providing memories of the significance of Venus in creating devastation. The ancient Mexicans sacrificed to the Morning Star (Venus), as did the Skidi Pawnee, and Quetzalcoatl was associated in mythology with Venus. Mexican traditions have Venus as "smoking"—that is, a comet.[77]

When it comes to the solar system, the nearby universe, Velikovsky rejects the idea of gradualism and the idea that the system has been in place for a very, very long time. On the contrary, "as we have learned from the records of ancient times, the order today is not the primeval order; it was established less than twenty-seven centuries ago." This truth is indeed reflected in the lines of the folk epic, the *Kalevala*:

> *when the moon was placed in orbit,*
> *when the silver sun was planted,*
> *when the Bear was firmly stationed.*[78]

The recycling of folklore as historical document to support unorthodox theories about history covers a wide range of efforts, from the spiritual interests of Theosophists to the efforts of someone like Immanuel Velikovsky which border on the scientific.

It is, of course, interesting to speculate as to why certain individuals and groups have been attracted to such alternative visions of the past as the existence of lost continents and a hollow earth, or the influence of alien visitors upon human civilization, or the powerful force cosmic catastrophes exerted upon our physical world. At the outset of this chapter I suggested that there is an "occult" element at work here, at least in the sense that some people have a fondness for "secret" or "suppressed" knowledge. In the case of the Theosophists and other seekers after the mystical, the "occult" universe has spiritual dimensions and involves a belief in spiritual masters who teach the great truths of life but who are hidden away in hard-to-reach places like Tibet, who only appear in chance encounters, or who perhaps live in a spiritual realm little penetrated by mortals. Lost continents become an aspect of the secret universe from which the masters came or the hollow earth may be part of that in which they operate today. In the case of alien visitations, or civilizations inside the earth, or even ancient catastrophes, the knowledge is secret in a more secular sense, representing truths scorned by a blind, orthodox establishment but known to a few emerging seekers. It is not difficult to see the appeal of "secret" knowledge; those who possess it or seek it gain a certain moral and intellectual superiority, can see themselves as intellectual pioneers, can cast aspersions on scientific and scholarly establishments, can perhaps feel a bit like martyrs to a cause when their truth goes unrecognized.

Velikovsky evidently likened himself to Giordano Bruno, the Renaissance Italian scientist who was persecuted for his ideas, and thought of himself as a "suppressed genius."[79] We can only wonder whether Donnelly's political populism was a factor in his long-standing interest in writing unorthodox books (in addition to his Atlantis and catastrophist volumes, he wrote others arguing that he had found ciphers in Shakespeare's plays which indicated that Francis Bacon was their true author); populists opposed political and economic elites, perhaps Donnelly took pleasure and justification in opposing intellectual elites as well. In writing about ancient gold artifacts which to him represent aircraft but which conventional archaeologists have identified as religious in nature, von Däniken sniffs: "I'm sorry for the archaeologists, but that simply won't do."[80]

The appeal of folklore as document may stem from a latent euhemerism that wants to believe that simpler historical realities lie behind fantastic oral narratives, or that, say, old, familiar British nursery rhymes conceal messages about more esoteric, long-ago political trends. Or folklore, always shifting textually and whose meanings are not always clear or agreed upon, may be so conveniently malleable as to be open to various alternative historical interpretations. Certainly historians usually have ignored folklore or been actively suspicious of what it could possibly tell them about the past. Indeed Velikovsky deliberately excludes "all references to ancient literature, traditions, and folklore" from Earth in Upheaval lest "careless critics . . . decry the entire work as 'tales and legends.'"[81] For writers themselves sparring with historians or scientists, the temptation to rely on sources largely rejected by historians and irrelevant to scientific interpretation may be irresistible. And, indeed, because folklore may be little known beyond its own cultural contexts and the obscure work of a few scholars, it may itself glow with a certain aura of being "secret" knowledge. Hence it gets recycled as documentary, brought however unsuccessfully from a world of oral culture into a world of scientific discourse.

Chapter 6

AMERICANS AND THE FOLK ARTS IN MEXICO

Tourism, Fine Art, Architecture, Interior Decoration, International Relations

◇◇

Folklore frequently has played a central role in cultural nationalism movements for various and complex reasons, but at a most fundamental level folklore comes to be seen as the expression of "the people" who are in turn viewed as possessing the essence of a national character or spirit. Herder developed this view in the eighteenth century, and folklore came to have an important symbolic place in the Finnish nationalist movement that called attention to the *Kalevala* epic. Such was also the case in the Irish movement, which eventually brought about the independence of the Republic of Ireland from the United Kingdom and in which not only language revival was a significant factor but which, "stirred by the English threat to Irish culture, developed a concern for Irish folklore."[1]

Folklore likewise came to a prominent position in Mexico following the Mexican Revolution, which began in 1910. Here the leftist tilt of the revolution glorified the common and indigenous people and produced an atmosphere in which folk materials, associated with those social strata, came to be of particular interest. Interestingly, this intense focus on Mexican folklore became important for many Americans (that is, "*North* Americans," citizens of the United States) who came to Mexico just after the revolution, drawn by cultural and political developments taking place there.[2] How these Americans (and later ones) perceived and used Mexican folklore to their own ends is the subject of this chapter.

The Mexican Revolution created not only American interest in Mexico but also tensions between the United States and Mexico. Some in American government and business circles feared that the revolution would bring about a Bolshevik state on America's borders (a fear not unlike that of the Cuban state that took shape some years later), while the immigration of large numbers of Mexicans into the United States at the time caused other anxieties for Americans, whose stereotypes of Mexicans equated them with *banditos* or saw them as people of "ignorance, filthy habits, and high fertility."[3] To counter negative attitudes, the postrevolution Obregón and Calles regimes sought to influence the course of American opinion in positive directions, establishing, for example, the Summer School for Foreigners at the National University, which brought American students, particularly teachers of Spanish from the American Southwest, to Mexico City, for courses in language and literature but also Mexican culture, including archaeology and folklore. American intellectuals, such as John Dewey, were also invited to lecture, so that the Summer School attracted not only teachers improving their language skills and cultural knowledge but also prominent members of the American cultural establishment. However, Mexico as a place simply exerted a powerful appeal for many Americans intrigued by the possibilities for a new, emerging society and new cultural developments as well as a growing awareness of the existence of ancient wonders and of sympathetic traditional ways of life in a nearby nation. American writers, artists, and social observers and commentators began to gravitate "south of the border" to experience Mexican life.

These Americans took note of various aspects of Mexico: political transformations, pre-Columbian civilizations, the artistic renaissance particularly centered around the production of public murals, a society very different from that of the United States. Mexican folk art and folk crafts became an important focus of interest. Such was the case for several reasons. In the 1920s and 1930s in both the United States and Mexico there was growing interest in folk art and the indigenous arts of Native Americans, leading in the United States for example, to such developments as Lincoln Kirstein's "American Folk Painting" exhibition at Harvard and Abby Aldrich Rockefeller's collecting activities. In Mexico the cultural renaissance that followed the revolution "was based on the exaltation of Mexico's indigenous and popular traditions in the arts. . . . National songs and dances became popular overnight, and every home had examples of popular crafts, a gourd from Olinalá or a pot from Oaxaca."[4] In 1921 the Mexican government celebrated the centennial of Mexican independence with among other things "a major exhibition of folk art [and] a demonstration of *charro* cowboy skills. . . . The celebration culminated with Mexican Night in Chapultepec Park . . . enlivened by fireworks and folk dances and music."[5]

The Americans picked up on these nationalistic Mexican uses of folklore, but also were influenced by their own romantic ideas about Mexican

traditional society as less materialistic and happier than the American society from which they came and as stressing the beauties of the handmade
as opposed to the machine-made goods of modern societies. The form and
functions of Mexican folk art and traditions, so very different from anything
known in the United States, served to stress the very novelty of this place.
And the development of conceptions of the "folk society" and the "folk-
urban continuum" in the context of the Mexican research of such anthropologists as Robert Redfield and Oscar Lewis, though their notion of "folk"
was not precisely that of folklore, gave the term folk further centrality. Folk
art and crafts and rituals (which indeed were available in great variety or
which could be successfully revived where they had become dormant) were
colorful and often ingenious and could be seen as beautiful manifestations
of a powerful premodernity and of a strikingly original aesthetic. Folklore
could symbolize social norms and ideas in opposition to those of modern,
materialistic, machine-obsessed America, a sense of community foreign to
the American visitors, and a contented, aesthetically satisfied place, as well
as a connection to the Mexico in which these Americans found themselves.
They would collect and deal in folk art, write about it, incorporate it into
their own art, decorate with it, even design and build houses congruent with
it. That is, they would come to use it in a variety of ways, recycling it to suit
their own needs and intentions. If Whitehead's *John Henry Days* looks liter-
arily at a variety of fictional uses of folklore, set in the context particularly
of tourism, these Americans in Mexico incorporated similarly various uses
of folklore into their relationship with a foreign country.

A number of Americans in Mexico wrote about folklore in one context
or another, and, indeed, one of America's most celebrated twentieth-century
writers, Katherine Anne Porter, wrote the introductory essay for the catalog
of the Mexican folk art exhibit that went to the United States in 1922; in it
she sketches out many of the ideas that reflect or establish the ways in which
the Americans interested in Mexican culture were to reenvision the folk
traditions of their host country. Of course, there was "native quaintness" and
"rude and healthful vigor" in Mexican folk creations, but in addition to such
characterizations Porter positions folk art in clear opposition to American
and modern culture. Mexican painted chests and trays point to the "ugli-
ness of our kind of civilization." The Mexican materials in the exhibition do
not show the "*artifices* of modern progress." In writing of a Mexican myth
Porter notes that (in contrast to puritanical America) "there is no death
nor sin in it." Mexican folklore becomes the convenient antithesis for what
the Americans have left behind, reflection of an alternative worldview to

which Porter and her fellow expatriates are more sympathetic than that of their own culture. This attitude is further anchored by an insistence on tying present-day folk to ancient Mexican civilizations, thus further divorcing Mexico from the European contexts that inform the United States and much of the modern world. The entire first section of Porter's essay is about ancient Mexico and how to approach it with understanding, and she manages to draw a few connections to modern folk materials, noting, for example, how a contemporary Guadalajara jug in the exhibition traces its design to ancient Mexican use of the "bold flaring circle," or that designs from Aztec codices may be worked into present-day weavings.[6]

The opposition to American and modern culture is likewise emphasized in looking at the authenticity and supposed purity of the Mexican materials, as well as the localness of the arts and crafts traditions. The Mexican artisan makes his or her wares "to sell them to his own people," for him- or herself or "near-by markets." They are "untainted by . . . popular tastes" and "beautiful and useful [but] not costly." That is, they are, in one way or another, indigenous and accessible, and stand against outside forces, whether aesthetic or commercial. The Mexicans even transformed the Spanish influence into something their own and we have today traditions surviving "with a steadfastness that is *anachronism* in this fluctuating age."[7] Mexican folk art represents something with a rootedness absent from modern society, particularly the America of mass production and constant change, something resistant to European influence (which it can nonetheless coopt).

Writing of a visit he made in 1927 to Tehuantepec, the town which lies in the isthmus of the same name, Carleton Beals took note not of arts and crafts but of dance and fiesta, but what he called attention to echoes some of what Porter says (though she would savage one of his several books about Mexico in the *New Republic* and use him unkindly in a short story). The dance and ritual are, like the folk objects, indicative of things that contrast with America and American culture: "Compared to life in rural American towns in the South and Mid-West, the world of Tehuantepec is rich indeed. . . . one of Tehuantepec's joys is not struggling with New York subway turnstiles." The "creative power" of the dance in particular is something which "the industrial age has . . . destroyed."[8]

More than a dozen years after Porter published her catalog essay, Heath Bowman and Stirling Dickinson would spend a chapter of their book *Mexican Odyssey* on the "craft towns" of Mexico; that is, on "little villages hidden away among the mountains or in valleys," each of which specialized in a certain kind of folk ware. Bowman was a writer, Dickinson a visual artist and they motored into Mexico in 1934, among the first to use the still uncompleted Pan American Highway, and spent several months looking around, though Dickinson would later return and settle in San Miguel de Allende where he eventually directed Instituto Allende, the American-style college there. Their book is a travel book, chronicling their journey and what they saw while on it, and despite Dickinson's being an artist, they gave little close attention to how local crafts were made or their style and design. But clearly they were intrigued by some of the things that had struck Porter: the localness of the wares ("we are interested chiefly in the local crafts" at the great Oaxaca market; the "perfect" craft town is one "solely dependent on its one ware"), the "dignity and self-sufficiency" the crafts represent, the continuity of Mexican tradition (the religious masks of Guerrero are "not anachronisms, but the link between the past and the present"). They draw contrasts between the traditional crafts and creeping modern elements ("gaudy" innovations or local youth wearing bell-bottom trousers who thus are "presaging a new and less picturesque Mexico") and the final sections of the chapter deal with not the craft towns at all but with the ruins at San Agustin Acolman and Teotihucan (respectively colonial and pre-Columbian), as though to connect the crafts tradition with older elements in Mexican civilization. And they fear a "breakdown of Mexican crafts" when they discover an artisan who is exporting his production of high-quality serapes directly to New York, perhaps indirectly causing many peons to buy "hideous store blankets of plaid."[9] The traditional crafts represent what Bowman and Dickinson establish at the outset of their book, that Mexico provides a remarkable and sudden transition from America to another reality, the very ideological proposition that had brought so many *yanquis* to Mexico in the first place.

In 1934 journalist Erna Fergusson published her *Fiesta in Mexico*, a whole volume about Mexican celebrations, which perhaps because of their public nature had obtained much attention from the Americans. She traveled to various festivals and her book is primarily descriptive, but she touches on certain themes suggestive of how Americans conceptualized Mexican folklore vis-à-vis their own position and cultural background: Mexico (perhaps unlike the United States) is a place of cultural purity ("The people who make the fiestas ... do not know they are quaint and picturesque survivals") which enjoys a continuity with the ancient civilizations of the place (the people of Oaxaca are "walking so easily out of antiquity into today"). It is a place of community (Mexicans seem genuinely startled that she is attending a fiesta at Tixtla all by herself; this festival is attended by "everybody

who can get there"). Yet upper-class, Europeanized Mexicans themselves
have disdain for anything having to do with the Indians, including their
fiestas (one was "amazed that anybody should go anywhere to see Indians
dance"[10]). Thus the Americans become the ones who truly appreciate certain
important aspects of Mexican culture, using folklore to establish themselves
as a sympathetic avant-garde (the poet Witter Bynner would organize an
American protest in Chapala when the government threatened the wearing of native dress there, and Fergusson herself expresses concern over the
anticlerical government's dismay over the religious connections of fiestas).

Neither Beals nor Bowman and Dickinson nor Fergusson nor even Porter is trying to develop a theoretical conception of Mexican folklore, and
their writings are primarily simply descriptive of Mexico and its creations.
Nonetheless, they suggest the construction of an ideology about the purity, authenticity, and continuity of folk materials and most particularly
that Mexican folk things—whether crafts or rituals—are emblematic of a
culture decidedly and appealingly not American or even "modern." That attitude toward folklore seems especially appropriate for a group of expatriates trying not only to come to terms with the society in which they find
themselves but also to separate themselves from their very different (and
for them problematic) home culture in the United States. Folklore, inher-
ently Mexican (and so presented through the nationalistic lens Mexico had
adopted and which the Americans could hardly fail to notice), becomes a
convenient marker of difference.

Of course, if certain folklore is distinctively Mexican, that fact can be
exploited not only by expatriates abandoning their own society but also to
promote tourism to Mexico. People travel to see things not familiar to them
at home, wherever home may be, and promoters of tourism will emphasize
the geographically or culturally different in trying to lure visitors. The visitors in turn will seek to bring home souvenirs which seem both typical of
the place they have been and at variance with what is available at home. For
Mexico, colorful and (for Americans and other foreigners) unusual folklore
would be a perfect draw for tourists, and it is interesting to see the development of the idea that Mexican folk arts, crafts, festivals, and dances were
among the principal attractions for tourists.

American writers in Mexico in the 1920s and 1930s, then, were attracted
to folklore from early on not only as something emblematic of their expa-
triation but also as a means of drawing temporary visitors to Mexico and
satisfying their touristic impulses for experiencing the exotic and for souvenirs. As Americans began to produce early guidebooks to Mexico, they

invariably included information on dances, festivals, and arts and crafts as of central importance to the tourist, and in fact this trend continued into recent years. In doing so they were partaking in a practice common in many places, recycling folklore in the context of tourism.

One of the early guidebooks which was very popular, undergoing frequent revisions and reprintings, was Frances Toor's *Guide to Mexico*.[11] Interestingly, Toor is remembered primarily *as* a folklorist who established the periodical *Mexican Folkways* and whose carefully researched book, *A Treasury of Mexican Folkways*, continues to be an important English-language source for information on Mexican folklore. However, Toor also catered to tourists for a living, operating a studio and gallery in the Zona Rosa, then and later an upscale and foreigner- and tourist-centric Mexico City neighborhood,[12] a gallery where visitors to the capital could purchase work by Diego Rivera, Rufino Tamayo, and others, obtain the services of a professional shopper ("the trick of finding the RIGHT THINGS at the RIGHT PRICE"[13]), or even rent a furnished studio apartment, and she published not only several guidebooks and maps (notably one designed by Carlos Merida) but also *Spanish for Your Mexican Visit*.

Toor's guidebook, in addition to fold-out maps with tiny drawings of important sites and caricatures of Mexicans, contains the usual information of guidebooks, mostly brief entries on places to see in Mexico City, the vicinity of Mexico City, and then locations further afield. But she also includes a special section on festivals, listing a number of them by date and giving also some basic information on Mexican festivals ("A feature of all festivals are marvelous fireworks, made by the Indians in the form of little bulls, wheels, huge castles and others. Immense balloons are also popular."[14]). There is also information on festivals in connection with particular places discussed in the guidebook, and Toor includes information about some crafts and photographs of regional dances. Thus the seemingly ubiquitous popular celebrations emerge as an important element in the tourist's experiencing Mexico. Toor emphasizes this also in her other guidebook, *Motorist Guide to Mexico*, written for the increasing number of Americans driving down into Mexico. This likewise contains a chapter on "Festival Dates and Holidays," where Toor provides a general outline of the shape of religious festivals (beginning in the morning with the singing of *mañanitas*—"the good morning song to the saint"—and proceeding on to dances and evening fireworks), though she also includes mention of many secular festivals as well. As with her other guide, Toor also includes information on festivals and dances (including photographs of a Yaqui deer dancer and the Oaxacan plume dance) when she discusses particular places, as well as information on folk crafts, folk music, and folk dance and dress.[15]

Around the same time Toor's guides began to appear, another influential guidebook was brought out by New York publisher G. P. Putnam's Sons, authored by another of the figures active in the expatriate community in Mexico, Anita Brenner. (Brenner was born in Aguascalientes, the daughter of a Latvian Jewish emigrant to Mexico, and considered herself Mexican; however, her father took the family back and forth between Mexico and Texas during the revolution, and Brenner entered Columbia University in 1927 and spent much of the subsequent period of her life based in New York, with journeys to Mexico.) In *Your Mexican Holiday: A Modern Guide* (1932), Brenner offers, in addition to chapters that are oriented to particular regions ("The Valley of Mexico") or places suited for particular interests ("Honeymoon Places," "Hunting, Fishing and Exploring"), chapters concerned with Mexican society and culture, including one on fiestas and one on arts and crafts. "There are so many fiestas in so many places in Mexico, that the subject could easily be a book," Brenner writes (perhaps foreshadowing Ferguson's work), providing then as full a calendar as possible. Though she writes that these celebrations "are worth your while only if you are much in sympathy with peasant Mexico," because they are very difficult to access, the space she accords them suggests that they are important to the tourist experience. Folk crafts, in her view, are rather a different matter, for Mexico "is one of the great craft and popular art countries, comparable only to China and Japan,"[16] and obviously crafts are more easily acquired than remote festivals accessed. Brenner notes the various types of wares made (ceramics, textiles, laquer, and so forth) and where they can be found, having established the considerable significance of the folk art tradition as world class (and, as such, worthy of interest and purchase).

These early guidebooks[17] set the folkloric, then, as important to tourism, and later American guidebooks continued this tradition of interest. Mexico was presented as a place in which certain forms of folk culture were integral to appreciating a visit. In the 1960s and 1970s, for example, James Norman's *Terry's Guide to Mexico* (it had originally appeared in 1909, the work of T. Philip Terry, and had gone through several editions) and Kate Simon's *Mexico: Places and Pleasures*[18] were very popular guidebooks for English-speaking tourists, particularly Americans. Norman includes sections on "Folk Arts and Handicrafts" ("Mexico is a land of gay and meaningful handicrafts"), music, including much on folk music, and folk dance (these in the context of a longer cultural chapter), and a chapter on fiestas ("one of Mexico's most fascinating social activities"), as well as one called "Traditional Food and Drink." Norman takes a somewhat romantic approach to some of what he says about the folkloric (a fiesta "encompasses an enchanted world in which almost everything takes place as if it were not so, or as in a dream"; the *zandunga*, the dance of the Tehuantepec region, has "a touch of melancholy"), but certainly strives to present the reader/tourist with a briefly comprehensive view of the folkloric (and romantic attitudes are perhaps particularly attractive to tourism). Simon presents folk crafts as an especially prominent focus for tourist shopping, often providing practical information about where kinds of folk wares can be purchased (she notes, for example, the Mexico City shop of Victor Fosado V, prominent dealer in folk arts, who was a disciple of the American Fred Davis, whose work in promoting the sale of Mexican folk objects is discussed below).[19]

In 1959 James Norman, the reviser of Terry's well-established guidebook and a writer who had lived and worked in San Miguel de Allende in Guanajuato state for a number of years, also produced a book devoted to Mexican folk art and crafts, like Simon's guidebook oriented toward the purchase of such items by tourists. It is a rather remarkable work, being a fairly comprehensive book devoted to contemporary Mexican folk art but slanted toward tourists and other visitors to Mexico and toward how to acquire various kinds of folk artifacts, purposes made clear by the book's very title, *In Mexico: Where to Look, How to Buy Mexican Popular Arts and Crafts*[20] (at one time reprinted in paperback simply as *The Shopper's Guide to Mexico*). Norman sees such purchases as essential to the Mexican tourist experience:

> *It is customary while vacationing abroad to sight-see, to loaf.... Occasionally you interrupt an itinerary to buy something, but shopping is usually incidental to the main purpose of travel.*
>
> *But in Mexico this is reversed.*
>
> *After you cross the Rio Grande you suddenly chuck aside the travel poster attractions.... These no longer seem important. Instead, you head for the nearest curio shop or street market and you indulge in the principal below-the-border tourist sport ... shopping....*
>
> *... If you are at all well-traveled you'll probably repeat what other travelers have said, that nowhere, except in China, have you ever seen such an abundance of noteworthy popular arts and handicrafts.*[21]

That is, folk art (particularly the acquisition of folk art) is central to the experience of being a tourist in Mexico as it is almost nowhere else. Folk art provides a kind of cultural authenticity (as opposed to "the travel post-er attractions") that allows the visitor to go beyond the superficial. Once you've come to appreciate Mexican folk art, "you'll have broken through the tourist-belt barrier and you'll have met Mexico," Norman writes.[22] Norman maintains a kind of cultural nationalism in his perspective (though it is directed to outsiders, intended to influence the visitor to see folk art as em-blematic of a Mexico that can literally be taken home, souvenir not merely of a place but of a cultural experience). He goes on to survey a variety of kinds of wares (textiles and dress, pottery, lacquer and masks, even furni-ture), always with practical considerations, such as auctions at the national pawnshop in Mexico City as a source of collectanea; the second section of the book is specifically a guide to shopping, directing the reader to particu-lar outlets for popular arts and crafts and even to particular craftspeople (with an appendix on market days).[23]

Norman's specialized guidebook might be seen as one culmination[24] of earlier appreciation of Mexican folk contexts and of earlier interest in acquiring and collecting the folkloric. Perhaps the book could be viewed then as representing and promoting a level of mass interest in collecting the products of folkloric Mexico and particularly their use in home decoration, an interest which, on a much different scale, goes back at least to the Ameri-cans in 1920s Mexico and which continued, gradually picking up steam, in subsequent decades. Although many American visitors to Mexico acquired folk objects as the odd souvenir, Mexico and Mexican folk art inspired sev-eral major collectors to amass important assemblies of artifacts. Notable in this respect were Nelson Rockefeller, Alexander Girard, and Elizabeth and Dwight Morrow, and the ideas behind and the uses to which they put their collections are of importance in understanding the recycling of the folkloric to suit nontraditional ends.

Of course, these collectors were not the first to take an interest, as the earlier existence of several businesses in Mexico City to sell folk art attests, businesses operated by both Mexicans and Americans. The Sonora News Company, which worked closely with the Southern Pacific Railway's Mexi-can subsidiary and which produced a variety of printed material including postcards for American visitors, sold folk art as "curios," and some time after he arrived in Mexico around 1910 hired Fred Davis to run an operation selling popular arts and crafts and silver as well as antiquities[25] (Davis was, among other things, a silversmith). Davis took over the Sonora Company's Mexico City showroom, was able to take advantage of the revolution, as Mexican antiquities came on the market during the turmoil, and for many years played a central role in introducing folk art to American visitors, later making his shop an important gathering place and exhibition space for such major figures in the arts as Rivera, Orozco, and Tamayo. He also showed work by such American artists as New Orleans-born printmaker Caroline Durieux, whose husband ran the Mexico City Ford dealership, and William Spratling, whose work is discussed below. Davis also employed others who would play prominent roles in dealing in folk art, not only Victor Fosado V but also René d'Harnoncourt, who would go on to become the director of the Museum of Modern Art in New York. In 1933 Davis moved from Sonora to work for Sanborns, the drug store/restaurant/emporium that had been founded in 1903 by the Sanborn brothers from California and which included folk art and crafts among the wares it sold, particularly to American visitors.[26] Several similar establishments in Mexico City and elsewhere also did business as dealers in Mexican popular arts and crafts (sometimes combined with dealing in antiquities), including Artes de Mexico, Artculos Regionales "Sol" (managed by Fred Liebig), and Native Arts in Mexico City, and J. Gordon Forbes in Oaxaca and the Kelly Curio Shop in Monterrey.[27]

That by 1930 there was an American awareness of Mexican folk art is made clear by the appearance in that year of Susan Smith's book, *Made in Mexico*.[28] It appeared as part of a children's series published by Knopf, Borzoi Books for Children about Art and Handicraft, which included Smith's well-received *Art in America*, as well as books about French and Russian decorative art. Smith emphasizes the everyday reality of Mexican folk art. "In Mexico," she writes, "art isn't something that is kept in museums and is spoken of only by critics. It is a part of everyday life, and Mexicans make beautiful things as a matter of course. . . . You find it in the market-places, on the street-corner, on station platforms, by the roadside. . . ." And, interestingly and in line with her view of Mexican folk art as everyday, she attempts to set folk arts and crafts in their cultural contexts by, for example, describing how artisans may bring their wares to markets and how they sell them there. But that Mexico should have been prominently included in the series (and that the book should have gone through three printings by 1933) is indicative of a high level of awareness of Mexican folk art by that time. So it is not surprising that important collectors should begin to appear on the scene.

Nelson Rockefeller's interest in, indeed passion for, art went back to his college days, and he was influenced strongly by his mother, art patron Abby Aldrich Rockefeller. Abby Rockefeller had begun to take an interest in American folk art in the 1920s, eventually giving her collection of hundreds of objects to Colonial Williamsburg, a Rockefeller-supported project, which established the Folk Art Center and Museum named after her. However, she was also vitally interested in Mexican art, perhaps because of her interest in contemporary art and the prominence of modern Mexican artists (she was one of the founders of the Museum of Modern Art). Her interest extended to Mexican folk arts, and she is known to have several times visited an exhibition of Mexican art, both fine and folk, at the Art Center in New York, which itself had been created by the Education Fund, founded by John D. Rockefeller Sr. to promote American education. The exhibition included objects for sale, and she bought some, mostly pottery and tiles, which were incorporated into one of the family houses on the Pocontico Hills estate in Westchester. The exhibition had been organized by Frances Flynn Paine, an American who had grown up in Mexico, and the Rockefeller Foundation soon gave Paine a grant to study Mexican folk art; Abby Rockefeller purchased Mexican folk art through Paine (as well as Spanish colonial pieces that she saw as complementing the American colonial objects she intended for Williamsburg). The Museum of Modern Art gave its second one-man show to Diego Rivera in 1931, and in the early thirties René d'Harnoncourt, eventually to become director of the Modern, moved from Mexico to New York, bringing with him his extensive knowledge of Mexican folk art. In October 1930 what has been called a "nearly encyclopedic" exhibition of Mexican art opened at the Metropolitan Museum in New York, originally organized in Mexico by Dwight Morrow and William Spratling and curated by d'Harnoncourt; it included many artists "whose works . . . called on indigenous folk forms, colors and themes"[29] as well as a variety of folk art itself.

Rockefeller himself went to Mexico, with his wife, Mary, in 1933,[30] and, guided by Paine, toured a number of folk art centers, acquiring a number of examples. Though he also met modern artists (including the painter Roberto Montenegro, an artist who looked to folk art for inspiration and who sought its recognition) and took in pre-Columbian sites, "it was folk art—and the people who made and used it—that made the deepest impression on him."[31] Rockefeller returned to Mexico several times in the 1930s and in 1942 brought his family for a five-week vacation spent mostly in Oaxaca, guided by Montenegro (figure 6.1). By all accounts Rockefeller continued throughout his trips to Mexico to be an avid field collector, finding his way to many markets, befriending noted artisans like Teodora Blanco, carefully considering what to acquire. In 1939 he had become president of the Museum of Modern Art and set about bringing a major Mexican exhibition into

Figure 6.1: Nelson A. Rockefeller (*left*) in Mexico in the 1940s, with Rosa Covarubbias, William Spratling, and Roberto Montenegro. Courtesy Rockefeller Archive Center. American-born Covarubbias was married to Mexican artist and ethnographer Miguel Covarubbias. Spratling is best known for his revival of silver jewelry making in Mexico, though he also helped the Morrows build Casa Mañana. Artist Montenegro influenced Rockefeller's interest in folk art.

being, "20 Centuries of Mexican Art," putting Montenegro in charge of the folk art section and commissioning him to collect pieces for the exhibition, pieces which would become part of Rockefeller's personal collection.[32] In 1954 he founded the Museum of Primitive Art as a home for his collection of tribal art. Then in 1968 he stumbled upon a New York shop that showed Mexican folk art, rekindling his interest in his own Mexican collection. In 1969 the Museum of Primitive Art mounted an exhibition of his Mexican materials. In 1978 Rockefeller returned to Oaxaca for further investigation and collecting, but he died not long after this visit. His Mexican collections were given by his family to two American museums.

Rockefeller's motives were in many respects typical of avid collectors. He himself would write that "I have sensed something strong, imaginative, and beautiful about her [Mexico's] popular arts," and clearly, like many collectors, he had an abiding appreciation for the aesthetic of the pieces he sought to acquire and enjoy. His daughter has also said that "The Mexican people and their art connected father with a deep part of himself. . . . Through his folk art collection, Father could savor the Latin joy in life."[33] Indeed, probably like other Americans drawn to Mexico and Mexican folk art, coming out of a more subdued, more restricted American context, he may have been attracted to the color and seeming excess of many Mexican artifacts. Mexican folk art may have provided for him, as his daughter's remarks at least suggest, something quite personal, a sort of psychic release and a chance to commune with a more free, more "abandoned" aesthetic and way of life (a perspective he would have had in common with many of the Americans who went to Mexico in the 1920s and 1930s). That is, as a collector (and perhaps many collectors of folk art do this), he recycled the folk psychologically according to his own needs and perspectives, giving what he acquired personal meanings. We might also wonder if one aspect of this personal meaning was giving this man of vast wealth, power, and social status some connection to a humbler world.

However, in addition to whatever personal uses Rockefeller may have made of his folk art, he also used it, if indirectly, for political ends. Over many years Rockefeller had an important political career, becoming vice president of the United States. Although his career in elective office had begun with nothing less than his four terms as governor of New York, he had also held various high appointive positions, including several relating to Latin America. President Roosevelt appointed him coordinator for Inter-American Affairs, and Rockefeller certainly saw the "20 Centuries of Mexican Art" exhibition "as an excellent opportunity to shore up relations between Mexico and the United States . . . an initial expression of his commitment to inter-American cooperation."[34] Although this exhibition included much more than folk art, we can imagine that Rockefeller saw his involvement in folk art as expressing his commitment to Latin American culture and as thus further cementing American-Mexican relations. (We do know that he worked to ease U.S. tariffs on Mexican silverwork, and that he was "elated" when Kaufmann's department store in Pittsburgh used Mexican popular crafts in a merchandising campaign.[35]) Yet it was Dwight Morrow, who collected folk art along with his wife, Elizabeth, for whom folk art was even more central to his involvement in American-Mexican diplomacy.

Dwight Morrow became the United States ambassador to Mexico in 1927. The Morrows did not command the vast wealth the Rockefellers did, but they might be said to have been members of the same American social and political establishment. Morrow was a corporate lawyer who became a partner in J. P. Morgan and Company (and when he finally left

Mexico became the Republican senator from New Jersey). Morrow was an Amherst classmate and a backer of Calvin Coolidge and expected to be offered an important government post when Coolidge became president; indeed, many of Morrow's friends and associates viewed him as exceptionally talented and destined for great things. He did not expect to be offered the Mexican ambassadorship; at the time some saw Mexico as a diplomatic backwater (as well as a still dangerous place[36]), although Morrow accepted and probably viewed Mexico as an intriguing challenge. When they arrived, the Morrows were charmed by the country and soon became highly important figures in the diplomatic, political, and cultural scenes there. In Mexico Morrow's influence with high Mexican officials was well known. He was able to shape government policies and actions, partly because he was seen as a sympathetic friend of the nation and its endeavors and ideas, including its discovery of indigenous art. And he was thought to respect Mexican sovereignty.

Morrow's predecessor as ambassador had been James Sheffield, who had offended the Mexicans with what was perceived as his anti-Mexican rhetoric and his attempts to intimidate Mexico especially over the conflict between Mexico and the American oil companies operating in the country, a prime dispute of the times. Morrow, however, immediately recognized the need to smooth over relations, and the Morrows perceived cultural matters as one way to do so. They realized the importance of the relationship between nationalism and culture, made friends with many influential Mexican artists and American expatriates who supported Mexican cultural endeavors ("crucial translators," as Rick López has termed them, of Mexican ideas and impulses[37]), and even served as art patrons. And they made sure that Mexicans were aware of their interests and their sympathies. Although their support of the arts was broad ranging (as a "farewell" gift to the people of Cuernavaca, for example, they commissioned a now-celebrated mural by Diego Rivera depicting the history of the region, despite the fact that Rivera was well known as a communist), they became well aware of *mexicanidad* and of the current recognition of Indianness and an "ethnicized national identity."[38] Hence folk art, and its collection, became an important aspect of their artistic interests. Ultimately this led to the prominence of popular arts in the 1930 Mexican arts exhibition at the Metropolitan Museum in New York, which Morrow played a key role in organizing, seeing it as a major step in making Americans aware of the cultural glories of their neighbor to the south and stimulating positive images and relations. Susan Danly notes, for example, that the *Brooklyn Eagle*, at the time a prominent New York City

Figure 6.2: One of William Spratling's illustrations showing a room of the Morrows' house, Casa Mañana, with pottery used as decoration. From Elizabeth Morrow, *Casa Mañana;* original in private collection; used by permission.

newspaper that had once been edited by Walt Whitman, put the exhibition in its list of the top-ten exhibitions of 1930, and she quotes the paper's article about it as having shown a clear awareness of the exhibition's purpose in "promoting international understanding," something which accounted for "its special significance." "The Morrows' collection of popular arts made a great impression on the American public in the 1930s," Danly also says.[39]

Of course, folk art was not something the Morrows saw only in terms of its political and diplomatic value. Elizabeth in particular was personally taken by the folk art she encountered practically from the moment of her arrival. In the early weeks after her arrival she discovered the candy *calaveras* which were sold for the Days of the Dead, and she soon began collecting folk art, haunting markets and visiting shops, and she made the acquaintance not only of Mexican artists and intellectuals interested in the popular arts but also Fred Davis and René d'Harnoncourt, who guided her, as they did others, in the acquisition of prime examples. Davis and d'Harnoncourt helped Mrs. Morrow in using Mexican folk artifacts in decorating her residence, and indeed the Morrows' creation of a house in Cuernavaca, Casa Mañana, as a weekend retreat allowed them to use their folk art in interior decoration while showing their devotion to Mexican culture by creating a house in an indigenous style to which they could invite their artist friends and others interested in the popular arts.

Not only was Casa Mañana built (working from a small original house on the property the Morrows acquired) in a style that accorded with Mexican colonial architecture, it was constructed using folk techniques, so that it might be said that the Morrows borrowed from the tradition of Mexican folk structures in conceiving it. Rather than hire an architect to design it, they hired Francisco "Pancho" Rebello, a local mason, to put it together according to their ideas, and he in turn used Mexican craftsmen to make various parts of the house, such as the tiles and the wrought-iron grill work. (William Spratling, who *was* trained as an architect and who had taught architecture at Tulane, made drawings of various parts of the house [figure 6.2] which Elizabeth Morrow published in the book she wrote about it.[40] Indeed, Spratling served as something of a consulting architect on the house, and the Morrows also consulted with Fred Davis on design matters, while René d'Harnoncourt was commissioned to do a fresco for the garden and helped with aspects of the furnishings and decoration.) Not only was the house itself, then, a recycling of Mexican folk design, but it was created in part to provide a backdrop for the Morrows' folk art collection. In her book about the house Elizabeth Morrow would write of how she selected those pieces she used to furnish the house "not . . . as collector's pieces but . . . to show how easily the native handicraft wares . . . lend themselves to decoration and daily use." She goes on to say:

> Mexican art has a continuous tradition, and there is no clash between modern pottery made by the Indians today and the plates and platters of two hundred years ago. We used both on our table and mixed old and modern lacquer with them. Serapes of all kinds served for bedspreads and blankets. The water jars made wonderful flower pots for patio and verandah. The gay old painted chests were not bought simply for their color but to hold household linen. These things made the atmosphere of the place . . . and without them the house would not be Casa Mañana.[41]

Folk art becomes a key element in house decoration, amplifying the "atmosphere" of a folk-inspired structure in introducing a mood of Mexicanness. For the Morrows architectural structure and art[42] join to translate personal feelings for Mexican culture into something tangible, whether for the

Morrows' own pleasure or to communicate their regard for Mexico to those to whom they sought to make that position clear.[43]

Elizabeth Morrow's interest in Mexican folk art certainly extended further than decorating, however, and she also produced a children's book based in her love for and knowledge of folk art, a book which "truly reached a broad audience,"[44] appearing in print the same year as Susan Smith's *Made in Mexico*, also intended for young readers. The book was *The Painted Pig*, which was illustrated by d'Harnoncourt (who had, earlier, written a related story he had been unable to publish). It tells the story of two Mexican children, sister and brother Pita and Pedro. Pita possesses a clay pig "piggy bank" and Pedro, rejecting many other possible toys, wants one just like it and asks local toy maker Pancho to create a duplicate. Pancho agrees but clearly is put off by the idea of just duplicating an original and procrastinates, leaving Pedro to construct his own clay pig, though his turns out to be rather elephant-like. Finally Pancho produces a "duplicate" pig, though in rather different colors from Pita's. Elizabeth Morrow had access to illustrator d'Harnoncourt's extensive collection of Mexican folk toys (figure 6.3), and she used her book not merely as a vehicle for telling a pleasant story but for running through a panoply of Mexican folk art, not only clay pigs but also straw figures, a bird made out of a gourd, clown and animal figurines, and the paper cut-outs hung for fiestas.[45] One of d'Harnoncourt's illustrations in fact depicts a huge assortment of *piñatas* and other toys. And Morrow was able to work into her story experiences she had had with some of the folk craftsmen she had dealt with in constructing Casa Mañana. Pancho the toy maker gives the children fantastic excuses for his failure to produce a pig, just as the Morrows' mason Pancho Rebello had done when he did not complete his work. And the toy maker expresses the same folk aesthetic that a furniture maker did to Mrs. Morrow when she asked him to make a number of identical chairs for the dining room at Casa Mañana: "it would be very stupid to make two pigs exactly the same." The furniture maker had asked for more than his usual fee to make twelve chairs "Because it is so dull to make twelve chairs exactly alike."[46]

Hence Morrow produced a literary work based on her knowledge of folk art and on the particular examples collected by her illustrator. Further, she worked into her narrative her experiences of having worked with craftspeople and having encountered their perspectives and lives, and she attempted to put the folk art into other, larger contexts; the toy maker has a place at the local market, where he interacts with other vendors; the children seek him out there, a place to which they naturally gravitate. René d'Harnoncourt's

Figure 6.3: René d'Harnoncourt's illustration from Elizabeth Morrow's *The Painted Pig* of an array of folk toys, mostly piñatas, thought to be an affectionate portrait from his own collection of toys; the little girl in the foreground represents a main character in the story. Used by permission of the d'Harnoncourt estate.

illustrations not only depict folk objects but pick up on the style and colors of Mexican folk art, as he displayed his "ability to absorb 'the native genius of Mexican folk art.'"[47] Though we tend to dismiss children's literature as unimportant, Morrow and her collaborator produced a literary work of significance, using folk art as the virtual essence of the story they chose to tell, recycling their collecting, their artifacts, and their experiences into narrative art.

Nor were they alone in looking to Mexican folklore to create art, though in fact relatively little of the fiction or poetry produced by American writers in Mexico focused on the folk arts, though several famous American poets and fiction writers (Hart Crane, Langston Hughes, Katherine Anne Porter) were expatriates in Mexico.[48] Witter Bynner, at the time a poet of considerable prominence though today largely forgotten, wrote a number of Mexican poems, some of which were collected in his *Indian Earth*.[49] Several of these poems certainly suggest that Bynner was observant of Mexican folk culture.[50] "Street Musicians," for example, evokes a picture of traditional "men of music" and of one in particular with "gentle kingliness," while "A Weaver of Jojotepec" details the poet's relationship with a craftsman and moves on to musing on serapes. "A Guitarist" tells of music and dancing that reminds us of a "blind guitarist" centuries and continents away, while "Fiesta" uses a celebration to call attention to a prisoner and criminal in the local jail. "Folk-Song" only muses on differing human perspectives and situations. This is all to suggest that even Bynner, despite his evident awareness of Mexican folk culture, did not much incorporate the folk into his work except for quite general background to be jumped off from. Visual artists, however, were much more apt than literary ones to make use of folklore in creating work.

A prime example is Howard Cook's 1933 watercolor (a study for a mural), "Fiesta—Torito," (figure 6.4) today in the collection of the Roswell (New Mexico) Art Center.[51] The subject is indeed a *torito*, that is, one of the bull-like structures customarily packed with fireworks; at fiestas and on other occasions the fireworks are lit and an individual dances with the structure over his head; the effect, needless to say, is far more daring and exciting than any produced by even the most spectacular pyrotechnics normally seen in the United States. In Cook's watercolor the *torito* and its bearer dominate the center of the picture, the trails of sparks generated by the turning wheels of the structure arcing out like comet tails. Knots of spectators, mostly excited children, draw back from the moving conflagration. Behind and to the left a local band is playing, obviously adding a loud overlay of sound to the scene if not literally to the image. Behind and to the right is the door of the local church, reminding that the celebration is probably religious, despite the secular associations of the fireworks. In the foreground other spectators sit, more calmly looking on, further removed from the action of the *torito* and the more excited, closer-up spectator/participants who playfully cringe from the flaming sparks. Although Frances Toor, Erna Ferguson, and others could call attention to Mexican fiestas as a draw for our attention, Cook visually impels us to confront a potent representation of the real thing. Fiestas are complex performances and, indeed, Latin American folklorists sometimes study them in teams, as no one person can take in all the elements involved. As an artist, however, Cook imagines the totality, the center of interest that is the *torito*, the band, the church with its religious possibilities,

Figure 6.4: Howard Cook, *Fiesta—Torito*. Watercolor and ink on paper, 1933, final study for fresco in Hotel Taxqueño, Taxco. Roswell Museum and Art Center, Roswell, New Mexico. Gift of Mr. and Mrs. Howard N. Cook.

the levels of participation from excited engagement to cooler observing. The folk activity, the fiesta, provides Cook with a dynamic subject with layers of possibilities.

D'Harnoncourt took rather a different approach to fiestas in some of the drawings which appear in the book he published in 1931, *Mexicana: A Book of Pictures,*[52] a volume close on the heels of *The Painted Pig*. Perhaps to suggest how difficult it can be to capture the multifaceted action of such ritual celebrations, d'Harnoncourt provides a succession of images (although he *is* offering studies of several different fiestas) and sometimes a series of images within one drawing. Thus he provides "Way to the Fiesta," simply a landscape in which many people, presumably fiesta goers, make their way along a road, while "Fiesta" itself gives us an overview of a town, particularly its church, with crowds and the arcs of fireworks to suggest the occasion. "The Child Jesus" shows us a child dressed as Jesus with an elaborate folk art crown, reinforcing the religious heart of many fiestas, but a child sitting because he is clearly tired out after his participation. "Carnival in Huejotzingo" presents five tableaus of costumed dancers, mostly ritually armed, as if to show the viewer several connected but separate actions that take place in succession or simultaneously; although background is lightly sketched in in most of the tableaus, in one scene four dancers possibly chasing a towns-woman are set against a blank background as if to abstract them in space as pure carnivalesque energy. "The Moors and the Christians," depicting one of the most famous of dances, fills the frame with elaborate figures lunging with swords, suggesting that their playful power fills the world around them like the drawing fills the page. If Cook creates the totality of a fiesta in a single image, d'Harnoncourt stretches out his interest over a succession.

Other American artists approached folk artifacts because of their in-triguing forms. Mexican pots, for example, provided a number of artists with shapes around which to build images. Howard Cook's watercolor "Market, Oaxaca" (Philadelphia Museum of Art) poses stalls full of pots, some gap-ing circles as we look into them, others presenting solid rotundity as they sit waiting to be sold. Though clearly intrigued by these shapes and others (Cook also includes less regularly round baskets and counterposes the an-gularity of market umbrellas), his picture also looks at a moment of Mexi-can folklife, a small number of vendors and buyers congregating as the life of the market takes shape. Other artists featured Mexicans, notably Mexican women, with pottery, the shapes of jars providing a regularity of shapes to set off graceful human forms. Lowell Houser's "Ajijic Maidens Carrying Wa-ter Jars" (c. 1925) sets women against a wall of banana fronds, stressing their tropicalness while the jars suggest the everydayness of their lives. "Indian Woman with Jug," an oil on canvas by Jean Charlot (who was of French-Mexican ancestry but who spent much of his career in the United States) stresses the abstract shape of a carried jug, a shape which meshes with the curves of the woman herself, while behind her vignettes of Mexican folklife widen the interest of the image. Henrietta Shore's c. 1927 oil painting is not unlike Houser's, a line of women, water pots (according to James Oles in the style of San Bartolo Coyotepec) here carried on their heads and topping off their almost languid bodies set against a dry landscape of black mountains. James Oles sees the painting as emphasizing a lack of running water, not to suggest poverty but rather "as evidence of continuing traditions"[53]; that is, as a mark of the premodern continuity that fascinated many of the Americans who came to Mexico.

Mexican religious traditions also intrigued American artists. Perkins Hanley, for example, did a watercolor around 1933 of "A Mexican Coun-try Church Image of Christ," a rendering of one of the probably life-size wooden, assembled folk carvings of Jesus with crown of thorns and marks of having been scourged, perhaps too calmly seated upon a box. Lowell

Houser's woodcut "Devotion before a Crucifix" (c. 1927) suggests the reason such scenes appealed, indicative as they were of a kind of religious fervor largely unknown to Americans and seen as a part of the cultural difference that brought Americans to Mexican culture in the first place. Paul Strand's "Christo with Thorns, Huezotla" (1933) is a photograph of a Christ figure similar to the one depicted by Hanley (though clothed and standing here). Mexican folk art and artifacts offered a particularly striking subject for photographers and such artists as Strand and Edward Weston produced a number of images rooted in the creativity of Mexican popular artists and craftspeople.

Weston and his lover Tina Modotti went to Mexico in 1923 planning an extended stay, following a shorter visit when Modotti had initially joined another lover Robo de Richey, who had earlier arranged exhibitions in Mexico for Weston and other photographers. Though known today as an eminent photographer, earlier Modotti (born in Italy, she had emigrated to California) was known primarily as an actress and she was one of Weston's first nude models. Drawn to Mexico by the burgeoning cultural life (and, indeed, by folk art; Weston had seen in California the very exhibit for which Porter wrote the catalog), Weston, whose interest in shapes would lead to his famous images of seashells and vegetables, began to photograph every-day objects, and this interest brought him to the folk objects which were abundant in the Mexican context and in which many of the Americans and Mexicans he came to know were interested. Modotti had agreed to be his darkroom assistant in return for being taught photography by Weston, and many of her photographs show his strong influence upon her work such that she photographed many of the same subjects as he and in similar style. At one point Weston and Modotti collaborated with Anita Brenner on a project involving "an investigation of Mexican art,"[54] and many of Weston's and Modotti's photographs appear as illustrations in Brenner's monumental book, *Idols behind Altars*.

Weston was highly averse to photographing "the picturesque" ("I might call my work in Mexico a fight to avoid its natural picturesqueness," he would write[55] in his Daybooks, the journals he kept at certain times in his life, including Mexico), so his attraction to folk artifacts was not because of their "color" or exotic characteristics, or so he argued. He recognized folk art as expressing something fundamental about Mexico (he also writes of using folk art to decorate his Mexican residences, and he was pleased when Mexicans said that his work captured their country), and probably, as he sought out what he liked to refer to as "elemental form,"[56] he must at least have been intrigued by the differentness of these objects which he would photograph with a kind of purity of form where there is virtually nothing else in the image to detract from the object itself. It is difficult to imagine that Weston saw Mexican folk objects as merely shapes, and we can certainly imagine that he appreciated them as part of a cultural context even if his photographs isolate them from that context. We know from his Daybooks that he particularly liked the black clay ware from Oaxaca ("The black clay toys and pottery from Oaxaca, I like extremely well."[57]), and one of his best-known photographs, "Tres Ollas de Oaxaca" (c. 1926), is of three Oaxacan black pots, arranged against each other in a trinity of form. They have a special vivid quality in their darkness against what seems to be a concrete surface (possibly Weston's roof), their round openings mirroring their round bodies, the lightly scratched decorative designs dully reflecting some remote light source. "Palma Santa" (1926) is an image of palm strands woven into strips for Good Friday, in this case lightly colored straw against an inky black background, and here the very fact of the palm having been woven, however simply, suggests the hand of a craftsperson (and hence a cultural context). "Hand of Amado Galvan" (1926) gives us another pot, but here the hand of the craftsman, the potter, is literally included, holding the pot up to the sky as if in triumph or worship. "Pájaro Blanco" (1926) is a picture of a gourd fashioned to look like a bird, a simple but common form of Mexican folk art.

In all of these images, Weston clearly is intrigued by shapes, and in isolating the objects from larger contexts he emphasizes shape and form.[58] He means to, as he phrased it, "present objectively the texture, rhythm, form in nature ... to record the quintessence of the object or element ... rather than an interpretation, a superficial phase, a passing mood."[59] Yet in choosing man-made objects, here folk artifacts, he cannot entirely escape the cultural context. The scratched designs on the pots remind us of a cultural need for decoration. The very fact that the palms are "sacred" calls attention to a religious context. The very hand of Galvan the potter introduces a human, cultural element, calling attention to maker and even the setting of making. The fact that the bird is not really a bird, a thing of nature, but rather a human fashioning of a bird-like artifact reminds us that this object was culturally made and must have human meanings. This inevitably suggests at least the possibility of interpretation, an interpretation relating to the use of specific folk art objects, which in themselves convey meaning. Further, though Weston saw himself as "not searching for unusual subject matter, but making the commonplace unusual," in using the artifacts of one (folk) culture in a medium really projected to another (elite) one, he inevitably faces the problem that what may be commonplace in its own context may seem quite exotic to the other. Those who look at his photographs may inevitably see, in addition to the elemental object, something strange and asking for interpretation.

The same questions might be posed about Modotti's photographs of folk artifacts, which closely resemble Weston's and which clearly show his influence. In two photographs she depicts piñatas hanging for sale, perhaps in a market. She comes in close on them as objects, but in one shot in particular she catches a group of men and boys, perhaps customers or at least market browsers, who seem to gaze upon the piñatas with interest or perhaps even awe. That is, we get something of the cultural context, of the marketing situation, of human attitudes; we can imagine the bustle of this place looked down upon by the hung-up figurines waiting to be taken away and burst open. The photographer cannot avoid including something beyond the object to pique our interest in the larger context. The fact that the piñata figures have a certain grotesqueness to them (also the case with masks Modotti photographed) inevitably lifts these objects from everydayness to something beyond, to a situation where the viewer from another culture wants to ask about the context in which these exotic things were created and in which they have their existence.[60]

When it comes to another, related subject which much occupied Weston, the murals used to decorate *pulquerías* (the cheap saloons whose staple drink was *pulque*), another problem arises. These murals, though popular art, have a certain complexity that a simple pot, for example, may lack. And, of course, they are found in an obvious context, on the wall of a particular establishment where particular activities take place. Weston not only saw these as presenting possibilities for photographically expressing the essence of something, he was quite enthusiastic about them as forms of art:

> *The aspiring young painters of Mexico should study the unaspiring paintings—popular themes—popular art—which adorn the humble and often—most often—filthy pulqueria. This he should do, instead of going to the degraded impotent art of the self-glorified academician.*[61]

Weston may have attempted to isolate such murals. Certainly they are central to his photographs of them. "Pulquería, Mexico, D.F." (1926),[62] perhaps the best known of Weston's *pulquería* photographs (figure 6.5), gives us the front of the establishment called Charrito, whose mural depicts a Mexican

Figure 6.5: Edward Weston, *Charrito (Pulquería) Mexico*. 1926, gelatin silver print. Collection Center for Creative Photography, The University of Arizona, Tucson. Copyright 1981, Center for Creative Photography, Arizona Board of Regents.

cowboy (a *charro*) and his horse in a landscape, while curtains at the borders of the picture suggest the very artificial nature of the "staged" scene. Weston gives us not only the mural but also the shop's commercial sign, a dozing man, perhaps a patron of the establishment, and a woman in an upper window next to the sign. That is, we get a whole (if tightly enclosed) cultural context, from advertising which makes clear the nature of the place to human habitation and patronage to the curtains that suggest something about a creator's aesthetic. Or another image of a mural depicts a bullfighter facing a bull, but it is located on the corner of a building, such that we see a street to the side with its web of electric wires and the face of a boy walking, as well as a municipal street sign on the edge of the building itself.

Modotti also photographed *pulquería* murals (as she did other folk art, closely following Weston's lead), and it can be difficult to distinguish her photos from Weston's. Her "Exterior of a Pulquería" (c. 1926)[63] gives us not only two murals but passersby, a standing patron at a table, the large sign with the name of the shop, a posted menu board, and bits of electrical wiring on the facade. Though Modotti may mean to give us a tightly circumscribed image of popular art, she suggests a whole world open to interpretation. When it comes to *pulquería* murals, Weston and Modotti are giving us not only an objectively presented record of the quintessence of something, but also images which do interpret a scene and which present subjects which most viewers will not find commonplace at all.

Certainly by including Weston's and Modotti's photographs in *Idols behind Altars* Anita Brenner assigned interpretations to their subject matter. Brenner's book is not easy to characterize. It spends chapters considering Mexican art, including José Guadalupe Posada's popular broadsides, but it might best be characterized as a book about Mexico's complexity and the cultural continuity within that complexity which unites various historical phases and developments with the Mexican spirit and consciousness. In a chapter called "Earth, Straw, and Flesh," Brenner ties together pottery, ballad-making, and Aztec history to suggest the importance of the Mexican "earth," and here she uses Weston-Modotti photographs[64] of pottery (a clay horse figurine which seems ready to gallop through the image; a vase by Galvan), pottery of course coming from the earth and having some fundamental connection to it. In "The Dark Madonna," Brenner writes of the merging of ancient religions with that brought by the Spanish conquerors and uses photographs of a folk figure of Our Lady of Soledad and a simple carving of "Our Lord of the Tree," suggestive of ancient nature worship adapted to Christianity. Whatever Weston and Modotti sought to do with their pure and objective images, Brenner reminds us that these folk artifacts have meanings in a larger context. Weston would write:

> *These several years in Mexico have influenced my thought and life. Not so much the contact with my artist friends as the less direct proximity of a primitive race. Before Mexico I had been surrounded by the usual mass of American burgess—sprinkled with a few sophisticated friends. Of simple peasant people I knew nothing. And I have been refreshed by their elemental expression,—I have felt the soil.*[65]

That is, he was in Mexico like many other Americans, to appreciate the cultural differences provided by the "primitive race" who created, among other things, the folk art he photographed. He and Modotti both used folk art not merely to provide objects to be presented in their elemental forms but also to remind them and those who viewed their work of the culturally different place to which they had come, a place that indeed produced "elemental expression" in art objects that had both a simplicity and a powerful beauty.

In that respect folk art was the perfect subject, displaying a "primitiveness" that immediately catches our attention and intrigues us with its different aesthetic.

But other American artists would use Mexican folk art in other ways. The architect and designer Alexander Girard was, with Nelson Rockefeller and the Morrows, another great collector of Mexican folk art. He was in Mexico buying folk art in the 1930s, though his collection seems to have been put together over many years, and though it started with Mexico, it came to include folk art from many cultures. Eventually he needed to build a warehouse to contain it all, so vast had it become. In 1978 he and his wife gave the collection to the Museum of International Folk Art in Santa Fe, which constructed an additional wing to house the collection (which contained over a hundred thousand pieces). Further, Girard designed the exhibition that would be called "Multiple Visions," and he would arrange the folk artifacts not in conventional museum fashion but in what might be called dioramas or tableaus, in "scenes" that used the folk art pieces to recreate fanciful contexts like whole villages. Girard may originally have started buying folk art in Mexico with the idea of creating "vignettes" of Mexican village life for which he would "need quantities of houses, park benches, and trees for his villages as well as people to populate them,"[66] and he certainly used folk art in interior design installations over the years.[67]

His museum dioramas are of a piece with such uses, and they have been controversial with scholars, who have sometimes objected to the mixing of artifacts from quite different traditions, the incorporation of non-folk objects, and what may seem more like playing with artifacts than seriously presenting them. However, we can construe Girard's constructs as in themselves works of art which quite literally use folk objects to create meaning, as a sort of hybrid form which mixes museum display and aesthetic recreation and which are thus another creative, artistic use of folklore (albeit one which only someone like Girard, with a truly vast collection of objects, including dozens or more similar objects, could indulge in). In terms of his Mexican materials, for example, Girard uses a number of pottery figures from Tlaquepaque in Jalisco state to create a market scene, and figures and structures made by a particular workshop in Acatlán de Osorio in Puebla state to create a village (figure 6.6).[68] The first gives the viewer a sense of the crowded bustle of a marketplace, the second, replete with sand to suggest the local earth, gives off an array of color and a hint of the extreme heat that might be hitting the walls and ground of this make-believe place. We certainly may criticize Girard's installations as not very effectively conveying

Figure 6.6: Alexander Girard's construction of a Mexican village tableau from materials made by artisans from Acatlán de Osorio in Puebla state, Museum of International Folk Art, Santa Fe, New Mexico.

information about folk art objects and as suggesting that folk art objects are the playthings of collectors, not objects with their own profound meanings.[69] But they no doubt charm many visitors in a way that conventional museum exhibits do not, and they are Girard's own art form, a unique use of folk objects as the building blocks of an aesthetic of miniaturization.

Clearly the influence of interior decoration can be seen in Girard's installations, and in that he follows in the footsteps of the Morrows and even Edward Weston, who writes of one of his residences in Mexico:

My present effort to make the room livable consists in the placing and use of various native crafts: a serape over my bed, a petate for my floor, a lovely old flower-decorated chest to hold treasures, the caja de orinar for more treasures. . . . The bastones de Apizaco brighten one corner, and my chair is an "episcopal."[70]

There has been an ongoing tradition of using Mexican folk art in home decorating of course, particularly in such places as Santa Fe, where interest in both Mexico and folk art have been considerable. However, this trend certainly was popular in Mexico itself, going back to postrevolutionary interest in native crafts. The collections of Diego Rivera and Frida Kahlo, used to decorate their residences, have become particularly well known. But a book like the 1989 volume *Casa Mexicana*, geared to give decorating ideas to Americans, suggests an ongoing interest in the use of folk art as decoration, while it calls the reader's attention to how Mexican artists, for example, have used folk art in their homes. For instance, the bedroom of artist José Luis Cuervo is covered in retablos, the folk paintings, usually on tin, that depict miracles, and two photographs taken in the house of Rufino Tamayo show shelves bulging with Day of the Dead sugar skulls, Oaxacan carved animals, and clay *bateas*. A house in Zihuantejo, developed by Americans, contains a dining room shelf with painted gourds and tiny, figurative clay bells. In Los Angeles two British fashion designers have created a Mexican cottage full of Mexican ceramic coffee and tea pots and painted chairs.[71] Doubtless the folk art accents have different meanings in the differing contexts, but the book's very suggestion that such artifacts can be so used ties in with a long line of recycling the folk to make our nests enchanting and cozy and also indicates a desire to incorporate into our modern context of everyday living other cultural realities, borrowed from what we may even now think of as a "primitive race" which colorfully undercuts our modernity and prosaic existence.

It was in part a wish to escape modernity and escape American society that brought American expatriates to Mexico in the 1920s and 1930s. Once there, these expatriates often found the folk, whether through such manifestations as fiestas or such tangible creations as artifacts. The folk became important in ideological reuse, in being able to suggest an aesthetic and a worldview very different from the one that had been left behind in the United States. Folk art could be referenced in writings and in visual artworks to suggest a different cultural reality. It could be focused on for tourists, who seek souvenirs, striking physical reminders of other worlds encountered. And because Mexican elites were themselves into appreciating folk art (as, among other things, indicative of an ethnicized national identity), Americans like Ambassador Morrow and Nelson Rockefeller (who were hardly alienated by modernity or American culture) could use folk art collecting as a means of influencing Mexican opinion and fostering international relations. They might even build folk-inspired houses for themselves, and certainly the use of folk art to decorate their homes was taken up by many others, recycling colorful artifacts and "accents" to remind them of other cultural contexts or perhaps to suggest travels or psychic connections to other worlds. Though different motives may have inspired these attempts, Mexican folk art has found many uses recycled out of its native context, re-situated in a variety of ways.

CONNECTIONS

A Brief Conclusion

◇◇

One of the principal theoretical approaches to folklore in the twentieth century was functionalism, a perspective ultimately derived from British social
anthropology. Folklorists sought to explain the social meaning of the lore
they studied in terms of how it functioned for the group that performed
it; that is, what were its uses within the tradition where it circulated. Did it
promote social cohesion, provide a sense of group identity, pass on a certain kind of knowledge? Anglo-American sea shanties gave sailors a work
rhythm, Burmese law tales gave village magistrates a rudimentary knowledge of legal principles.[1] William Bascom would suggest that all folklore,
broadly speaking, served one (or sometimes more) of four possible social
functions, including validating culture and enforcing conformity.[2] To look
at the functions of a particular proverb, story, song, or ritual was to understand much about the social roles that folklore played in culture, and functionalism took an important place in the attempts to understand folklore
contextually that became increasingly important in folk studies.

Functionalism, then, looks at how those inside a culture use folklore.
This book has looked at some of the ways in which those outside the traditions in which folklore circulates have sought to make use of folklore.
Over many decades an educated public has become more and more aware
of folklore. The extent to which folklore has been understood by the general
public has varied greatly, but folklore has had considerable appeal to many
persons, and many writers, artists, and commentators have adapted folklore
in a variety of ways: to fit and bolster intellectual theories, to provide a basis
for artistic work, to sell goods, to promote an activity or a place. Because in
our globalized, commodity-centric, politicized, literate, mass culture-orient-
ed world, we are most likely to know folklore from sources other than the
direct circulation of the lore within its historical cultural context, it becomes
increasingly important for folklorists—however they may relate to the term
folklorism—to look at folklore outside those "natural" folk contexts.

Folklore has wide appeal beyond its historical cultural contexts for several reasons, including the assumption that folk materials—stories, rituals,

traditional sayings—have inherent meanings. Because folklore is presumed to be deeply rooted in cultures and their pasts, those inherent meanings are commonly seen as basic to humanity. Because folk traditions are somehow collectively formed, they have the potential to reflect the important human realizations and perceptions that provide meaning. Folklore is viewed positively as reflecting much that is basic to human experience and thus becomes a prime reference point to be mined and re-situated in other human expression. Folklore takes on symbolic and referential importance and becomes a useful tool in communication beyond the traditional communication in which folklore plays its historical cultural role. It becomes particularly important in terms of the cultural and social connections that can be made in terms of it, and much of the "use" made of folklore discussed in this book could be seen in the light of "connectivity." Folklore seems to connect—at a very basic level—to a variety of ideas, modes of expression, and meanings that inform many kinds of human endeavor.

The members of the Louisiana branch of the American Folklore Society and the later Lyle Saxon looked to African American folklore as giving them a connection to the plantation world that potentially conveyed social status. They continually presented the folklore they observed and collected within the context of the plantation and their ties to that world. Folklore was part of their nostalgic connection to a world that had been destroyed by the Civil War and its aftermath and which persisted in a much-diminished form.

Those Americans who went to Mexico in the 1920s and 1930s looked to Mexican folklore as something that could connect them to their new context. They were particularly attracted to folk art and other forms of material culture, which appealed because these were colorful and seemingly omnipresent. That these cultural forms were also radically different from what North American culture produced—not only in terms of styles and basic appearances but also modes of production and local social context—added to their appeal and provided a Mexican connection while also emphasizing an apartness from a United States that was being left behind. That these cultural forms might be rejected by some, more elite Mexicans, who possibly looked to the United States for their own models, gave folklore even greater cachet; the Americans could see themselves as having a special connection to Mexico, one that even some Mexicans did not share. If, for example, folk art could be used in interior decorating to suggest a specific connection to the people of Mexico, as it did for Edward Weston, so, too, could it—especially as taken out of Mexico and employed in the United States, as it was by Alexander Girard—suggest a wider connection to peasant cultures and noble savages. And insofar as folk culture actually appealed to some other Mexican elites, the American interest—that of Nelson Rockefeller and the Morrows, for example—could provide links for cultural understanding and political connections.

In his attempts to explain folklore to general readers, Lafcadio Hearn sought to draw his personal connections to places and cultures he was trying to bond with. Widely seen as a wanderer, Hearn certainly did enjoy a peripatetic life: born in the Greek Isles, "exiled" to the United States, where he spent long periods in both Ohio and New Orleans, moving on to Martinique and finally to the Japan with which he has been particularly associated. Repelled by modernity, however, he was not simply a wanderer but rather a man in search of more congenial cultural settings, and when he thought he had found one, he tried to dig in, to become as much an insider to that culture as possible. His understanding of local folklore, and his abilities in explaining it to others, provided him with a means of feeling insiderness, of connecting to the local contexts where he found himself.

The photographers who documented Louisiana folklife for the Farm Security Administration or Standard Oil saw folklore as connected to their missions, whether promoting government programs to rebuild the nation in a time of crisis or documenting the social value of petroleum production and use. For the FSA photographers, folklife offered glimpses of the good, traditional ways that deserved protection and support; for the Standard Oil photographers it offered the chance to show how traditional ways coexisted with and benefited from petroleum. Earlier photographers had seen how photographing folklife offered a connection to locality, often to the romanticism that a locality might be seen as projecting, and they took images of folklife because it did seem to capture a spirit of place, folklore often being seen as inextricably connected to locale.

That presumed connection to locale is a primary factor in connecting folklore to tourism, the focus for Colson Whitehead's novel *John Henry Days*. The John Henry Days of the title are a local festival rooted in the presumed connection between a place in West Virginia and a folk hero whose exploits figure in folksong and oral history. The novel itself examines fictionally how many interests, notably those hooked into tourist industries and tourism possibilities, relate to the festival and its hero, using the folklore to promote a sense of place and visits to that place. The John Henry Days festival acts as a stand-in for many events that seek to attract visitors by connecting place to a vaunted tradition, while it also in the novel gives other fictional characters other kinds of connections.

Those commentators like Erich von Däniken and Ignatius Donnelly, who have sought to use folklore as evidence in propounding "occult" theories, have assumed folklore to be a sort of historical document. Nonetheless, folklore has had particular appeal in that context as connecting modern writers and readers to ancient ideas and observations, to taking them back to "contemporary" sources. Those sources become more than documents and put us practically in the presence of the conditions, providing not only the intellectual possibilities of documents but also an emotional connection to past times.

The appeal of folklore to those outside particular folk traditions has been multifaceted. Folklore has seemed to offer a variety of connections that can be exploited and pressed into the service of artistic creation or ideological positioning or commercial use. Folklore has been seen as useful in the service of tourism, politics, personal perspectives, social messages, even unorthodox ideas. Obviously other folklorists have thought and will continue to think of contexts other than those discussed in this book in which folklore has been used and communicated beyond the oral tradition. In fact, in our postmodern world, it is essential that folklorists do so, for so many of our postmodern understandings of the traditional are played out in nontraditional contexts, and I predict that folk studies will increasingly look to discussions of nontraditional uses of folklore.

NOTES

INTRODUCTION

1. A definition passed to me solely through oral tradition. I heard it in the 1960s or 1970s from, I think, my fellow *Folklore Forum* editor, Jim Durham.

2. Regarding the animated cartoon commercials, I refer to the TV commercials for Quilted Northern paper, a brand made by Georgia Pacific. The elderly quilting ladies appeared in advertising material from circa 2003 until late in 2007. In the initial commercial the animated ladies appeared to be knitting, suggesting that neither the producers of the advertising nor the manufacturers of the paper towels actually had any idea what quilting was or what were its processes. This was corrected for later commercials. Alessandro Falassi, *Folklore by the Fireside: Text and Context of the Italian Veglia* (Austin: University of Texas Press, 1980) discusses Italian nighttime tale-telling sessions; although certainly folktales are not only told around the fire at night in traditional European societies, this has been one very important context for them. For one discussion of aristocratic French uses of fairytales, see Jack Zipes, *Fairy Tale as Myth, Myth as Fairy Tale* (Lexington: University Press of Kentucky, 1994), 19ff.

It is entirely possible to hear a New Orleans brass band in its regular, street context, and many Americans have firsthand acquaintance with quilting traditions, but, except for mostly revivalist contexts, folktales are almost exclusively known through non-oral contexts such as books and cartoons and in Britain at any rate, as Jennifer Shackler's recent work has reminded us, through the theatrical event of the Christmas pantomime, a popular but non-folk context largely unfamiliar to Americans and American folklorists (Jennifer Shackler, "Unruly Tales: Ideology, Anxiety, and the Regulation of Genre," *Journal of American Folklore* 120 [2007]: 381–400). The extent to which folktales—despite our contemporary remove from them as oral materials—are well known is perhaps remarkable, to the extent that numerous cartoon, joke, and children's book parodies of traditional tales are possible and widespread. On folktale parodies, see Ellen A. Greever, "Fractured Fairy Tales: Parody in Literary Fairy Tales for Children" (Ph.D. dissertation, University of North Carolina at Chapel Hill, 1995).

3. Roger D. Abrahams and Barbara A. Babcock, "The Literary Use of Proverbs," *Journal of American Folklore* 90 (1977): 414–29; Frank de Caro and Rosan Augusta Jordan, *Re-Situating Folklore: Folk Contexts and Twentieth-Century Literature and Art* (Knoxville: University of Tennessee Press, 2004).

4. Regina Bendix, "Folklorism: The Challenge of a Concept," *International Folklore Review* 6 (1988): 5.

5. Guntis Smidchens, "Folklorism Revisited," *Journal of Folklore Research* 36 (1999): 52; Hermann Bausinger, *Folk Culture in a World of Technology*, trans. Elke Dettmer (Bloomington: Indiana University Press, 1990), 127.

6. Smidchens, 52.

7. Smidchens, 52.

8. Barbara Thornbury, "Folklorism and Japan's Performing Arts," *Journal of Folklore Research* 32 (1995): 207.

Thus folklorism and other uses of folklore might be said to do something similar to folklore what the concept of "heritage" is said to do to the past, that is, celebrate it and "reshape what we inherit for current needs" (David Lowenthal, *The Heritage Crusade and the Spoils of History* [Cambridge: Cambridge University Press, 1998], xv). Writing from the perspective of a historian, Lowenthal has treated extensively the subject of "heritage"—that is, what are perceived to be legacies from the past, often but not exclusively fixed on physical objects that come to have iconic significance and may be central in commemorations, ceremonies, visitations, or reenactments that may have nationalistic significance; Lowenthal includes "intangible folkways" (19) as a focus for heritage. Heritage, he argues "is not history at all; while it borrows from and enlivens historical study, heritage is not an inquiry into the past but a celebration of it, not an effort to know what actually happened but a profession of faith in a past tailored to present-day purposes" (x). Whether or not heritage includes folklore and other aspects of "tradition" (see Lowenthal, 3), Lowenthal notes that heritage, which of course he does not see in the same way a folklorist might (see Lowenthal, 3), "is the chief focus of patriotism and a prime lure for tourism" (xiii). The same might be said for folklore re-situated. Patriotism and nationalism are, of course, closely interlinked, and we can see how central folklore has been in nationalistic endeavors. Likewise, folklore and folklorism play an important role in tourism.

9. Bendix, 1.

10. Linda Dégh, "Uses of Folklore as Expressive of Identity by Hungarians in the Old and New Country," *Journal of Folklore Research* 21 (1984): 188.

11. Dorson discussed fakelore in a number of places, but see his *American Folklore and the Historian* (Chicago: University of Chicago Press, 1971), 3–14.

12. Vilmos Voight, "The Concept of Today's Folklore as We See It from Budapest, Hungary, Europe," *Journal of Folklore Research* 21 (1984): 167.

13. Dégh, 189.

14. See chapter 1, below, 31–50.

15. Richard M. Dorson, *Folklore and Folklife: An Introduction* (Chicago: University of Chicago Press, 1972), speaks in his discussion of current theoretical approaches to folklore of a contextual approach, which he saw as a "growing movement among energetic younger folklorists" (45). This approach saw folklore as embedded in a social and cultural context and to be understood only within an appreciation of that context. The term contextual approach did not catch on with folklorists, however, although they increasingly stressed the importance of context. Gradually they came to view folklore in terms of its use in a context as being a king of performance and to consider folklore under the aegis of performance theory; see Richard Bauman, *Verbal Art as Performance* (Prospect Heights, Ill.: Waveland Press, 1984).

16. Some of these are discussed in de Caro and Jordan, 14–18. Other kinds of artists have also had various reasons for looking to folklore, as de Caro and Jordan try to indicate for the visual arts, although folklorists have given rather little attention to folklore in other

art forms (but see Willard B. Moore, "The Intersection of Folk and Fine Arts," *Journal of Folklore Research* 36 [1999]: 71–82). Oddly enough, given their often-intense interest in folk music, they have given little attention to folklore and the work of classical composers, though as a *New York Times* reviewer (Allan Kozinn, "The John Henry Who Might Have Been," *New York Times,* November 23, 2009, C4), recently expressed it:

> *Most listeners accept it as a given that folk song has been a powerful influence on composers of art music, from the authors of the parody Masses of the 1500s through Haydn, Beethoven and Bartok to Aaron Copeland and George Crumb. Often composers drawn to folk melodies either provide accompaniments in their own styles or simply allude to them, weaving strands of their musical DNA into larger structures.*

See also C. K. Szego, "The Sound of Rocks Aquiver? Composing Racial Ambivalence in Territorial Hawai'i," *Journal of American Folklore* 123 (2010): 31–62.

17. See Mary Ellen Brown, "Ballad," and Frank de Caro, "Literary Ballad," in Mary Ellen Brown and Bruce A. Rosenberg, eds., *Encyclopedia of Folklore and Literature* (Santa Barbara: ABC-CLIO, 1998), 47–48, 382–84, for information and for further references.

18. See de Caro and Jordan, 94–98, 170–78.

19. Shalom Staub, "Folklore and Authenticity: A Myopic Marriage in Public Sector Programs," in *The Conservation of Culture: Folklorists and the Public Sector,* ed. Burt Feintuch (Lexington: University Press of Kentucky, 1988), 166.

20. David Whisnant, *All That Is Native and Fine: The Politics of Culture in an American Region* (Chapel Hill: University of North Carolina Press, 1983).

21. Robert Cantwell, "Conjuring Culture: Ideology and Magic in the Festival of American Folklife," *Journal of American Folklore* 104 (1991): 148–63; Robert Cantwell, *Ethnomimesis: Folklife and the Representation of Culture* (Chapel Hill: University of North Carolina Press, 1993); Inta Gale Carpenter, Richard Bauman, and Patricia Sawin, *Reflections on the Folklife Festival: An Ethnography of Participant Experience* (Bloomington: Indiana University Folklore Institute Special Publications, No. 2, 1992); Richard Price and Sally Price, *On the Mall: Presenting Maroon Tradition Bearers at the 1992 Festival of American Folklife* (Bloomington: Indiana University Folklore Institute Special Publications, No. 4, 1994); Barbara Kirshenblatt-Gimblett, "Objects of Ethnography," in *Exhibiting Cultures: The Poetics and Politics of Museum Display,* ed. Ivan Karp and Steven D. Lavine (Washington: Smithsonian Institution Press, 1991), 386–443; Barbara Kirshenblatt-Gimblett, *Destination Culture: Tourism, Museums, and Heritage* (Berkeley and Los Angeles: University of California Press, 1998). A special issue of the *Journal of American Folklore* devoted to the Smithsonian Festival edited by Heather A. Diamond and Ricardo D. Tremillos appeared as issue no. 479 (121 [2008]). Christine Garlough, "Folklore and the Potential of Acknowledgment: Representing 'India' at the Minnesota Festival of Nations," *Western Folklore* 70 (2011): 69–98, deals with ethnic folk performances at another festival.

22. Charles Camp and Timothy Lloyd, "Six Reasons Not to Produce Folklife Festivals," *Kentucky Folklife Record* 26, 1–2 (1980): 67–74. Quotations below are from p. 74.

23. Whisnant, 184, 185, 247.

24. Helen A. Regis and Shana Walton, "Producing the Folk at the New Orleans Jazz and Heritage Festival," *Journal of American Folklore* 121 (2008): 428.

25. Regis and Walton, 427.

26. Emily Satterwhite, "Imagining Home, Nation, World: Appalachia on the Mall," *Journal of American Folklore* 121 (2008): 23, 28, 29.

27. Quoted in *Putting Folklore to Use*, ed. Michael Owen Jones (Lexington: University Press of Kentucky, 1994), 11.

28. Marjorie Bard, "Aiding the Homeless: The Use of Narratives in Diagnosis and Prevention," in Jones, 76–93.

29. David Shuldiner, "Promoting Self-Worth among the Aging," in Jones, 214.

30. Michael Owen Jones, "A Folklorist's Approach to Organizational Behavior (OB) and Organization Development," in Jones, 179.

31. Sara Selene Faulds, "Designing Public Spaces for People's Symbolic Uses," in Jones, 150–61.

32. David J. Hufford, "Folklore and Medicine," in Jones, 117–35.

33. James Westfall Thompson and Bernard J. Holm, *A History of Historical Writing*, 2 vols. (New York: Macmillan, 1942), II: 143.

34. See Robert T. Clark, *Herder: His Life and Thought* (Berkeley and Los Angeles: University of California Press, 1955); Alexander Gillies, "Herder's Approach to the Philosophy of History," *Modern Language Review* 35 (1940): 193–206; Eugene E. Reed, "Herder, Primitivism and the Age of Poetry," *Modern Language Review* 60 (1965): 553–67; F. M. Barnard, ed., *Herder on Social and Political Culture*, trans. from the German (Cambridge: Cambridge University Press, 1969).

35. Quoted in Ruth Michaelis-Jena, *The Brothers Grimm* (New York and Washington: Praeger, 1970), 52.

36. Michaelis-Jena, 50, 51.

37. See Jacob Grimm, *Teutonic Mythology*, trans. James Steven Stallybrass, 4 vols. (London: George Bell, 1882–1888), II: 647, 784–85.

38. Peter Assion, "Eugen Fehrle and 'The Mythos of our Folk,'" in *The Nazification of an Academic Discipline, ed.* James R. Dow and Hannjost Lixfeld (Bloomington and Indianapolis: Indiana University Press, 1994), 119, 122.

39. Anka Oesterle, "The Office of Ancestral Inheritance and Folklore Scholarship," in Dow and Lixfeld, 195.

40. Sandra Eminov, "Folklore and Nationalism in Modern China," in *Folklore, Nationalism and Politics*, ed. Felix J. Oinas (Columbus: Slavica Publishers, 1978), 169.

41. Felix J. Oinas, "The Political Uses and Themes of Folklore in the Soviet Union," in Oinas, 78.

42. Robert B. Klymasz, "Folklore Politics in the Soviet Ukraine: Perspectives on Some Recent Trends and Developments," in Oinas, 102.

43. William A. Wilson, "Kalevala," in Brown and Rosenberg, 350.

44. William A. Wilson, *Folklore and Nationalism in Modern Finland* (Bloomington: Indiana University Press, 1976), 119.

45. Wilson, *Folklore and Nationalism*, 131.

46. David Kerr, "On Not Becoming a Folklorist: Field Methodology and the Reproduction of Underdevelopment," *Folklore* 102 (1991): 50.

47. Simon J. Bronner, *Following Tradition: Folklore in the Discourse on American Culture* (Logan: Utah State University Press, 1998), 75, 81.

48. Bronner, 85, quoting Stewart Culin.

49. Knapp is quoted by Bronner, 89, Mason by Bronner, 90.

50. Bronner, 100, 117, 121; Booker T. Washington quoted by Bronner, 102.

51. Richard Reuss, "American Folksongs and Left-Wing Politics: 1935–56," *Journal of the Folklore Institute* 12 (1975): 94, 95, 99.

52. Robert Cantwell, *When We Were Good: The Folk Revival* (Cambridge, Mass.: Harvard University Press, 1996), 189, 190.

53. Bruce Jackson, "The Folksong Revival," in *Transforming Tradition: Folk Music Revivals Reconsidered*, ed. Neil V. Rosenberg (Urbana: University of Illinois Press, 1993), 75, suggests that the folksong revival "audience seemed more willing to sing about political causes than it was willing to be involved in any of them"; Neil Rosenberg's interview with folklorist Kenneth S. Goldstein (Kenneth S. Goldstein, "A Future Folklorist in the Record Business," in Rosenberg, 107–21) about his work as a record producer gives keen insight into some of the commercial aspects of the revival. Goldstein, 113–14, says: "I tried to see that it was financially viable for the companies to issue the records, and when necessary I would issue other things that could make money for them . . . I was a well-trained M.B.A. I knew how to deal with markets, with sales, with market research."

54. Ellen Stekert, "Cents and Nonsense in the Urban Folksong Movement: 1930–66," in Rosenberg, 98; Stekert's essay originally appeared in *Folklore and Society: Essays in Honor of Benjamin A. Botkin*, ed. Bruce A. Jackson (Hatboro, Pa.: Folklore Associates, 1966), 153–68, where her terminology differs.

55. Jackson, 78.

56. Kay Stone, *Some Day Your Witch Will Come* (Detroit: Wayne State University Press, 2008), 84. This aspect of the revival of traditional folktales is also dealt with by Richard Alvey, "The Historical Development of Organized Storytelling in the United States" (Ph.D. dissertation, University of Pennsylvania, 1974). See Joseph Sobol, *The Storyteller's Journey: An American Revival* (Urbana: University of Illinois Press, 1998), for various aspects of the storytelling revival.

57. Stone, 97, 90.

58. Although some "revivals" have involved a recycling process in which folk traditions are relocated to non-folk contexts, certainly not all revivalistic processes should be so seen or labeled as folklorism. Some may create new forms of folk tradition and may be akin to older forms of cultural borrowing that have been part of the historical processes of tradition. Sabina Magliocco suggests that *reclamation* can be a better term to use in some contexts, such as neopagan movements which have revalued "discarded" older traditions (discussion list communication, H-Folk @ H-Net, November 16, 2008; see also her *Witching Culture: Folklore and Neopaganism in America* [Philadelphia: University of Pennsylvania Press, 2004]).

59. Priscilla Denby, "Folklore in the Mass Media," *Folklore Forum* 4 (1971): 113–25.

60. Wolfgang Mieder and Barbara Mieder, "Tradition and Innovation: Proverbs in Advertising," in *The Wisdom of Many: Essays on the Proverb*, ed. Wolfgang Mieder and Alan Dundes (New York: Garland Publishing, 1981), 311.

61. Mieder and Mieder, 317.

62. Linda Dégh, *American Folklore and the Mass Media* (Bloomington: Indiana University Press, 1994), 36–39.

63. For example, K. Bernice Stewart and Homer A. Watt, "Legends of Paul Bunyan, Lumberjack," *Transactions of the Wisconsin Academy of Sciences, Arts and Letters* 18 (1916): 639–51.

64. Daniel Hoffman, *Paul Bunyan: Last of the Frontier Demigods* (Lincoln: University of Nebraska Press, Bison Books, 1983), 7. See Hoffman for the development of the Paul Bunyan "story" and for references to sources noted in this and the following paragraph.

65. See B. A. Botkin, ed., *A Treasury of Mississippi River Folklore* (New York: Crown, 1955), 35–36.

66. Eric Hobsbawm and Terence Ranger, eds., *The Invention of Tradition* (Cambridge: Cambridge University Press, 1983).

67. Alan Dundes, "Nationalistic Inferiority Complexes and the Fabrication of Folklore: A Reconsideration of Ossian, the *Kinder-und* Hausmärchen, *the Kalevala* and Paul Bunyan," *Journal of Folklore Research* 22 (1985): 11ff.

68. Bausinger, 129.

69. Bausinger, 137.

70. Bausinger, 136.

71. Demetrios Loukatos, "Folklore and Tourism in Greece," *International Folklore Review* 2 (1982): 69.

72. Loukatos, 66.

73. Rosenberg, 5.

74. For a sampling of scholarship relating to these particular authors and folklore, see Carl Lindahl, *Earnest Games: Folkloric Patterns in the Canterbury Tales* (Bloomington: Indiana University Press, 1987); Philip C. Kolin, "Bibliography of Scholarship on Shakespeare and Folklore," *Mississippi Folklore Register* 10 (1976): 210–33; Daniel R. Barnes, "The Bosom Serpent: A Legend in American Folklore and Culture," *Journal of American Folklore* 85 (1972): 111–22; Sharon Rose Wilson, *Margaret Atwood's Fairy Tale Sexual Politics* (Jackson: University Press of Mississippi, 1993); de Caro and Jordan, 53–71, 170–74.

75. Linda Dégh, *American Folklore and the Mass Media*, argues for "folklore communication through new media" (1), that the mass media have created "a new communality" and their "interference" "not only accelerates the folklore process but also contributes to . . . a never-before-experienced inflation of folklore. . . . It is closer to the truth to admit that the media have become a part of folklore" (24–25). Bruce Jackson argues (in denying Alan Dundes's assertion that the folksong revival was folklorismus, though they may be working from differing conceptions of the less than clearly defined folklorismus) that the revival created "a real community" (81). Ronald L. Baker, "*Miracle Magazine* in the Sixties: Mass Media Narratives of Healings and Blessings," *Journal of American Folklore* 118 (2005): 204–18, provides legend narratives that were presented in print, implying that the magazine that printed them was an actual conduit for folkloric transmission. Diane E.

Goldstein, Sylvia Ann Grider, and Jeannie Banks Thomas, *Haunting Experiences: Ghosts in Contemporary Folklore* (Logan: Utah State University Press, 2007), discuss the overlap between older traditions of the supernatural and such modern manifestations as ghost tours and pop-cultural haunted houses. Of course, the Internet presents a relatively new challenge for folklorists concerned with the nature of folklore and its transmission. Robert Glenn Howard, "Electronic Hybridity: The Persistent Process of the Vernacular Web," *Journal of American Folklore* 121 (2008): 201, notes that folklorists' earlier considerations of the Internet tended to treat them [on-line communications] as if they were just some novel form of media object . . . traditional forms being communicated, if in somewhat modified ways," and argues that, "If we exchange the media object approach for that of persistent process, the folklorist is equipped to document something far more complex and powerful." He insists that "there is a class of on-line discourse that is properly termed 'vernacular'" (195) and that "an increasing prevalence of participatory media extends into growing webs of network-based folk culture" (192). Certainly the recycling of folklore historically transmitted through traditional channels via such new conduits as the Internet differs from the creation of new on-line folk communities and communications, though these two processes are related ones and ought to be considered in conjunction.

76. Dégh, *American Folklore and the Mass Media*, 28.

77. Rosenberg, 5.

78. Stekert, 100.

CHAPTER 1

1. Colson Whitehead, *John Henry Days* (New York: Doubleday, 2001). In the rest of this chapter page references are cited in the text.

2. This actual set of stamps included Paul Bunyan, Mighty Casey, and Pecos Bill in addition to John Henry. They were issued at Anaheim, California, July 11, 1996.

3. Michael Caesar, *Umberto Eco: Philosophy, Semiotics and the Work of Fiction* (Cambridge: Polity Press; Malden, Mass.: Blackwell, 1999), 18.

4. Barthes is quoted by David Seed, "The *Open Work* in Theory and Practice," in *Reading Eco: An Anthology*, ed. Rocco Capozzi (Bloomington: Indiana University Press, 1997), 74.

5. Guy Johnson, *John Henry: Tracking Down a Negro Legend* (Chapel Hill: University of North Carolina Press, 1929), 151.

6. There are other claimants. Recently John Garst, "Chasing John Henry in Alabama and Mississippi: A Personal Memoir of Work in Progress," *Tributaries: Journal of the Alabama Folklife Association* 5 (2002): 92–129, has argued for a location in Alabama, marshaling an array of evidence. Earlier MacEdward Leach, "John Henry," in *Folklore and Society: Essays in Honor of Benj. A. Botkin*, ed. Bruce Jackson, 93–106 (Hatboro, Pa.: Folklore Associates, 1966), discussed possible Jamaican origins and a Jamaican venue for events precipitating the tradition.

Most recently, in a well-received and often fascinating book, historian Scott Reynolds Nelson, *Steel Drivin' Man: John Henry, the Untold Story of an American Legend* (New York: Oxford University Press, 2006), argues that John Henry's "contest" took place not at the

Big Bend Tunnel but at the nearby Lewis Tunnel; he determines that no steam drills were ever used at Big Bend. Furthermore he locates the John Henry saga in the context of the widespread use of convict labor in building the railroads in question and finds the record of an actual John Henry leased from the Virginia State Penitentiary and put to work on the West Virginia tunnels; such convicts were in effect forced to do the work in question, having no option to strike or leave; the work was of course very dangerous, so that a term in the penitentiary could be a virtual death sentence, and many of the African American convicts died, sometimes of silicosis from dust stirred up by steam drills. Even dead convicts had to be returned to the penitentiary, however, to prove they had not escaped, a fact giving rise to the well-known line that says John Henry was taken to the white house (at the Virginia prison) and buried in the sand (a number of convict bodies having been recently excavated by archaeologists there).

Although he is not interested in considering the John Henry story an "open text" as such, Nelson is, like Whitehead, intrigued by the development of the tradition in a variety of directions. "Nailing down the song to a single interpretation is impossible," Nelson says, "making his story almost infinitely mutable" (172). He discusses several aspects of the expansion of the tradition in terms of versions of the song collected and in terms of how such figures as Carl Sandburg, Fiddlin' John Carson, and left-wing commentators worked with the song and story. Probably most interesting and significant, however, are his insights into early functions and meanings of the songs (though folklorists may find his ideas about the development of American folk musical traditions in the relevant time period to be quite speculative and overly dependent on imaginative reconstructions and his not always clearly distinguishing between ballad and hammer songs possibly confusing). He argues that the song was not initially the story of a heroic man of great prowess who could defeat a machine but a cautionary tale and stresses the function of the hammer songs in helping to preserve workers from injury and death as well as noting different uses of the songs by different groups of workers and hence using different permutations of the song.

7. Zora Neale Hurston adamantly asserts that there is no John Henry tradition outside the songs, but see Alan Dundes, ed., *Mother Wit from the Laughing Barrel: Readings in the Interpretation of Afro-American Folklore* (Jackson: University Press of Mississippi, 1990), 561–67.

8. Johnson, 69.

9. See Norm Cohen, *Long Steel Rail: The Railroad in American Folksong*, 2nd ed. (Urbana: University of Illinois Press, 2000), 70–72.

10. Louise Rand Bascom, "Ballads and Songs of Western North Carolina," *Journal of American Folklore* 22 (1909): 249–50; E. C. Perrow, "Songs and Rhymes from the South," *Journal of American Folklore* 26 (1913): 163–65; Perrow's John Henry ballad was collected in 1912, but the article includes hammer songs collected as early as 1905.

11. Johnson; Louis Chappell, *John Henry: A Folk-Lore Study* (Jena: Frommannsche Verlag, 1933).

12. Cohen notes that "much of the national awareness of John Henry stems from a revival of interest in the late 1920s, following the research of Guy B. Johnson, rather than from direct survival from the nineteenth century" (64).

13. Johnson, 150.

14. Brett Williams, *John Henry: A Bio-Bibliography* (Westport, Conn.: Greenwood Press, 1983), 61. Chappell's study she sees as "most helpful to those seeking substantive information on the Big Bend Tunnel community." I am indebted to Williams's excellent survey of the materials relating to John Henry in my own consideration of the development of the "legend."

15. Guy Johnson, "A Mighty Legend," *Nation*, October 7, 1931, 367.

16. Roark Bradford, *John Henry* (New York: Harper, 1931).

17. Williams, 79.

18. Roark Bradford, *Old Man Adam and His Chillun* (New York: Harper, 1928).

19. See Jeffrey Hadler, "Remus Orthography: The History of the Representation of the African-American Voice," *Journal of Folklore Research* 35 (1998): 99–126.

20. Williams, 79.

21. Whitehead takes these words from an actual interview with Robeson by Julia Dorn that appeared in 1939 in *CAC* (a publication of the Theatre Arts Committee); it is reprinted in Philip S. Foner, ed., *Paul Robeson Speaks: Writings, Speeches, Interviews, 1918–1974* (New York: Brunner/Mazel Publishers), 131. See pages 81–82, 136–37, 211–17, and 300 for other comments made by Robeson about folk music. He discusses the pentatonic scale in "The Related Sounds of Music," which originally appeared in the *Daily World*, April 7, 1973, and is reprinted in Foner, 443–48. See also Sheila Tully Boyle and Andrew Bunie, *Paul Robeson: The Years of Promise and Achievement* (Amherst: University of Massachusetts Press, 2001), 288ff, 303, 321, 400–401.

22. Richard M. Dorson, *Folklore and Fakelore: Essays toward a Discipline of Folk Studies* (Cambridge, Mass.: Harvard University Press, 1976), 288; Dorson's discussion of John Henry originally appeared as "The Career of John Henry," *Western Folklore* 24 (1965): 155–63. Williams, pp. 141–61, provides a discography of John Henry recordings. Cohen also provides extensive discographical information.

23. The earliest sheet music Williams lists was published in the 1930s although Nelson, p. 116, notes that W. C. Handy copyrighted sheet music for the song in 1922; however, Nelson seems to have in mind "John Henry Blues," which appears in the volume of his work Handy later edited, *Blues: An Anthology*, intro. Abbe Niles, illus. Miguel Covarrubias (New York: Albert and Charles Boni, 1926), 135–39; in the notes to *Blues: An Anthology* Abbe Niles affirms that this song is "founded on a very famous ballad-worksong" (45); it is not, however, the traditional "John Henry." Whitehead seems to have an earlier date than the 1930s in mind for the character Jake Rose.

24. Williams, 119.

25. Williams, 119.

26. References in the text indicate that this episode is taking place a few years after the death of Lemon Jefferson (which took place in 1929) and while Paramount was a premier blues label (Paramount ceased operations in 1933).

27. Williams notes several (85) and also a weekly CBS radio series on which Juan Hernandez played John Henry and sang songs based on folk materials, and Dennis G. Jerz has noted other plays produced for the Federal Theatre Project; see the abstract of his conference paper, "Protesting and Patronizing: John Henry Stories in Two Little-known Federal Theatre Project Plays," at http://uwec.edu/jerzdg/research/johnhenr.htm.

28. Williams, 86ff.

29. John Oliver Killens, *A Man Ain't Nothin' But a Man* (Boston: Little, Brown, 1975).

30. Archie Green, "John Henry Depicted," *JEMF Quarterly* 14 (1978): 30–37.

31. In the novel Pamela Street explains to J that the statue at the tunnel is referred to as the one built by Jim Beam and that the local sponsors got the whiskey company to pay for it in exchange for being allowed to use the same design for their bottle. This story adds an interesting dimension by creating an overlap between local and larger economic forces, but in fact the actual whiskey bottle's design is quite different from that of the Hinton statue. Nelson (6, 172) states that the Jim Beam Distillery and country singer Johnny Cash did both contribute funds toward building the statue, which he places in Talcott.

32. And indeed Whitehead's outsiders come from very outside the local context; Lucien considers this job "a weird gig" (293) and marvels that the attendees "can wear a T-shirt and a baseball cap and not consider it an ironic gesture" (292), that they are "normal folks, what they call families" (293).

CHAPTER 2

1. But see Alan Dundes, *Folklore Matters* (Knoxville: University of Tennessee Press, 1989), 1–39.

2. Elliott Oring, "The Arts, Artifacts, and Artifices of Identity," *Journal of American Folklore* 107 (1994): 211–33.

3. See Miriam Camitta, "Gender and Method in Folklore Fieldwork," *Southern Folklore* 47 (1990): 21–31; James Clifford and George E. Marcus, eds., *Writing Culture: The Poetics and Politics of Ethnography* (Berkeley and Los Angeles: University of California Press, 1986); John Dorst, "Rereading *Mules and Men*: Toward the Death of the Ethnographer," *Cultural Anthropology* 2 (1987): 305–18; Rosan Augusta Jordan, "Folklore Study in New Orleans' Gilded Age: The 'Louisiana Association,'" *Louisiana Folklore Miscellany* 7 (1992): 109–31.

4. Rosemary Lévy Zumwalt, *American Folklore Scholarship: A Dialogue of Dissent* (Bloomington: Indiana University Press, 1988).

5. The use of the term *Creole* is complicated. Today in Louisiana the word is largely used to refer to people who are culturally and socially Afro-French, *when* it refers to *people* (it may also be used to apply to local products, such as Creole tomatoes, and to a cuisine and a language) in a contemporary context. At the end of the nineteenth century, there was a movement among white New Orleanians to insist that "Creole" properly referred only to Louisianians of pure European (principally French and Spanish) descent; this usage is often continued today in making historical reference to such people. We use the term "Creole" to refer to such whites and "Creole of color" to refer to the Afro-French because this usage was probably that preferred by the society in which the people we are discussing moved, although their own actual usage of the term in some cases differs.

6. Alcée Fortier, *Louisiana Folk-Tales in French Dialect and English Translation* (Boston: Houghton Mifflin, American Folklore Society Memoirs, no. 2, 1895).

7. Glenn R. Conrad, gen. ed., *A Dictionary of Louisiana Biography*, 2 vols. (New Orleans: Louisiana Historical Association in cooperation with the Center for Louisiana Studies, University of Southwestern Louisiana, 1988), II: 719.

8. Unless otherwise noted, all quotations relating to association meetings and business are from the minutes preserved at Tulane University. Quotations from these minutes are identified by the designation Typescript with the relevant page numbers and are drawn from a typed version of the original handwritten minutes; dates of meetings are given in the text or in citations. This material is used by the kind permission of Tulane University and the authors wish to express their appreciation for permission to quote from this source. See the Acknowledgments for further information. This source is cited as Typescript (although in some cases the date only is given in the text); this first quotation is from p. 2.

9. "Louisiana Association of the American Folk-Lore Society," *Journal of American Folklore* 5 (1892): 160.

10. Typescript, 6–7.

11. Typescript, 11–12.

12. Typescript, 19.

13. Alcée Fortier, "Louisiana Nursery Tales," *Journal of American Folklore* 1 (1888): 140–45.

14. Cecilia Viets Jamison, "A Louisiana Legend Concerning Will o' the Wisp," *Journal of American Folklore* 18 (1905): 250.

15. Mollie Evelyn Moore Davis, "De Witch-'ooman an de Spinnin'-Wheel. The Witch Prevented from Entering Her Skin: A Tale from Louisiana," *Journal of American Folklore* 18 (1905): 251–52.

16. Mrs. William Preston Johnston, "Two Negro Tales," *Journal of American Folklore* 9 (1896): 194–98.

17. Johnston, 194.

18. Sara Avery McIlhenny, "Stories Mammy Told Me," *Atlantic Monthly* 151 (1933): 382.

19. "On the Field of Work of a Journal of American Folk-Lore," *Journal of American Folklore* 1 (1888): 3–7.

20. Joseph G. Tregle Jr., "Creoles and Americans," in *Creole New Orleans: Race and Americanization*, ed. Arnold R. Hirsch and Joseph Logsdon (Baton Rouge: Louisiana State University Press, 1992), 168.

21. William Ivy Hair, *Carnival of Fury: Robert Charles and the New Orleans Race Riot of 1900* (Baton Rouge: Louisiana State University Press, 1976), 119.

22. William Ivy Hair, *Bourbonism and Agrarian Protest: Louisiana Politics, 1877–1900* (Baton Rouge: Louisiana State University Press, 1969), 68.

23. Hair, *Carnival of Fury*, 89.

24. Joy Jackson, *New Orleans in the Gilded Age: Politics and Urban Progress, 1877–1900* (Baton Rouge: Louisiana State University Press for the Louisiana Historical Association, 1969), 20.

25. Dale A. Somers, "Black and White in New Orleans: A Study in Urban Race Relations," *Journal of Southern History* 40 (1974): 38.

26. Jackson, 318.

27. Richard Bauman, "Differential Identity and the Social Base of Folklore," *Journal of American Folklore* 84 (1971): 31–41.

28. Alcée Fortier, *Louisiana Studies: Literature, Customs and Dialects, History and Education* (New Orleans: F. F. Hansell and Brother, 1894), 128–31.

29. Fortier's passage may be subject to alternate interpretation, but our reading is that his friend is a (white) Creole who spares the family the anxiety African Americans would supposedly feel upon discovering the magical objects on their doorstep. He thus demonstrates that the enlightened Creoles are dismissive of voodoo (while sympathetic to the problems of poor, superstitious blacks).

30. Somers, p. 23, quoting a newspaper item of 1869.

31. In fact, "C. C. Antoine, Negro lieutenant governor of the state, appeared regularly in his [J. W. Durel, founder of the Creole journal *Le Carillon*] sketches pictured as an 'orangoutan' mouthing the 'gumbo' French Durel ascribed to all native black political leaders" (Tregle, 171).

32. George Washington Cable, *Old Creole Days* (New York: Scribner's, 1879).

33. Edward Larocque Tinker, *Creole City: Its Past and Its People* (New York and London: Longmans, Green, 1953), 215.

34. Tinker, 215.

35. Tinker, 218, 219.

36. Louis D. Rubin, *George W. Cable: The Life and Times of a Southern Heretic* (New York: Pegasus, 1969), 197.

37. Tinker, 219.

38. Jackson, 302.

39. Fortier, *Louisiana Folk-Tales*, x.

40. Typescript, 11, 46; Jamison, 250; Johnston, 194.

41. Fortier, *Louisiana Studies*, 125–26; continuing page numbers are cited in the text.

42. The published minutes for February 12, 1893, refer to this story ("New Orleans Association," *Journal of American Folklore* 6 [1893]: 157–58), but the text is taken from a separate manuscript filed with the Minutes at Tulane University.

43. Ruth McEnery Stuart, *A Golden Wedding and Other Tales* (New York: Harper, 1893), 137.

44. Stuart, 153, 154.

45. Mollie Evelyn Moore Davis, "Throwing the Wanga (St. John's Eve)," in *The Louisiana Book: Selections from the Literature of the State*, ed. Thomas M'Caleb (New Orleans: R. E. Straughan, 1894), 558.

46. Davis, 558.

47. Davis, 559.

48. Tregle, 169.

49. Bauman, 41.

50. Richard M. Dorson, *American Folklore and the Historian* (Chicago: University of Chicago Press, 1971), 10; Zumwalt; Simon J. Bronner, *American Folklore Studies: An Intellectual History* (Lawrence: University of Kansas Press, 1986).

51. For example, in *Old Louisiana* (New York and London: Century, 1929) he lampoons the widespread lovers' leap legends. This section is amusing but obviously shows little understanding of the nature of legend or the desire to understand it.

52. Lyle Saxon, Robert Tallant, and Edward Dreyer, eds., *Gumbo Ya-Ya: A Collection of Louisiana Folk Tales* (Boston: Houghton Mifflin, 1946).

53. James W. Thomas, *Lyle Saxon: A Critical Biography* (Birmingham: Summa Publications, 1991), 111, 119.

54. Cathy Chance Harvey, "Lyle Saxon: A Portrait in Letters, 1917–1945" (Ph.D. dissertation, Tulane University, 1980), 448.

55. Lyle Saxon and Edward Dreyer, *The Friends of Joe Gilmore and Some Friends of Lyle Saxon* (New York: Hastings House, 1948), 116.

56. Frank de Caro, *Folklife in Louisiana Photography: Images of Tradition* (Baton Rouge: Louisiana State University Press, 1990), 61.

57. Joseph Blotner, *Faulkner: A Biography* (New York: Random House, 1984), 222.

58. Edmund Wilson, *The Twenties: From Notebooks and Diaries of the Period* (New York: Farrar, Straus and Giroux, 1975), 258.

59. Saxon and Dreyer, 99.

60. Thomas, xii, ix.

61. Harvey, 11.

62. Lyle Saxon, *Children of Strangers* (Boston: Houghton Mifflin, 1937).

63. Harvey, 213.

64. Lyle Saxon, *Old Louisiana*, illus. E. H. Suydam (New York: Century, 1929).

65. Lyle Saxon, *Fabulous New Orleans*, illus. E. H. Suydam (New York: D. Appleton-Century, 1928), 16.

66. Saxon, *Fabulous New Orleans*, 25, 27.

67. Saxon, *Fabulous New Orleans*, 59.

68. Among other things, the Zulu parade that Saxon claimed to have seen as a boy did not exist until a later time.

69. Harvey, 494.

70. Lyle Saxon, *Father Mississippi* (New York: Century, 1927).

71. Saxon, *Father Mississippi*, 3.

72. Saxon, *Old Louisiana*, 13.

73. Saxon, *Old Louisiana*, 31.

74. Saxon, *Old Louisiana*, 316, 320, 321.

75. Saxon, *Old Louisiana*, 353, 367.

76. Saxon, *Old Louisiana*, 345–46.

77. Saxon, *Father Mississippi*, 39.

78. Saxon, *Old Louisiana*, 368.

79. Saxon, *Old Louisiana*, 320–21, 380.

80. Horace Beck, "Our Popular Traditions," in *American Folklore and Legend*, ed. The Editors of Reader's Digest (Pleasantville, N.Y.: Reader's Digest Association, 1978), 8.

81. Barbara Kirshenblatt-Gimblett, "On Difference," *Journal of American Folklore* 107 (1994): 236.

82. Henry Glassie, "On Identity," *Journal of American Folklore* 107 (1994): 240.

83. Kirshenblatt-Gimblett, 237.

CHAPTER 3

1. Lafcadio Hearn, *Occidental Gleanings*, ed. Albert Mordell, 2 vols. (New York: Dodd, Mead, 1925), I: 160.

2. Hearn, I: 160–61.

3. Hearn, I: 174.

4. Paul Murray, *A Fantastic Journey: The Life and Literature of Lafcadio Hearn* (Ann Arbor: University of Michigan Press, 1993), 52.

5. W. K. McNeil, "Lafcadio Hearn, American Folklorist," *Journal of American Folklore* 91 (1978): 966–67.

6. F. A. de Caro, "A History of Folklife Research in Louisiana," in *Louisiana Folklife: A Guide to the State*, ed. Nicholas R. Spitzer (Baton Rouge: Louisiana Folklife Program and Center for Gulf South History and Culture, 1985), 13–15.

7. This count is that of Jonathan Cott, *Wandering Ghost: The Odyssey of Lafcadio Hearn* (New York: Alfred A. Knopf, 1991), of material published since 1906 and does not include his own biography or Paul Murray's in 1997.

8. Alan Dundes, "The Study of Folklore and Literature in Culture: Identification and Interpretation," *Journal of American Folklore* 78 (1965): 136–42.

9. Murray, 92, 99.

10. S. Frederick Starr, "The Creole Japan of Lafcadio Hearn," unpublished manuscript, 9.

11. Quoted by Cott, 21.

12. Murray, 32ff.

13. Lafcadio Hearn, *Stray Leaves from Strange Literatures* (Boston: James R. Osgood & Co., 1884); Lafcadio Hearn, *Some Chinese Ghosts* (Boston: Roberts Brothers, 1887).

14. Simon J. Bronner, ed., *Lafcadio Hearn's America: Ethnographic Sketches and Editorials* (Lexington: University Press of Kentucky, 2002), 2.

15. Lafcadio Hearn, *Children of the Levee*, ed. O. W. Frost, intro. John Ball (Lexington: University of Kentucky Press, 1957), 32.

16. Hearn, *Children of the Levee*, 56, 21.

17. Lafcadio Hearn, *Two Years in the French West Indies* (New York: Harper, 1890).

18. Hearn, *Two Years in the French West Indies*, 37; subsequent references to this volume give only page numbers in the text.

19. Lafcadio Hearn, *Gombo Zhèbes: Little Dictionary of Creole Proverbs* (New Orleans: Will H. Coleman, 1885), 4.

20. S. Frederick Starr, ed., *Inventing New Orleans: Writings of Lafcadio Hearn* (Jackson: University Press of Mississippi, 2001), xxiv, xix, xxv.

21. Lafcadio Hearn, *An American Miscellany*, ed. Albert Mordell, 2 vols. (New York: Dodd, Mead, 1924–1925), II: 164.

22. Hearn, *Gombo Zhèbes*, 3.

23. Lafcadio Hearn, *Creole Sketches*, ed. Charles Woodward Hutson, illus. The Author (Boston: Houghton Mifflin, 1924).

24. Bronner, 1.

25. Hearn, *An American Miscellany*, II: 203.

26. Starr, *Inventing New Orleans*, 67.

27. The material appears in the *Historical Sketch Book and Guide to New Orleans* (New Orleans: Will H. Coleman, 1885), whose title page says only "edited and compiled by several leading writers of the New Orleans press." P. D. and Ione Perkins in their standard bibliography of Hearn's writings (*Lafcadio Hearn: A Bibliography of His Writings*, intro. Sanki

Ichikawa [Boston and New York: Houghton Mifflin, 1934]) are only willing to definitely attribute "The Scenes of Cable's Romances" and "Père Antoine's Date Palm" to Hearn.

CHAPTER 4

1. Susan Sonntag, *On Photography* (New York: Farrar, Straus and Giroux, 1977), 153.

2. The term *folklife* can, according to Simon Bronner, *American Folklore Studies: An Intellectual History* (Lawrence: University of Kansas Press, 1986), 13, be traced back to 1847 (via its Swedish source term *folk-liv*), but its precise meaning is difficult to delineate. It refers to the sum total of traditional materials passed down by the folk process; it overlaps with *folklore* but includes a variety of traditional ways of life, material culture, processes.

3. The work of Emerson, Sutcliffe, and Stone is discussed in Ian Jeffrey, *Photography: A Concise History* (New York: Oxford University Press, 1981), 67–71; Gail Buckland, *Reality Recorded: Early Documentary Photography* (Newton Abbot, England: David and Charles, 1974), 95–95; and Editors of Time-Life Books, *Documentary Photograpy* (New York: Time-Life, 1972), 22–27.

4. See Buckland on Bourne, 44–45, and Thomson, 51ff.

5. Jeffrey, 182.

6. For a selection of Inha's photographs, see Urpo Vento and Pekka Laaksonnen, eds., *I. K. Inha 1894: Valokuvaaja Vienen Karjalassa/A Photographer in Viena Karelia* (Helsinki: Academia Scientiarum Fennica, 1968). Curtis published his work as *The North American Indian*, ed. Frederick Webb Hodge, 20 vols. (Seattle and Cambridge: E. S. Curtis and The University Press, 1907–1939). It has often been noted that Curtis commonly created posed pictures rather than documenting culture as it existed.

7. On stereographs, see William Culp Darrah, *The World of Stereographs* (Gettysburg: National Stereoscopic Association, 1977).

8. Mugnier's photographs have been published in two books, Lester Burbank Bridaham, ed., *New Orleans and Bayou Country: Photographs (1880–1910) by George François Mugnier* (New York: Weathervane, 1972), and John R. Kemp and Linda Orr King, eds., *Louisiana Images, 1880–1920* (Baton Rouge: Louisiana State University Press for the Louisiana State Museum, 1975).

9. The photographs referenced appear in Kemp and King, 17, 107, 109, 9.

10. Charles Alan Watkins, "The Blurred Image: Documentary Photography and the Depression South" (Ph.D. dissertation, University of Delaware, 1982).

11. Ralph A. Graves, "Louisiana, Land of Perpetual Romance," *National Geographic Magazine* 57 (1930): 393–491.

12. Interview with Fonville Winans, April 23, 1986.

13. Interview with Elemore Morgan Jr., May 4, 1986.

14. Frances Parkinson Keyes, *All This Is Louisiana: An Illustrated Story Book* (Lafayette: Sans Souci Press, n.d. [originally New York: Harper, 1950]). The photographs of the St. Amico procession, with Keyes's commentary, appear on pp. 204–7. Other folklife photos mentioned appear on pp. 27, 57, 143, 184–85.

15. Arnold Genthe, *As I Remember* (New York: Reynal and Hitchcock, 1936), 212–13.

16. Arnold Genthe, *Impressions of Old New Orleans: A Book of Pictures*, foreword Grace King (New York: George H. Doran, 1926).

17. Genthe, *Impressions*; see plates 39, 51, 64, 69, 74, 79, 84.

18. Genthe, *Impressions*, plates 69, 79, 81.

19. Watkins, 52.

20. F. Jack Hurley took the phrase as the title of his important history of Roy Stryker's work, *Portrait of a Decade: Roy Stryker and the Development of Documentary Photography in the Thirties* (Baton Rouge: Louisiana State University Press, 1972).

21. Watkins, 121.

22. Saxon's work is also discussed in chapter 2. For other discussion of *Gumbo Ya-Ya*, see Frank de Caro and Rosan Augusta Jordan, *Re-Situating Folklore: Folk Contexts and Twentieth-Century Literature and Art* (Knoxville: University of Tennessee Press, 2004), 73–91.

23. Russell Lee to Roy Stryker, September 20, 1938, in Roy Stryker Papers, 1912–72, Photographic Archives, University of Louisville.

24. The photograph of unloading oysters appears in Frank de Caro, *Folklife in Louisiana Photography: Images of Tradition* (Baton Rouge: Louisiana State University Press, 1990), 66; *Folklife in Louisiana Photography* provides a more detailed discussion of the photography that is the subject of this chapter and reproduces images discussed but not reproduced here.

25. Russell Lee to Roy Stryker, September 16, 1938, in Stryker Papers.

26. Robert Flaherty's celebrated film *Louisiana Story* does something similar, telling the story of how a noisy drilling rig and its crew interact with a Cajun family living a traditional life in the Louisiana swamp country. The film was not part of the SONJ photography project but was also supported by Standard Oil and the film crew was visited by a project photographer while production was being undertaken.

27. The Rosskams were a husband/wife team who worked for the SONJ project. Just how they as a team managed to take single images is not clear.

28. The term is used by Fred B. Kniffen and Malcolm Comeaux, *The Spanish Moss Folk Industry of Louisiana* (Baton Rouge: Louisiana State University School of Geoscience, 1979).

CHAPTER 5

1. Erich von Däniken, *Chariots of the Gods?,* trans. Michael Heron (New York: Putnam's, 1969).

2. Von Däniken, 44, 10.

3. According to the *Oxford English Dictionary* the word derives from the Latin occulere, meaning to cover over. The English word as used to mean secret or hidden appears in the sixteenth century (earliest use cited is 1533, though as a verb meaning to hide or conceal 1527); its use to mean those "sciences" dealing with such aspects of the supernatural as magic and alchemy appears in the seventeenth century (earliest use cited 1633). It is, of course, not difficult to see the connection between both uses of the word, and they are certainly related uses.

4. See Frank de Caro, "Euhemerism," in *Folklore: An Encyclopedia of Beliefs, Customs, Tales, Music, and Art,* ed. Thomas A. Green, 2 vols. (Santa Barbara and Oxford: ABC-CLIO, 1997), I: 259–60.

5. I do not mean to imply that folklore cannot be legitimately a historical document. In "Folklore as an 'Historical Science': The Anglo-American Viewpoint" (Ph.D. dissertation, Indiana University, 1972), I trace various approaches to folklore as yielding historical knowledge.

6. Von Däniken, 33.

7. Von Däniken, 29, 47, 70, 110.

8. Von Däniken, 83.

9. Erich von Däniken, *Gods from Outer Space: Return to the Stars or Evidence for the Impossible,* trans. Michael Heron (New York: Putnam's, 1970), originally published in German as *Zurück zu den Sternen.*

10. Von Däniken, *Gods from Outer Space,* 16, 7; the latter references a foreword by Wilhelm Roggersdorf.

11. Von Däniken, *Gods from Outer Space,* 63, 73ff, 148ff.

12. Von Däniken, *Gods from Outer Space,* 176, 146.

13. Erich von Däniken, *The Gold of the Gods,* trans. Michael Heron (New York: Putnam's, 1973).

14. Von Däniken, *Gold of the Gods,* 181.

15. Von Däniken, *Gold of the Gods,* 116, 141, 79, 85.

16. Von Däniken, *Gold of the Gods,* 119, 98.

17. Josef F. Blumrich, *The Spaceships of Ezekiel* (New York: Bantam, 1974); it was originally published in Germany in 1973 as *Da tat sich der Himmel auf.*

18. Barry H. Downing, *The Bible & Flying Saucers* (New York: Avon, 1968).

19. Jacques Bergier, *Extra-Terrestrial Visitations from Prehistoric Times to the Present* (Chicago: Henry Regnery, 1973).

20. Jean Sendy, *The Coming of the Gods,* trans. Lowell Bair (New York: Berkley Medallion, 1973.

21. Andrew Tomas, *We Are Not the First: Riddles of Ancient Science* (New York: Bantam, 1973), 11, 31, 1.

22. W. R. Drake, *Gods or Spacemen?* (Amherst, Wisc.: Amherst Press, 1964), 8, 10, 14, 15, 16.

23. Drake, 95, 99, 100, 110, 106; Drake writes of fairies or apparitions on pages 32 and 111, and refers to "many" photographs of fairies, perhaps a reference to the Cottingley fairy photographs hoax, although if so he seems to have accepted the genuineness of the Cottingley photographs; on the Cottingley photos, see S. F. Sanderson, "The Cottingley Fairy Photographs: A Re-Appraisal of the Evidence," *Folklore* 84 (1973): 89–103.

24. W. Raymond Drake, *Gods and Spacemen in the Ancient East* (New York: New American Library, 1973), 91, 101.

25. Clifford Wilson, *Crash Go the Chariots: An Alternative to* Chariots of the Gods (New York: Lancer: 1972); Barry Thiering and Edgar Castle, eds., *Some Trust in Chariots: Sixteen Views of Erich von Däniken's* Chariots of the Gods? (New York: Popular Library, n.d.; original publication 1972); although the publication of the latter volume had Australian

origins, in the United States it was reprinted as a mass-market paperback; the included essays cover a number of issues but none address the matter of the historicity of folklore. On von Däniken's being influenced by H. P. Lovecraft, alluded to above, see Jason Colavito, "Charioteer of the Gods: H. P. Lovecraft and the Invention of Ancient Astronauts," *eSkeptic* April 26, 2004 (www.skeptic.com/eskeptic/04-04-26).

26. Drake, *Gods or Spacemen?* 22.

27. Daniel Cohen, *Mysterious Places* (New York: Dodd, Mead, 1969), 4. Cohen provides (1–25) a very useful short account of interest in the Atlantis story. For a more detailed account, see L. Sprague de Camp, *Lost Continents: The Atlantis Theme in History, Science, and Literature* (New York: Dover, 1970), especially 1–50.

28. Cohen, 10.

29. Cohen, 11.

30. Ignatius Donnelly, *Atlantis: The Antediluvian World*, modern rev. ed., ed. Egerton Sykes (New York: Gramercy Publishing, 1970; originally published 1882).

Marjorie Ingle, *Mayan Revival Style: Art Deco Mayan Fantasy* (Salt Lake City: Peregrine Smith, 1984), 76ff, suggests that popular interest in lost continents, stimulated by Donnelly's long-in-print book and James Churchward's later Mu books, influenced the development of the Mayan Revival style in American architecture.

31. Donnelly, 1–2.

32. Donnelly, 111.

33. Donnelly, 115, 117, 118, 119, 123, 126–27.

34. Donnelly, 116.

35. Donnelly, 53–106.

36. Blavatsky has attracted several biographers and is the subject of a number of other books as well, some of them highly critical, including S. L. Cranston, *HPB: The Extraordinary Life and Influence of Helena Blavatsky, Founder of the Modern Theosophical Movement* (New York: Putnam, 1994); Marion Meade, *Madame Blavatsky, the Woman Behind the Myth* (New York: Putnam, 1980); Peter Washington, *Madame Blavatsky's Baboon: A History of the Mystics, Mediums, and Misfits Who Brought Spiritualism to America* (New York: Schocken, 1994).

37. Cohen, 26.

38. This lecture is reprinted in Hans Stefan Santesson, *Understanding Mu* (New York: Paperback Library, 1970), 169–87.

39. Churchward himself seems never to have gone to Mexico and never saw Niven's tablets. Niven made rubbings and took photographs of the tablets and made a limited number of these available for publications, which Churchward must have seen initially. Then after the appearance of Churchward's first book, in which he discusses a few of the tablets, Niven sent him a larger number of rubbings to examine. In 1970 a book by Tony Earll appeared, *Mu Revealed* (New York: Paperback Library, 1970) in which the author claimed that the tablets were in a museum in Mexico and that he saw some of them, though his own information about Mu came from a series of scrolls excavated by a Professor Reesdon Hurdlop at Niven's site. According to David Hatcher Childress, *Lost Cities of North and Central America* (Kempton, Ill.: Adventures Unlimited Press, 1992), 252, the Earll book was a hoax (the name Tony Earll being an anagram for "Not really" and Hurdlop's name an

anagram for "Rednose Rudolph"). In his book, a narrative account of his travels, Childress tells someone that the tablets are said to have gone to a private museum in Mexico City but that no one even knows what this museum is called, let alone where it is. This assertion may stem from the fact that Niven himself maintained private museums. Robert S. Wicks and Roland H. Harrison, *Buried Cities, Forgotten Gods: William Niven's Life of Discovery and Revolution in Mexico and the American Southwest* (Lubbock: Texas Tech University Press, 1999), 241ff, indicate that Niven sought to export the tablets to the United States but ran into difficulties with Mexican authorities in his attempts to do so and buried the tablets for safe keeping in Tampico. Niven had sent some rubbings to the American Museum of Natural History in New York, which was unable to provide him with a determination about them. Some archaeologists questioned the legitimacy of Niven's finds (thinking that he might have been, for example, bamboozled by his diggers who provided fake artifacts), although others thought them genuine. Wicks and Harrison refer to the tablets as "problematic" (259).

40. James Churchward, *The Children of Mu* (New York: Paperback Library, 1968), 11.

41. James Churchward, *The Lost Continent of Mu* (New York: Paperback Library, 1968), 19–20, 80, 156, 187, 181, 74, 184.

42. Churchward, *Lost Continent of Mu*, 233, 68, 83; Churchward, *Children of Mu*, 186, 145.

43. Quoted from Symmes's 1818 circular by David Standish, *Hollow Earth: The Long and Curious History of Imagining Strange Lands, Fantastical Creature, Advanced Civilizations, and Marvelous Machines Below the Earth's Surface* (New York: Da Capo, 2006), 40. Much of my discussion of the history of the hollow earth idea is drawn from this excellent treatment.

44. Standish, 65.

45. Standish, 95.

46. Standish, 278.

47. Standish says that Hitler "supposedly" heard some lectures on Cyrus Teed's ideas and became interested in the hollow earth for purposes of military strategy (275). Standish says that there is only the "slimmest substantiation" of this interest. However, the more credulous Eric Norman, *This Hollow Earth* (New York: Lancer Books, 1970), devotes a chapter, 129–44, to Hitler's interest and the subsequent actions of the Nazis. Norman traces the interest to the British occult group the Golden Dawn and claims that Himmler's S.S. even collected folktales about European caves, tunnels, and mines in attempts to locate entrances to the interior world.

48. The Polish Ossendowski (1876–1945) is best known for books on Lenin and the Russian civil war, in which he fought. As a young man he traveled in India and around 1920 accompanied a group of Poles and white Russians fleeing communist-controlled Siberia who were trying to reach India through Mongolia and Tibet; he wound up sojourning in Mongolia. His book *Beast, Men and Gods*, about his travels during and after the Russian civil war, was a bestseller in English. The Russian Roerich (1874–1947) is well known as a painter and stage designer. In the 1920s he accompanied a scientific expedition to Central Asia and he remained interested in Asia, both as artist and philosopher, the rest of his life. He died in India, where he is buried. There is a Nicholas Roerich Museum in New York.

According to Robert Ernst Dickhoff, *Agharta* (Boston: Bruce Humphries, 1951; reprinted Mokelumne Hill, Calif.: Health Research, 1964), 25:

> When speaking of Agharta one will have to visualize a vast underground terminal
> city, being a branch of a subterranean, suboceanic network of tunnels radiating from
> what is now called the Continent of Antarctica, where one of seven icebound cities is
> now open again for operation, a city made out of colored plastic blocks and therefore
> called the Rainbow City.

Dickhoff is identified as Sungma Red Lama and Messenger of Buddha. He also says that "Shamballah is not a City of Mystery located somewhere in Tibet . . . but . . . Spiritual Communion for all Buddhists" (15).

49. Fawcett came back into the public eye with the 2009 publication of the book by David Grann, *The Lost City of Z: A Tale of Deadly Obsession in the Amazon* (New York: Doubleday, 2009). Grann deals with Fawcett primarily as an explorer of the Amazon region, fixated on the idea that the ruins of a great civilization could be found in the jungles of that area. Grann, the latest of a number of people interested in Fawcett's fate, notes (though rather in passing) Fawcett's interest in the occult, including spiritualism and Madame Blavatsky (167, 186, 206), and Fawcett's interest in native traditions, though as a means of learning about possible physical ruins (203, 271, 272). He does not indicate any interest on Fawcett's part in traditions about an underground world (he does say that "by 1924 Fawcett had filled his papers with reams of delirious writing about the end of the world and about a mystical Atlantean kingdom" [260]), though he notes being told there are "religious cults" "in the area" which "believed Fawcett had entered a network of underground tunnels and discovered . . . a portal to other realities" (261). Grann does not indicate whether these "cults" might be Theosophists or what the relevant "area" might be.

50. See, for example, Norman, 150ff.

51. Originally published in Chicago by Forbes in 1908 *The Smoky God* was reprinted in 1964 by Fieldcrest Publishing in New York.

52. Many of these points were brought up by William Reed, *The Phantom of the Poles* (New York: Walter S. Rockey, 1906; reprinted Mokelumne Hill, Calif.: Health Research, 1964), and Marshall S. Gardner, *A Journey to the Earth's Interior; or, Have the Poles Really Been Discovered* (Aurora, Ill.: The author, 1920; reprinted Mokelumne Hill, Calif.: Health Research, 1964). Reed and Gardner filled in the gap in interest in the hollow earth as real between the nineteenth century and Shaver and Palmer. Gardner brings up Eskimo legends, 304ff.

53. Raymond Bernard, *The Hollow Earth: The Greatest Geographical Discovery in History* (New York: University Books, 1969), 165. According to Standish, Raymond Bernard was a pen name for Walter Siegmeister, a member of the occult Rosicrucians who wrote his M.A. thesis on Rudolph Steiner, who broke away from the Theosophists to found his own Anthroposophical movement. Standish says that Siegmeister/Bernard appears to have "had a lifelong devotion to esoteric ideas of every sort" (276) and he did indeed publish works on such topics as constipation, the Dead Sea scrolls, vegetarianism, the secret life of Jesus, and the occult figure St. Germain. For his 1969 book Bernard recycled material published earlier in mimeographed volumes, such as *Flying Saucers from the Earth's Interior* (Joinville, Santa Catrina, Brazil, n.d.), *Nuclear Age Saviors: Flying Saucers and the Subterranean World* [called *Agharta, the Subterranean World* on its cover] (Mokelumne Hill, Calif.: Health

Research, 1960), and one with the same title as the 1969 book (Mokelumne Hill, Calif., 1963).

54. Bernard, *Hollow Earth* (1969), 168, 169; Bernard, *Flying Saucers*, 34.

55. Norman, 87, 14, 144, 85, 55.

56. Norman, 86–87.

57. Stephen Jay Gould, "Velikovsky in Collision," in *Ever since Darwin: Reflections in Natural History* (New York: Norton, 1977), 153. Martin Ridge, *Ignatius Donnelly: The Portrait of a Politician* (Chicago: University of Chicago Press, 1962), 203, notes of the earlier *Atlantis* that Donnelly himself "did not associate . . . with eccentric fringe groups which established mystical Atlantean cults. . . . [The book] had nothing mysterious or occult in its content or method."

58. Though *Ragnarok* would never be as popular as *Atlantis*, Donnelly actually had some difficulty in placing his second book with a publisher and in getting it the attention he sought; he eventually bought the plates from his original publisher and produced copies himself; it did have nineteen printings by 1899.

59. See Ridge, 197.

60. Ignatius Donnelly, *Ragnarok: The Age of Fire and Gravel*, intro. Leslie Shepard (New York: University Books, 1970), 1.

61. Donnelly, *Ragnarok*, 37.

62. Donnelly, *Ragnarok*, 91, 108, 112, 118, 251.

63. Donnelly, *Ragnarok*, 252, 113–14, 118.

64. Donnelly, *Ragnarok*, 137; the emphases are his.

65. Donnelly, *Ragnarok*, 168; the emphases are his.

66. Donnelly, *Ragnarok*, 169, 172, 173, 181.

67. Donnelly, *Ragnarok*, 192–93.

68. Donnelly, *Ragnarok*, 196–97; the emphases are his.

69. Donnelly, *Ragnarok*, 208, 209, 215, 239.

70. Although primarily using folk narratives, Donnelly does look to rituals for evidence. He notes widespread sacrifice to ensure the return of the sun (111), suggests that May Day festivities also have to do with the return of the sun after the clearing of the comet dust (240–41), and sees a ritual performed by Native Americans in Texas as mirroring the life in the caves of refuge (200).

71. Leslie Shepard, "Introduction," to Donnelly, *Ragnarok*, v.

72. In addition to the footnote, Velikovsky says the same thing at somewhat greater length in his essay "Precursors." This document is available on-line in the Velikovsky Archive (www.varchive.org/).

73. Immanuel Velikovsky, *Worlds in Collision* (New York: Pocket Books, 1977), 11. Originally published by Doubleday, 1950.

74. In 1952 Velikovsky published his *Ages in Chaos*, in which he posited chronology for ancient events different from that accepted by historians, and he would later publish other books not discussed here. In addition to his ideas about the influence of Venus and Mars upon earthly catastrophes, he developed ideas about influences exerted by Jupiter, Saturn, and Mercury, though these ideas remained largely unpublished and my discussion in this chapter is limited to his ideas about Venus and Mars (indeed, mostly about Venus) to demonstrate his interest in folkloric sources.

75. Velikovsky, *Worlds in Collision*, 12, 45, 101, 195, 311; emphasis added.

76. Velikovsky, *Worlds in Collision*, 48, 52, 67, 68.

77. Velikovsky, *Worlds in Collision*, 69–70, 76, 77, 143, 84, 85, 164, 166, 173.

78. Velikovsky, *Worlds in Collision*, 361.

79. At least according to the Wikipedia entry on Velikovsky. The Velikovsky essays cited as the source for this idea ("The Acceptance of Conventional Ideas in Science," "My Challenge to Conventional Ideas in Science," and "Claude Schaeffer," available at varchive. org/) do not entirely bear it out. In "My Challenge," his address to the American Association for the Advancement of Science in 1974, Velikovsky does offer justifications for his ideas in terms of recent discoveries, notes attempts to suppress his work by pressuring his publisher to drop it, suggests that the "entire scientific community" has opposed him, and does quote Bruno, perhaps implying a comparison. (He notes in this essay that *Worlds in Collision* had gone through 72 printings.) In "The Acceptance of Conventional Ideas in Science" he does speak of "persecution to which innovators are subject," notes that his books caused "great anxiety" and were judged to be "work of no worth," and refers to Bruno's burning at the stake for heresy.

80. Von Däniken, *Gold of the Gods*, 31.

81. Immanuel Velikovsky, *Earth in Upheaval* (New York: Pocket Books, 1977), xvii.

One might note that since the 1980s geologists and other scientists have come to accept the limited significance of certain catastrophes, such as the falling meteor that may have ended the existence of dinosaurs, in the history of the earth.

CHAPTER 6

1. Richard M. Dorson, "Foreword," in *Folktales of Ireland*, ed. Sean O'Sullivan (Chicago: University of Chicago Press, 1966), xiii.

2. This chapter does not, however, attempt to discuss the interests of Mexican Americans; that is, citizens of the United States of Mexican heritage, who have sometimes been interested in Mexican folklore, who may have seen themselves as culturally part of a Greater Mexico, and whose approach to Mexican culture and folklore has often been a sophisticated one but one rather different from that of other Americans who may have gone to Mexico.

3. Helen Delpar, *The Enormous Vogue of Things Mexican: Cultural Relations between the United States and Mexico, 1920–1935* (Tuscaloosa: The University of Alabama Press, 1992), 16. Delpar's book has been a valuable source of background information for this chapter.

4. Delpar, 12.

5. Delpar, 13.

6. Katherine Anne Porter, "Outline of Mexican Popular Arts and Crafts," in *Uncollected Early Prose of Katherine Anne Porter*, ed. Ruth M. Alvarez and Thomas F. Walsh (Austin: University of Texas Press, 1993), 180, 165, 166, 167 (emphasis added), 148, 151, 172.

7. Porter, 139, 168, 179, 156, 160–61, 187 (emphasis added).

8. Carleton Beals, *Glass Houses: Ten Years of Free-Lancing* (Philadelphia and New York: J. B. Lippincott, 1938), 290.

9. Heath Bowman and Stirling Dickinson, *Mexican Odyssey*, foreword José Mojica (Chicago and New York: Willett, Clark & Co., 1935), 169, 190, 177, 169, 174, 191, 189, 197.

10. Erna Fergusson, *Fiesta in Mexico* (New York: Knopf, 1934), 5, 87, 40, 30.

11. Frances Toor, *Guide to Mexico*, 3rd ed. (Mexico City: Frances Toor Studios, n.d.). Toor brought out revised editions frequently; she began publishing the guide around 1933. Quotations are from the edition cited.

12. It was not called the Zona Rosa until the 1950s, however, at which time it began to attract bohemians and artists and nightclubs and restaurants.

13. From an advertisement in Toor, 217.

14. Toor, 72.

15. Frances Toor, *Motorist Guide to Mexico* (Mexico City: Frances Toor Studios, 1938), 259, 191, 249–55, 164ff.

16. Anita Brenner, *Your Mexican Holiday: A Modern Guide* (New York and London: Putnam, 1932), 180, 190, 193.

17. These books by Toor and Brenner were not, of course, the first Mexican guidebooks to appear; see, for example, Reau Campbell, *Campbell's Complete Guide and Descriptive Book of Mexico*, rev. ed. (Chicago: n.p., 1908), originally published in the late nineteenth century, as were books by Thomas Janvier and Emil Riedel. They are, however, the first to appear in the context of the burst of American interest in Mexico that began with the 1920s. Campbell, who died in 1910, had been well known as a guide for parties of foreign tourists in Mexico. T. Philip Terry's 1909 guidebook is discussed briefly below for its revision by James Norman.

18. Simon's book was first published in 1962, though any references here are to the Harper Colophon paperback edition of 1984. References to Norman's revision of Terry's guide are to the edition of 1972.

19. James Norman, *Terry's Guide to Mexico*, rev. ed. (Garden City, N.Y.: Doubleday, 1972), 141, 160, 151; Kate Simon, *Mexico: Places and Pleasures* (New York: Harper and Row [Harper Colophon], 1984), 75.

20. James Norman, *In Mexico: Where to Look, How to Buy Mexican Popular Arts and Crafts* (New York: William Morrow, 1959).

21. Norman, *In Mexico*, 11–12.

22. Norman, *In Mexico*, 21.

23. Norman's guidebook, though intended for tourists and collectors, may be of particular interest to folklorists, as it does, though not scholarly in tone, provide a very full discussion of contemporary folk arts and crafts. Another relatively recent guidebook that should interest folklorists is Carl Franz, *The People's Guide to Mexico* (Santa Fe: John Muir Publications, 1972; 9th printing 1983). Coming out of "hippie" interest in Mexico as a destination, it is geared for the more bohemian traveler looking for a less than luxury experience possibly over an extended period of time. Franz and his coauthor, Lorena Havens, have imported Mexican folk objects for sale in the United States, although the book does not specifically single out the availability of crafts. It does, however, provide an interesting array of useful folk cultural information from acquiring and sleeping in a hammock to the various kinds of vessels traditionally used for serving alcoholic drinks.

24. Other culminations might include the establishment by the Mexican government of the Fonart chain of shops selling folk artifacts, the opening of shops devoted to selling Mexican folk objects in such places as Austin, Santa Fe, and New Orleans, the importation of folk objects for sale at special events by various individuals, and the popularity of Day of the Dead objects, as that annual festival has become more important in the American consciousness for a variety of reasons.

25. William Niven, discussed in chapter 5, was likewise a dealer in antiquities in Mexico, including those pre-Columbian pieces he unearthed as an archaeologist.

26. The author well remembers the variety of excellent folk art still available at Sanborns' main branch, the Casa de Azulejos, in the 1970s. Sanborns was sold to Walgreens in the 1940s and eventually became the Mexican firm Grupo Sanborn, in turn part of the conglomerate Grupo Carso. Sanborns still operates a number of retail outlets in Mexico City and elsewhere in Mexico and Central America.

27. Toor, *Guide* and *Motorist Guide*, list or carry advertisements for the following firms and individuals dealing in various kinds of folk art or traditional crafts, in addition to those mentioned: Casa Cervantes, Donaji, El Incendio, El Tesoro, Industrias Tipicas, Legorreta y Hernano, Native Arts, Riveroll, Sanborns, Weston's, La Dama Elegante, Mayan Art, Cuernavaca Curio Shop, Arte Popular, Garcia Hernanos, El Arte Tonaltateca, Esperanza Castellanos Lambley, Mexican Indian Art Craft, and Ramon Ambriz Garcia, as well as William Spratling's Taller de las Delicias in Taxco, which sold Spratling's famous silver jewelry but also such items as serapes and tinwork. (Toor's books do not necessarily include the proper accent marks.) Both books even carry ads for the shop of Fred Leighton in Greenwich Village in New York; Leighton's business, bought out by others in the 1950s, later became known for its own designs and for Native American and for high-end estate jewelry, but earlier had exported from Mexico a wide variety of popular arts and crafts ranging from jewelry to pottery and toys.

28. Susan Smith, *Made in Mexico*, illus. Julio Castellanos (New York: Alfred A. Knopf, 1930). James Oles, "For Business or Pleasure: Exhibiting Mexican Folk Art, 1820–1930," in Susan Danly, ed., *Casa Mañana: The Morrow Collection of Mexican Popular Arts* (Albuquerque: University of New Mexico Press for the Mead Art Museum, Amherst College, 2002), 10–29, discusses earlier and contemporaneous exhibits of Mexican folk materials, going back to two nineteenth-century London exhibitions, William Bullock's commercially motivated exhibits in 1823, and American anthropologist Frederick Starr's exhibit sponsored by the Folk-Lore Society in 1899. Oles's chapter in English is followed by a Spanish translation with one additional illustration.

Many of the Americans interested in Mexican folk materials in the 1920s and 1930s, though they might complain about the decline of authenticity, were essentially naive in their approaches, and often little aware of the history or contexts of the folk art they looked at and purchased, or little aware of the changes their very interest might bring about. For a recent and sophisticated approach to Mexican folk art and tourism, see Chris Goertzen, *Made in Mexico: Tradition, Tourism, and Political Ferment in Oaxaca* (Jackson: University Press of Mississippi, 2010).

29. Marion Oettinger Jr., *Folk Treasures of Mexico: The Nelson A. Rockefeller Collection* (New York: Harry N. Abrams, 1990), 47. Oettinger's informative book, with contributions

by several people, has been very helpful in discussing here Rockefeller's involvement in folk art collecting, including the surrounding context.

30. This is his first trip noted by Oettinger. However, James Griffith (see n. 46) mentions that Rockefeller "is said" to have told a story that has him as a "young boy" visiting Mexico with his mother and going to markets with Elizabeth Morrow, thus evoking his first interest in Mexican folk art. However, Rockefeller was nineteen years old when the Morrows went to Mexico, so he could not have visited them as a "young boy" and this story may be apocryphal; it may be meant as indicative of Elizabeth Morrow's influence generally, and Griffith sees the Morrows as important figures in a transition from looking at Mexican folk art as "curios" to seeing it as "art."

31. Oettinger, 49.

32. The exhibition borrowed materials from many sources, including folklorist Frances Toor, artist Miguel Covarrubias, and movie star Delores del Rio.

33. Oettinger, 19, 22–23.

34. Oettinger, 52.

35. Oettinger, 52–53. Kaufmann's principal, Edgar S. Kaufmann, was himself a noted patron of the arts who commissioned Frank Lloyd Wright to design the iconic house Fallingwater as a Kaufman family country retreat. Visitors to the house today will see sculpture by one of Rockefeller's favorite Mexican folk artists, Mardonio Magaña.

36. For example, the Morrows's granddaughters, in the Postscript they wrote to the 2001 edition of Elizabeth Morrow's *The Painted Pig* (see n. 46), mention that the road from Mexico City to Cuernavaca, where the Morrows built a weekend house, was still inhabited by bandits.

37. Rick A. López, "The Morrows in Mexico: Nationalist Politics, Foreign Patronage, and the Promotion of Mexican Popular Arts," in Danly, 55.

38. López, 55.

39. Susan Danly, "Casa Mañana," in Danly, 97.

40. Spratling was a notably talented illustrator. Not only did he do the portraits for the whimsical book he and William Faulkner jointly produced about New Orleans residents, *Sherwood Anderson and Other Famous Creoles: A Gallery of Contemporary New Orleans* (inspired by Miguel Covarubbias's *The Prince of Wales and Other Famous Americans*) (New Orleans: Pelican Book Shop, 1926), but he produced the sketches that illustrated the book he published in collaboration with Natalie Scott, *Old Plantation Houses in Louisiana* (New York: William Helburn, 1927).

Spratling is best known for having created the modern silver industry in Taxco and for his designs for jewelry and other silver artifacts. His use of pre-Columbian motifs in his designs is most apparent, but Penny C. Morrill ("Renaissance-Transformation," in *William Spratling and the Mexican Silver Renaissance, Maestros de Plata*, Penny C. Morrill guest curator [New York and San Antonio: Harry N. Abrams and the San Antonio Museum of Art, 2002], 17–19) argues that Spratling fused the folk with contemporary design:

> *In establishing silver as an artistic medium, what Spratling achieved was a delicate balance, a synthesis of abstract tendencies in existent folk art tradition and in contemporary fine art. . . . One of the threads that can be followed throughout William Spratling's life was his appreciation for the many aspects of Mexico's folk art traditions.*

See also Taylor D. Littleton, *The Color of Silver: William Spratling, His Life and Art* (Baton Rouge: Louisiana State University Press, 2000).

41. Elizabeth Morrow, *Casa Mañana*, drawings William Spratling (n.p.: privately printed, 1932), no pagination.

The Morrows' house does not seem to have had any influence on or to have been influenced by the Maya Revival style in American architecture. This minor but interesting style used elements of pre-Columbian architecture, notably Mayan and Aztec, in the design of contemporary buildings, but does not seem to have drawn upon folk styles or motifs. Marjorie Ingle, *The Mayan Revival Style: Art Deco Mayan Fantasy* (Salt Lake City: Peregrine Smith, 1984), finds the earliest examples of the style in the United States as dating from 1910 and 1912, though she sees it connected to art deco and notes its heyday as the 1920s and 1930s.

42. Morrow includes a number of photographs of the artifacts she used for decoration, ranging from contemporary pottery to seventeenth-, eighteenth-, and nineteenth-century lacquer, eighteenth-century serapes, and a seventeenth-century feather mosaic. Danly, *Casa Mañana*, 157–73, includes a catalog of the Mexican pieces given by the Morrow family to the Mead Art Museum at Amherst College.

43. The name of the house was not meant to evoke the stereotype of Mexicans' putting off action into the future but was a play upon the Morrows' name and the Spanish meaning of *mañana* as "tomorrow."

44. Danly, "Casa Mañana," 98.

45. The catalog of artifacts given by the Morrow family to the Mead Art Museum in Danly, *Casa Mañana*, 157–73, does not include any examples of clay pigs (those which the Morrows owned may have been passed on to children in the family), though it does include reference to several clay items called "Savings Bank" and in fruit form; these are from Tonalá in Jalisco state, a noted pottery center. The "piggy bank" illustrated in Morrow's children's book appears to be in the Tonalá style, and such pigs were at one time widely available.

46. Elizabeth Morrow, *The Painted Pig: A Mexican Picture Book*, illus. René d'Harnoncourt (New York: Alfred A. Knopf, 1930), 16; Morrow, *Casa Mañana*, no pagination. *The Painted Pig* was very popular and went through many editions. In 2001 the University of New Mexico Press published a facsimile edition with an Afterword ("A Historically Important Pig," 34–35) by folklorist James Griffith and a Postscript ("Elizabeth Morrow's Mexico," 36–37) by Morrow's granddaughters, writers Margaret Eiluned Morgan and Reeve Morrow Lindbergh.

47. Danly, "Casa Mañana," 100, quoting in part Mary Austin.

48. Delpar, pp. 175ff, discusses the literature produced by Americans in Mexico in this period. Barbara Kingsolver's novel *The Lacuna* (New York: HarperCollins, 2009) has as its main character an American (he has a Mexican mother) who grew up and lived in Mexico in the 1920s and 1930s and who becomes a noted writer of fiction about Mexico; it is, however, historical fiction that he writes.

49. Witter Bynner, *Indian Earth* (New York: Alfred A. Knopf, 1929).

50. In these poems Bynner was experimenting with *shih*, a form derived from Chinese poetry (in addition to his own poetry, Bynner published translations from the Chinese).

This form was understood to consist of eight lines, each with the same number of words, and with a certain rhyme scheme. In fact, the term *shih* is more complicated and may refer to poems that were originally derived from folk sources, although this does not seem to have been an element in relating Bynner's poetry to folk culture.

51. Except for some photographs, discussed below, visual arts works discussed here appear reproduced in James Oles, *South of the Border: Mexico in the American Imagination 1914–1947*, essay Karen Cordero Reiman (Washington: Smithsonian Institution Press, 1993), published in conjunction with the exhibition organized by the Yale University Art Gallery. Locations for original artwork are given in the text if they are in public institutions, not if they are in private hands or are multiples. In Oles, *South of the Border*, see figures 30, 50, 51, 52, 62, 114, 115.

52. René d'Harnoncourt, *Mexicana: A Book of Pictures* (New York: Alfred A. Knopf, 1931); there is no pagination but the images discussed are found toward the end of the volume. D'Harnoncourt also includes an illustration of folk toys and others related to folk art.

53. Oles, *South of the Border*, 87. Oles identifies the pottery as the black ware of San Bartolo Coyotepec, but according to Goertzen, pp. 39ff, the black ware was not invented until the 1950s, so Oles may be mistaken. Goertzen states that the San Bartolo black ware, fired for a limited period of time and intended for decorative use by tourists, would in fact not contain water.

54. Anita Brenner, *Idols behind Altars* (New York: Payson and Clarke, 1929), 7.

55. Nancy Newhall, ed., *The Daybooks of Edward Weston*, 2 vols. (Millerton, N.Y.: Aperture, 1973), I: 66.

56. Newhall, I: 150.

57. Newhall, I: 157.

58. See Newhall, II: figs. 24, 26; Oles, *South of the Border*, figs. 78, 114, 118. The photo of Galván's hand and pot appears in Brenner's *Idols behind Altars*.

59. Quoted, "Edward Weston" Wikipedia entry.

60. These photographs appear in Sarah M. Lowe, *Tina Modotti: Photographs* (New York and Philadelphia: Harry N. Abrams and the Philadelphia Museum of Art, 1995), as plates 54, 55, 60, 61.

61. Newhall, I: 161.

62. It is so titled in Newhall I: plate 17. It appeared in Brenner, *Idols*, plate 48, as "El Charrito." Oles, *South of the Border*, includes it as "Charrito (Pulquería), Mexico," plate 57.

63. Lowe, plate 17.

64. In the book, Brenner does not identify the work of the photographers as being by one or the other.

65. Newhall, I: 190; emphasis added.

66. Henry Glassie, *The Spirit of Folk Art: The Girard Collection at the Museum of International Folk Art* (New York and Santa Fe: Harry N. Abrams and the Museum of New Mexico, 1989), from an introduction, "Alexander Girard: Designer and Collector," by Stanley Marcus, 11.

67. Charlene Cerny in her Foreword to Glassie says that Girard "was one of the first to incorporate folk art into interiors" (8), though as he was evidently doing this in the 1950s

and 1960s, many years after the Morrows and Weston, among others, did, it's unclear what she means. Perhaps she refers to professional decorators in the United States.

68. These are shown as figures 9 and 11 in Glassie, 22. About the Acatlán de Osorio village, the Multiple Visions gallery guide (*The Girard Gallery Guide; Multiple Visions: A Common Bond*, 2nd ed. [Santa Fe: Museum of International Folk Art, Museum of New Mexico], installation 9-1) notes that the scene is "not unlike many Mexican towns which survive today," suggesting the conscious attempt to aesthetically recreate reality.

69. Of course, folk artisans may themselves create tableaux. One of Girard's installations (13–19 in the multiple Visions exhibit) recreates a funeral scene using figures made by the Aguilar family of Oaxaca. The Aguilars themselves create and sell funeral scenes.

70. Newhall, I: 56.

71. Tim Street-Porter, *Casa Mexicana: The Architecture, Design, and Style of Mexico*, intro. Marie-Pierre Colle (New York: Stewart, Chabori, and Chang, 1989), 150–51, 163, 245, 250–53.

CONCLUSION

1. For shanties, see, for example, Stan Hugill, *Shanties and Sailors' Songs* (New York: Praeger, 1969); for Burmese law tales, see Maung Htin Aung, *Burmese Law Tales* (Oxford: Oxford University Press, 1962).

2. William R. Bascom, "Four Functions of Folklore," *Journal of American Folklore* 67 (1954): 333–49.

SELECTED BIBLIOGRAPHY

Abrahams, Roger D., and Barbara A. Babcock. 1977. "The Literary Use of Proverbs." *Journal of American Folklore* 90: 414–29.

Alvey, Richard. 1974. "The Historical Development of Organized Storytelling in the United States." Ph.D. dissertation, University of Pennsylvania.

Baker, Ronald L. 2005. "*Miracle Magazine* in the Sixties: Mass Media Narratives of Healings and Blessings." *Journal of American Folklore* 118: 204–18.

Barnard, F. M., ed. 1969. *Herder on Social and Political Culture*. Cambridge: Cambridge University Press.

Barnes, Daniel R. 1972. "The Bosom Serpent: A Legend in American Folklore and Culture." *Journal of American Folklore* 85: 111–22.

Bascom, William R. 1954. "Four Functions of Folklore." *Journal of American Folklore* 67: 333–49.

Bauman, Richard. 1971. "Differential Identity and the Social Base of Folklore." *Journal of American Folklore* 84 (1971): 31–41.

———. 1984. *Verbal Art as Performance*. Prospect Heights, Ill.: Waveland Press.

Bausinger, Hermann. 1990. *Folk Culture in a World of Technology*. Trans. Elke Dettmer. Bloomington: Indiana University Press.

Bendix, Regina. 1988. "Folklorism: The Challenge of a Concept." *International Folklore Review* 6: 5–15.

———, and Galit Hasan-Rokem, eds. 2012. *A Companion to Folklore*. Oxford: Wiley-Blackwell.

Bronner, Simon J. 1986. *American Folklore Studies: An Intellectual History*. Lawrence: University of Kansas Press.

———. 1998. *Following Tradition: Folklore in the Discourse on American Culture*. Logan: Utah State University Press.

Brown, Mary Ellen. 1984. *Burns and Tradition*. Urbana: University of Illinois Press.

Brunvand, Jan Harold. 1998 [1968]. *The Study of American Folklore: An Introduction*, 4th ed. New York: W. W. Norton.

———, ed. 1979. *Readings in American Folklore*. New York: W. W. Norton.

Burns, Tom. 1969. "Folklore in the Mass Media: Television." *Folklore Forum* 2: 90–106.

Camp, Charles, and Timothy Lloyd. 1980. "Six Reasons Not to Produce Folklife Festivals." *Kentucky Folklife Record* 26, 1–2: 67–74.

Cantwell, Robert. 1991. "Conjuring Culture: Ideology and Magic in the Festival of American Folklife." *Journal of American Folklore* 104: 148–63.

———. 1993. *Ethnomimesis: Folklife and the Representation of Culture*. Chapel Hill: University of North Carolina Press.

———. 1996. *When We Were Good: The Folk Revival*. Cambridge, Mass.: Harvard University Press.

Carpenter, Inta Gale, Richard Bauman, and Patricia Sawin. 1992. *Reflections on the Folklife Festival: An Ethnography of Participant Experience*. Bloomington: Indiana University Folklore Institute Special Publications, No. 2.

Cashman, Ray, Tom Mould, and Pravina Shukla, eds. 2011. *The Individual and Tradition: Folkloristic Perspectives*. Bloomington: Indiana University Press.

Clark, Robert T. 1955. *Herder: His Life and Thought*. Berkeley and Los Angeles: University of California Press.

Cohen, Norm. 2000. *Long Steel Rail: The Railroad in American Folksong*. 2nd ed. Urbana: University of Illinois Press.

de Caro, Frank, and Rosan Augusta Jordan. 2004. *Re-Situating Folklore: Folk Contexts and Twentieth-Century Literature and Art*. Knoxville: University of Tennessee Press.

Dégh, Linda. 1984. "Uses of Folklore as Expressive of Identity by Hungarians in the Old and New Country." *Journal of Folklore Research* 21: 187–200.

———. 1994. *American Folklore and the Mass Media*. Bloomington: Indiana University Press.

Denby, Priscilla. 1971. "Folklore in the Mass Media." *Folklore Forum* 4: 113–25.

Dorson, Richard M. 1959. *American Folklore*. Chicago: University of Chicago Press.

———. 1971. *American Folklore and the Historian*. Chicago: University of Chicago Press.

———, ed. 1972. *Folklore and Folklife: An Introduction*. Chicago: University of Chicago Press.

———. 1976. *Folklore and Fakelore: Essays toward a Discipline of Folk Studies*. Cambridge, Mass.: Harvard University Press.

Dow, James R., and Hannjost Lixfeld, eds. 1994. *The Nazification of an Academic Discipline*. Bloomington: Indiana University Press.

Dundes, Alan, ed. 1965. *The Study of Folklore*. Englewood Cliffs, N.J.: Prentice-Hall.

———. 1965. "The Study of Folklore and Literature in Culture: Identification and Interpretation." *Journal of American Folklore* 78: 136–42.

———. 1985. "Nationalistic Inferiority Complexes and the Fabrication of Folklore: A Reconsideration of Ossian, the *Kinder-und Hausmärchen, the Kalevala* and Paul Bunyan." *Journal of Folklore Research* 22: 5–18.

———. 1989. *Folklore Matters*. Knoxville: University of Tennessee Press.

———, ed. 1990. *Mother Wit from the Laughing Barrel: Readings in the Interpretation of Afro-American Folklore*. Jackson: University Press of Mississippi.

Edmunds, Michael. 2009. *Out of the Northwoods: The Many Lives of Paul Bunyan*. Madison: Wisconsin Historical Society Press.

Falassi, Alessandro. 1980. *Folklore by the Fireside: Text and Context of the Italian Veglia*. Austin: University of Texas Press.

Feintuch, Burt, ed. 1988. *The Conservation of Culture*. Lexington: University Press of Kentucky.

Garlough, Christine. 2011. "Folklore and the Potential of Acknowledgment: Representing 'India' at the Minnesota Festival of Nations." *Western Folklore* 70: 69–98.

Glassie, Henry. 1989. *The Spirit of Folk Art: The Girard Collection at the Museum of International Folk Art*. New York and Santa Fe: Harry N. Abrams and the Museum of New Mexico.

Goldstein, Diane E., Sylvia Ann Grider, and Jeannie Banks Thomas. 2007. *Haunting Experiences: Ghosts in Contemporary Folklore*. Logan: Utah State University Press.

Greever, Ellen A. 1995. "Fractured Fairy Tales: Parody in Literary Fairy Tales for Children." Ph.D. dissertation, University of North Carolina at Chapel Hill.

Hobsbawm, Eric, and Terence Ranger, eds. 1983. *The Invention of Tradition*. Cambridge: Cambridge University Press.

Hoffman, Daniel. 1983. *Paul Bunyan: Last of the Frontier Demigods*. Lincoln: University of Nebraska Press, Bison Books.

Howard, Robert Glenn. 2008. "Electronic Hybridity: The Persistent Process of the Vernacular Web." *Journal of American Folklore* 121: 192–218.

Jones, Michael Owen, ed. 1994. *Putting Folklore to Use*. Lexington: University Press of Kentucky.

Kerr, David. 1991. "On Not Becoming a Folklorist: Field Methodology and the Reproduction of Underdevelopment." *Folklore* 102: 48–61.

Kirshenblatt-Gimblett, Barbara. 1991. "Objects of Ethnography." In *Exhibiting Cultures: The Poetics and Politics of Museum Display*, ed. Ivan Karp and Steven D. Lavine. Washington: Smithsonian Institution Press. 386–443.

———. 1998. *Destination Culture: Tourism, Museums, and Heritage*. Berkeley and Los Angeles: University of California Press.

Kolin, Philip C. 1976. "Bibliography of Scholarship on Shakespeare and Folklore." *Mississippi Folklore Register* 10: 210–33.

Lindahl, Carl. 1987. *Earnest Games: Folkloric Patterns in the Canterbury Tales*. Bloomington: Indiana University Press.

Loukatos, Demetrios. 1982. "Folklore and Tourism in Greece." *International Folklore Review* 2: 65–69.

Lowenthal, David. 1998. *The Heritage Crusade and the Spoils of History*. Cambridge: Cambridge University Press.

Magliocco, Sabina. 2004. *Witching Culture: Folklore and Neopaganism in America*. Philadelphia: University of Pennsylvania Press.

Michaelis-Jena, Ruth. 1970. *The Brothers Grimm*. New York and Washington: Praeger.

Mieder, Wolfgang, and Barbara Mieder. 1981. "Tradition and Innovation: Proverbs in Advertising." In *The Wisdom of Many: Essays on the Proverb*, ed. Wolfgang Mieder and Alan Dundes. New York: Garland Publishing. 309–22.

———, ed. 1985. *Disenchantments: An Anthology of Modern Fairy Tale Poetry*. University Press of New England.

Moore, Willard B. 1999. "The Intersection of Folk and Fine Arts." *Journal of Folklore Research* 36: 71–82.

Nelson, Scott Reynolds. 2006. *Steel Drivin' Man: John Henry, the Untold Story of an American Legend*. New York: Oxford University Press.

[Newell, William Wells]. 1888. "On the Field of Work of a Journal of American Folk-Lore." *Journal of American Folklore* 1: 3–7.

Oinas, Felix J., ed. 1978. *Folklore, Nationalism and Politics*. Columbus: Slavica Publishers.

Oring, Elliott, ed. 1986. *Folk Groups and Folklore Genres: An Introduction*. Logan: Utah State University Press.

———, ed. 1989. *Folk Groups and Folklore Genres: A Reader*. Logan: Utah State University Press.

———. 1994. "The Arts, Artifacts, and Artifices of Identity." *Journal of American Folklore* 107: 211–33.

Peppard, Murray B. 1971. *Paths through the Forest: A Biography of the Brothers Grimm*. New York: Holt, Rinehart and Winston.

Price, Richard, and Sally Price. 1994. *On the Mall: Presenting Maroon Tradition Bearers at the 1992 Festival of American Folklife*. Bloomington: Indiana University Folklore Institute Special Publications, No. 4.

Prosterman, Leslie. 1995. *Ordinary Life, Festival Days: Aesthetics in the Midwestern County Fair*. Washington: Smithsonian Institution Press.

Regis, Helen A., and Shana Walton. 2008. "Producing the Folk at the New Orleans Jazz and Heritage Festival." *Journal of American Folklore* 121: 400–440.

Reuss, Richard. 1975. "American Folksongs and Left-Wing Politics: 1935–56." *Journal of the Folklore Institute* 12 (1975): 89–111.

Rosenberg, Bruce. 1991. *Folklore and Literature: Rival Siblings*. Knoxville: University of Tennessee Press.

———, and Mary Ellen Brown, eds. 1998. *Encyclopedia of Folklore and Literature*. Santa Barbara: ABC-CLIO.

Rosenberg, Neil V., ed. 1993. *Transforming Tradition: Folk Music Revivals Reconsidered*. Urbana: University of Illinois Press.

Satterwhite, Emily. 2008. "Imagining Home, Nation, World: Appalachia on the Mall." *Journal of American Folklore* 121: 10–34.

Shackler, Jennifer. 2007. "Unruly Tales: Ideology, Anxiety, and the Regulation of Genre." *Journal of American Folklore* 120: 381–400.

Smidchens, Guntis. 1999. "Folklorism Revisited." *Journal of Folklore Research* 36: 51–70.

Sobol, Joseph. 1998. *The Storyteller's Journey: An American Revival*. Urbana: University of Illinois Press.

Stone, Kay. 2010. *Some Day Your Witch Will Come*. Detroit: Wayne State University Press.

Szego, C. K. 2010. "The Sound of Rocks Aquiver? Composing Racial Ambivalence in Territorial Hawai'i." *Journal of American Folklore* 123: 31–62.

Thornbury, Barbara. 1995. "Folklorism and Japan's Performing Arts." *Journal of Folklore Research* 32: 207–20.

Toelken, Barre. 1996. *The Dynamics of Folklore*. Rev. & expanded ed. Logan: Utah State University Press.

Voight, Vilmos. 1984. "The Concept of Today's Folklore as We See It from Budapest, Hungary, Europe." *Journal of Folklore Research* 21: 165–75.

Whisnant, David. 1983. *All That Is Native and Fine: The Politics of Culture in an American Region*. Chapel Hill: University of North Carolina Press.

Williams, Brett. 1983. *John Henry: A Bio-Bibliography*. Westport, Conn.: Greenwood Press.

Wilson, Sharon Rose. 1993. *Margaret Atwood's Fairy Tale Sexual Politics*. Jackson: University Press of Mississippi.

Wilson, William A. 1976. *Folklore and Nationalism in Modern Finland*. Bloomington: Indiana University Press.

Zumwalt, Rosemary Lévy. 1988. *American Folklore Scholarship: A Dialogue of Dissent*. Bloomington: Indiana University Press.

INDEX

96–98; chicken pox epidemic, 97–98; in Cincinnati, 86, 89–91, 102; *Creole Sketches*, 101; as folklorist, 86–87; *Gombo Zhèbes*, 99–100; interracial marriage, 86; in Martinique, 91–99; and mythology, 88–89; in New Orleans, 99–103; *Some Chinese Ghosts*, 89; *Stray Leaves from Strange Literature*, 89; Tanyard murders, 90; *Two Years in the French West Indies*, 88, 91–99

Henry, Cammie Garrett, 72

Henry, John, 22, 23–24, 27, 31–50, 192, 200–201n6, 201n12; and convict labor, 200–201n6; Jamaican origins for tradition, 200n6

Henry, William, 99

Herder, Johann Gottfried, 13–15, 16, 159

heritage, 195n8

Heritage Society, 23

Hesiod, 151

Himmler, Heinrich, 15–16, 212n47

Hinton, West Virginia, 31, 34

Historical Section (Farm Security Administration), 117, 123

Hitler, Adolf, 145, 212n47

Hobsbawn, Eric, 24

hollow earth, 143–49

Hollow Earth, The, 148

homeless culture, 12

hootenannies, 19

Houser, Lowell, 180

Hufford, David, 13

Hughes, Langston, 177

Hurston, Zora Neale, 201n7

Icosameron, 144

identity, 27–28, 51–83, 84–103, 108, 109–10, 113, 115, 128, 173

ideology and politics, 13–18, 19–20, 28, 40, 163, 164, 188, 193, 198n53, 201n6

Idols behind Altars, 106, 185

Impressions of Old New Orleans, 115

"Indian Woman with Jug," 180

Inha, I. K., 106

In Mexico: Where to Look, How to Buy Mexican Popular Arts and Crafts, 167–68

Instituto Allende, 163

Jamison, Cecilia Viets, 55, 59

John Henry Days, 27, 31–50, 51, 161, 192, 203nn31–32

Johnson, Guy, 32, 37–38, 201n12

Johnston, J. Preston, 54

Johnston, Margaret Avery, 58, 59

Jones, Michael Own, 12–13

Jones, Sam (Stovepipe No. 1), 37

Jonesboro, Tennessee, 20

Journey to the Center of the Earth, The, 144–45

Kahlo, Frida, 188

Kalevala, 16–17, 155, 156, 159

Kane, Harnett T., 111, 112

Kaufmann's department store, 172, 218n35

Kerr, David, 17

Kertesz, Andre, 106

Keyes, Frances Parkinson, 111, 112

Killins, John Oliver, 43

King, Grace, 64

Kingsolver, Barbara, 219n48

Kingston Trio, 20

Kirshenblatt-Gimblett, Barbara, 83

Kirstein, Lincoln, 160

Knapp, William I., 18

Knott, Sarah Gertrude, 9

Kolosimo, Peter, 129

Koreshans, 145

Krehbiel, Henry Edward, 92

Kritias, 136

Lacuna, The, 219n48

Lallemond and Hart, 106

Lang, Dorothea, 117

Laughead, W. B., 23

Lee, Russell, 71, 117, 119–23

legends, 4, 8, 92–93, 95–96, 131, 132, 133, 134, 135, 137, 140, 141–42, 143, 145, 147–48, 151, 153, 205n51, 213n52

"20 Centuries of Mexican Art" exhibition, 170–71, 172

Ulmann, Doris, 71
Unidentified flying objects, 145, 146, 147
University of North Carolina Press, 111
Untermeyer, Louis, 23

Velikovsky, Immanuel, 149, 154–56, 157, 214n74, 215n79; *Ages in Chaos*, 214n74; *Earth in Upheaval*, 155, 157; *Worlds in Collision*, 155–57
Verne, Jules, 144–45
von Däniken, Erich, 129–33, 157, 193; *Chariots of the Gods?*, 129–33; *Gods from Outer Space*, 131; *Gold of the Gods*, 132
voodoo, 67–68

Washington, Booker T., 18
Watkins, Charles Alan, 111
Weigel, Karl Theodor, 15
Weiner, Dan, 106
Weston, Edward, 106, 181–85, 191, 221n67; "Hand of Amado Galvan," 182; "Pájaro Blanco," 182; "Palma Santa," 182; "Pulqueria, Mexico, D. F.," 183–84; "Tres Ollas de Oaxaca," 182
Whisnant, David, 9, 10
Whiston, William, 154
Whitehead, Colson, 27, 31–50, 105, 161, 192, 202n21, 202n23
White Top folk festival, 9, 10, 22
Williams, Brett, 38, 42, 202n14, 202nn22–23, 202n27
Wilson, Clifford, 135
Wilson, Edmond, 71, 72
Winans, Fonville, 111–12, 114, 115
Wolcott, Marion Post, 117, 119
Wooten, Bayard, 111

Yeats, William Butler, 89
Your Mexican Holiday: A Modern Guide, 166

Zihuantejo, 188
Zohar, The, 132

zombis, 93, 94
Zona Rosa (Mexico City), 165, 212n12
Zulu (New Orleans Mardi Gras organization and parade), 74–75, 206n68
Zumwalt, Rosemary Lévy, 70
Zuñi, 142